Brazilian Bourgeoisie and Foreign Policy

# Studies in Critical Social Sciences

*Series Editor*
David Fasenfest
(*Wayne State University*)

VOLUME 241

---

# New Scholarship in Political Economy

*Series Editors*
David Fasenfest
(*Wayne State University*)
Alfredo Saad-Filho
(*King's College London*)

*Editorial Board*
Kevin B. Anderson (*University of California, Santa Barbara*)
Tom Brass (*formerly of SPS, University of Cambridge*)
Raju Das (*York University*)
Ben Fine ((*emeritus*) SOAS *University of London*)
Jayati Ghosh (*Jawaharlal Nehru University*)
Elizabeth Hill (*University of Sydney*)
Dan Krier (*Iowa State University*)
Lauren Langman (*Loyola University Chicago*)
Valentine Moghadam (*Northeastern University*)
David N. Smith (*University of Kansas*)
Susanne Soederberg (*Queen's University*)
Aylin Topal (*Middle East Technical University*)
Fiona Tregenna (*University of Johannesburg*)
Matt Vidal (*Loughborough University London*)
Michelle Williams (*University of the Witwatersrand*)

VOLUME 22

The titles published in this series are listed at *brill.com/nspe*

# Brazilian Bourgeoisie and Foreign Policy

*By*

Tatiana Berringer

*Translated by*

Martin Charles Nicholl

BRILL

LEIDEN | BOSTON

Funding for the translation has been provided with the support of the São Paulo Research Foundation (FAPESP) through grant #2021/00290-5.

Cover illustration: Bust of Karl Marx, 1939, by S.D. Merkurov, at the Fallen Monument Park (Muzeon Park of Arts) in Moscow, Russia. Photo courtesy of Alfredo Saad-Filho.

Library of Congress Cataloging-in-Publication Data

Names: Berringer, Tatiana, author. | Nicholl, Martin Charles, translator.
Title: Brazilian bourgeoisie and foreign policy / by Tatiana Berringer ; translated by Martin Charles Nicholl.
Other titles: Burguesia brasileira e a política externa nos governos FHC e Lula. English
Description: Leiden ; Boston : Brill, [2023] | Series: Studies in critical social sciences, 2666-2205 ; volume 241. New scholarship in political economy ; volume 22 | Original title "A burguesia brasileira e a política externa nos governos FHC e Lula Curitiba" published in Portuguese by Editora Appris in 2015. | Includes bibliographical references and index.
Identifiers: LCCN 2022057747 (print) | LCCN 2022057748 (ebook) | ISBN 9789004532687 (hardback) | ISBN 9789004532694 (e-book)
Subjects: LCSH: Brazil–Foreign relations–1985- | Cardoso, Fernando Henrique. | Lula, 1945-
Classification: LCC F2538.3 .B4713 2023 (print) | LCC F2538.3 (ebook) | DDC 327.81–dc23/eng/20230113
LC record available at https://lccn.loc.gov/2022057747
LC ebook record available at https://lccn.loc.gov/2022057748

Typeface for the Latin, Greek, and Cyrillic scripts: "Brill". See and download: brill.com/brill-typeface.

ISSN 2666-2205
ISBN 978-90-04-53268-7 (hardback)
ISBN 978-90-04-53269-4 (e-book)

Copyright 2023 by Tatiana Berringer. Published by Koninklijke Brill NV, Leiden, The Netherlands.
Koninklijke Brill NV incorporates the imprints Brill, Brill Nijhoff, Brill Hotei, Brill Schöningh, Brill Fink, Brill mentis, Vandenhoeck & Ruprecht, Böhlau, V&R unipress and Wageningen Academic.
Koninklijke Brill NV reserves the right to protect this publication against unauthorized use. Requests for re-use and/or translations must be addressed to Koninklijke Brill NV via brill.com or copyright.com.

This book is printed on acid-free paper and produced in a sustainable manner.

# Contents

**Foreword** IX
    *Armando Boito, Jr.*
**Preface** XIII
**Acknowledgements** XV
**List of Figures and Tables** XVI
**Abbreviations and Acronyms** XVII

**Introduction** 1

1 **Power Bloc: Brazilian Theory and Policy** 5
  1   Theory: The Power Bloc and International Relations 5
  2   Theory: Power Bloc and Foreign Policy Analysis 19

2 **The FHC Governments**
*Neoliberalism, Power Bloc and Foreign Policy* 35
  1   Neoliberalism 35
  2   Neoliberalism and the Power Bloc in Brazil 39
  3   Foreign Policy in the FHC Governments 46
      3.1  *FTAA, MERCOSUR and the Internal Bourgeoisie* 54
      3.2  *Regional Politics between 1998 and 2000: The MERCOSUR Crisis and the Launching of the IIRSA* 66
      3.3  *The Lafer Administration and the Brazilian State's Passive Subordination to Imperialism* 71
      3.4  *The 2002 Elections* 73

3 **The Lula Governments**
*Neo-developmentalism, Power Bloc and Foreign Policy* 82
  1   Neo-developmentalism and Power Bloc 82
      1.1  *A Brief Review of Some of the Analytical Literature on the Lula Governments' Social and Economic Policies* 90
  2   Foreign Policy during the Lula Governments 93
      2.1  *South-South Coalitions* 96
      2.2  *Haiti* 98
      2.3  *Regional Integration* 99
      2.4  *Africa* 102
      2.5  *The Middle East* 103
      2.6  *China* 104

        2.7   *European Union*   105
        2.8   *The IMF*   106
        2.9   *The United States*   107
        2.10  *Defense Policy*   109
        2.11  *The Lula Governments' Foreign Policy and the Neo-developmentalist Front*   110
        2.12  *The Brazilian State's Position in Regard to Imperialism*   110
        2.13  *The Political Organization of the Neo-developmentalist Front*   112
        2.14  *The Internal Bourgeoisie and the South-South Foreign Policy*   114
        2.15  *Contradictions among Sectors Composing the Internal Bourgeoisie*   122
        2.16  *The Unstable Equilibrium of Compromises and Foreign Policy*   123
        2.17  *The Party-Political Dispute and Foreign Policy*   127

4  **Brazil and South America**   132
    1   Brazilian State and South America: Imperialism, Sub-imperialism and Neo-developmentalism   132
        1.1   *Brazilian Imperialism*   132
        1.2   *Brazilian Sub-imperialism*   138
        1.3   *Neo-developmentalism and Regional Politics*   144
    2   People's Movements and Unionism in Relation to Regional Integration Processes in South America   145
        2.1   *Brazilian People's Movements and Unionism and Regional Integration in the 1980s and 1990s*   147
        2.2   *The People's Classes and Regional Integration during the PT Governments*   151

5  **Brazil under FHC and Lula**   159

6  **Power Bloc and Foreign Policy in the Dilma, Temer and Bolsonaro Governments**   162
    1   The Dilma Government: Foreign Policy, Political Crisis and Power Bloc   162
        1.1   *Foreign Policy in the Dilma Governments*   167
        1.2   *The Power Bloc, the Political Crisis and Foreign Policy*   175

2 The Temer Government and the Return to Passive Subordination 184
   2.1 *Brazil's Trade and Production Structures Compared with the World* 186
   2.2 *The Brazilian State's Re-embracing of Passive Subordination* 190
   2.3 *Decadent External Insertion and Dependent Productive Structure* 194
   2.4 *'Weak Meat'* 195

3 The Bolsonaro Government and Its Explicit Passive Subordination to Imperialism: The Neofascist Alliance 198
   3.1 *Foreign Policies of the Bolsonaro Government and the Trump Government: The Neofascist Alliance* 201
   3.2 *A New Stage in Brazil-USA Relations: The Biden Government* 207

**References** 213
**Index** 231

# Foreword

Tatiana Berringer offers the reader an innovative work on Brazilian foreign policy.[1] The innovation appears in the theory the author has used, the empirical information colligated with the material under study and the results she has obtained. New concepts raise new questions and these, in turn, require the use of previously neglected sources and obtaining previously neglected information. The originality of the results springs naturally from the originality of the process itself. The reader can rightly wonder whether the author of this preface might not be exaggerating in his insistence on so much originality in the book. After all there have been many foreign policy studies in Brazil in recent years and, as those who dedicate themselves to producing knowledge must be well aware, it is no mean task to add even the most modest brick to the magnificent edification of science. However, we firmly believe that it is not an exaggeration at all. Furthermore, we must add that all that is new in the book is well-founded and convincing and obliges one to think.

This book portrays the changes in Brazilian foreign policy that took place in the transition from the Fernando Henrique Cardoso administration to that of Lula da Silva; a change that stemmed from another, much more profound and less visible change in the Power Bloc of the Brazilian State that took place in that conjuncture. In consonance with the conceptualization of Nicos Poulantzas, Tatiana Berringer takes 'Power Bloc' to mean that contradictory unity of classes and class fragments which, distributed hierarchically, jointly exercise the power of the State. In the passage from the 1990s decade to the years 2000 and particularly, after 2003 when the Lula da Silva government took office, the bourgeois fraction that Tatiana Berringer, again inspired by Poulantzas, calls the 'internal bourgeoisie' replaced big international capital and that fraction of the Brazilian bourgeoisie that was integrated to it, in the post of hegemonic fraction within the power bloc. It is that change, the author argues, in detail and in her own diversified way, which explains the transition from what she refers to as a foreign policy of passive subordination to imperialism that typified the FHC administrations to one that she refers to as conflictive subordination which was to be the mark of the Lula government's international policy.

An important part of Berringer's book is dedicated to showing how that new foreign policy, while still prioritizing the interests of the Big Internal

---

1 Foreword to the Portuguese edition.

Bourgeoisie, also embraced, albeit secondarily, the demands of the grassroots social movements and lower classes. In other words, a fraction of the bourgeoisie integrated to the power bloc in office also integrated a broad political front in which sectors of the common people participated. The author uses the concept 'neo-developmentalist front' to delineate that unstable convergence of heterogeneous interests in the international plane. A particularly illustrative analysis of that thesis is when the author addresses the Lula da Silva Government's decision to abandon the FTAA negotiations. Both the grassroots social movements and important segments of the big internal bourgeoisie were against the great treaty proposal insofar as it would bring about the further opening of the Brazilian economy to an unprecedented extent. Both the upper and lower hierarchical classes acted successfully to bar the FTAA agreement. Berringer also shows how the economic, political and diplomatic support that the Brazilian State provided for left-wing governments in Latin America has been another point of convergence between the international policy of the big internal bourgeoisie and the interests of the common people's movements. The book is surprising even when it addresses well known facts. It is common knowledge that the FTAA is a dead letter. What is less well-known, however, is the convergence of the interests of the big bourgeoisie and those of the common people in opposition to the FTAA; the theoretical framework that Tatiana Berringer uses to support her explanation of that convergence is unprecedented. As the book shows, what is involved is a political front and not a mere coopting of social movement leaders by the State.

Figuratively speaking, we could say that Tatiana Berringer's research, in its use of the Power Bloc concept, has both outward and inward effects. In the outward direction, it shows how the concept can be extended to the international scenario. That scenario appears as a complex intertwining of different hierarchically distributed national power blocs, a tangle that creates relations of alliance, of struggle, of subordination and of resistance among the various bourgeois fractions of different countries' power blocs. Thus, the national State appears as an institution crisscrossed by contradictions among the various fractions of the bourgeoisie who oppose or draw closer to so many other bourgeois fractions of imperialist or dependent countries, according to each one's specific interests and according to the correlation of forces in the international scenario. The interests of Brazil's Big Internal Bourgeoisie are close to the interests of the bourgeoisies of Southern Hemisphere countries like the countries of Latin America, whereas the interests of that fraction of the bourgeoisie integrated to international capital are distant from them and are closer to those hegemonic bourgeois fractions within the power blocs in the imperialist countries. The effect directed inwards is because, as Tatiana Berringer's

FOREWORD                                                                                                          XI

research shows, the capitalist States' social and economic policies, elements that Marxists have traditionally used in their power bloc studies, are insufficient for that analysis. Foreign policy must be added to them if a more reliable conclusion as to the composition of the bloc and determination of its hegemonic fraction is to be attained.

Classes, fractions of classes, power blocs and political fronts: it is the Marxist tradition that inscribes itself in Tatiana Berringer's work. Prestigious authors have previously mooted that a theory of international relations would not fit into Marxist theory. Marxism, they said, was an economic theory, a theory whereby the State was mere reflex of the economic aspect and as such would be incapable of creating concepts for international policy. This book indicates a fertile pathway for showing how wrong that thesis is. It starts from the power bloc concept and thinks through State foreign policy as an extension of the interests of the hegemonic fraction of the power bloc in the international scenario and in that scenario's extant conditions. It is, as passages of Berringer's book make clear, a very different and far more sophisticated approach than that used by the dominant tendencies in the field of international relations studies which operate with a simplistic image of a homogeneous State that would supposedly represent an immutable national interest in the international scenario. Furthermore, regarding another kind of difference, it is a pathway quite distinct from the one that the majority of the scarce Marxist studies in the area of international relations have followed. Those studies, and Tatiana Berringer, make an elucidating comparison on this point, have been inspired by Gramsci's expanded State theory and not by the concept of the State traditionally accepted in Marxist theory.

Tatiana Berringer's book is polemical and that in itself captivates the reader. Part of the accumulated literature on Brazilian foreign policy in the 1990s and years 2000 suggests that the policy changed because of changes in the government team members and changes of their ideas. That explanation, as Berringer's work reveals, leaves out the most important part of the process which was the changes in the correlation of forces among the bourgeois fractions, that is to say, the internal changes in the power bloc, which then enabled the changes of members and ideas in the government teams to take place. No government can remain in power for very long unless it acts in conformity with the extant relations of force among the classes and fractions of classes in the political process. Another part of the literature unilaterally proposes that the change in Brazilian foreign policy stemmed from changes in the international scenario. Simplifying somewhat, it would be like saying that if Fernando Henrique Cardoso and his PSDB had been in power in the years 2000 he would have conducted the same policy as Lula da Silva did, and vice versa; if Lula had come to power in the 1994 presidential elections, he would have conducted the same foreign policy that Fernando Henrique Cardoso did. Albeit not explicitly, that kind of reasoning evokes a fundamental concept that Tatiana Berringer criticizes theoretically; the concept of the State as a homogeneous entity that represents what would be the 'country's permanent national interests' in the international scenario. As its first chapter makes very clear, the theoretical starting point for this book consists of breaking with that concept of the State inherited from the so-called realistic current in the area of international relations, and working, instead, with the concept of the State whereby it is seen as a representative and organizer of the interests of the power bloc and of the fraction that occupies the hegemonic position in that political condominium.

The reader will encounter other stimulating and thoughtful polemics in which the book engages with the accumulated thematic literature. Brazilian critical thinking has split in its analyses of the Fernando Henrique Cardoso and Luís Inácio Lula da Silva governments. There are so many polemics. Tatiana Berringer's book is part of a line of research that has been unfolded at Unicamp's Marxist Studies Center (*Centro de Estudos Marxistas* – Cemarx). The book problematizes theses and current interpretations in quite distinct ways. The systematic demonstration of the differences separating the FHC government's foreign policy from that of the Lula da Silva government questions a thesis that was current in the decade 2000 to 2010 whereby there was a supposed continuity between the FHC era and the Lula era; the signs of an actual discontinuity between the two eras stem from the conflicts, which albeit involving the lower classes, are in fact conflicts within the power bloc itself. That demonstration not only problematizes those analyses that take the bourgeoisie to be a homogeneous bloc with no splits, but also those that affirm or suggest that the Lula governments were 'workers governments'. Lastly, the identification of the coherence and constancy of the Lula government foreign policy contradicts a thesis present in more recent debates whereby the PT-run governments operated a Bonapartist foreign policy, in the sense of being a zigzagging policy which at one and the same time expressed and maintained an unstable and moving correlation of forces.

This book addresses foreign policy but in a way that inserts its research object in the great debates on contemporary Brazilian policy.

*Armando Boito, Jr.*

# Preface

This book is the consolidation of a research project I have pursued throughout the years since earning my degree: a Marxist interpretation of Brazilian foreign policy in the 1990s, and the years 2000 and 2010. It has taken eight years to get to the point of publishing it in English. During the coursework in international relations, I began to experience a certain uneasiness, as many international relations students do, on perceiving that the debates in this area were far removed from Latin American reality. Furthermore, there was little or no emphasis on critical studies and, particularly, on Marxism. In those years of my Master's degree courses, I embarked on theoretical research regarding the concepts of the State that studies of international relations use and compared them with Marxism. The respective readings and theoretical reflections enabled me to develop my ideas and acquire the means I would use to conduct the empirical analysis in my doctoral studies. Marxist Nicos Poulantzas has been the theoretical reference for my academic studies.

The rigor of his systematization of the Marxist theory of the State was highly important in enabling me to establish a dialogue between political science and international relations. When comparing realism and Marxism, I was able to discern the points on which the two approaches diverge and those on which they draw closer. I moved away from theses that criticized the centrality of the State, and instead preferred to problematize the function and representation of its class interests. Thus, the Power Bloc concept, the idea that the bourgeoisie is fractional but at the same time maintains its unity around political objectives, was the key to enabling my application of that theoretical arsenal to foreign policy analyses. The State is no longer viewed as a 'billiard ball', a homogeneous entity for organizing the interests of the hegemonic fraction within the power bloc.

I undertook my doctoral research in the ambit of the 'Neoliberalism and Class relations in Brazil' group, linked to Unicamp's Marxist Studies Center. The research also enjoyed the support of the FAPESP thematic project 'Policy and social classes in neoliberal capitalism' (*Política e classes sociais no capitalismo neoliberal*). In addition to reading papers, theses and books on the theme, I undertook a systematic research review of the documents, publications and declarations of the Brazilian internal bourgeoisie, namely, the Federation of Industries of the State of São Paulo (*Federação das Indústrias do Estado de São Paulo* — FIESP), the National Confederation of Industry (*Confederação Nacional da Indústria* — CNI) and the National Confederation of Agriculture (*Confederação Nacional da Agricultura* — CNA) to identify class interests related to Brazilian foreign policy in the period 1995 to 2020. Investigating a more recent period has enabled me to understand the interests of the internal bourgeoisie and the social conflicts present in the social formation of Brazil.

After having defended my PhD thesis, I joined the research project *O Brasil e a França na mundialização neoliberal* (Brazil and France in the neoliberal globalization) financed by the Capes-Cofecub agreement. In 2014, I had the opportunity to carry out a working mission at the Université de Lumiére – Lyon II. I then expanded my research to embrace the 'people's' classes as one of the readers of my doctoral work had challenged me to do. I was also able to further qualify my reflections after I matriculated in the competitive selection process for the post of lecturer in International Relations at the ABC Federal University, in January 2015. The pedagogical proposal of the Batchelor's Degree course was highly innovative, and I became responsible for the study discipline 'Global organized civil society', a situation that led me to a more profound investigation of the role of social movements and trade unionism in foreign policy.

Later, when I was a tutor for Master's degree and PhD students in two of the UFABC's graduate programs (Global Political Economics and International Relations) and coordinator of the research group 'Foreign Policy and social classes' (*Política Externa e classes sociais*) (CNPQ), I continued to review the documents and positions of Brazil's internal bourgeoisie and broadened the outreach of my studies to ponder the role of the middle sectors. In the last eight years I have dedicated myself to reflecting on the Brazilian political crisis and the impeachment of Dilma Rousseff. I conducted an analysis of the alliances among classes and class fractions in the 2016 *Coup d'état* and especially that of the upper middle class (civil servants, doctors, journalists, lawyers, etc.), a sector that has been the driving force behind the process of neofascist resurgence in Brazil. I have also registered some observations regarding the Temer and Bolsonaro governments. In short, I have endeavored to systematize and unify the research I have carried out in the years since I defended my PhD thesis as well as the work of the students I have tutored.

Research into the interests of classes and class fractions and into Brazilian foreign policy has long been a latent research object and aroused much interest both in the Brazilian academic world and beyond it. I hope it will have the same impact on the English-speaking audience.

# Acknowledgements

This book is the result of exchanges and debates with colleagues and students over the last few years, especially those devoted to the study of Brazilian politics and the work of Nicos Poulantzas. I would like to highlight the excellent supervision and friendship of Armando Boito, Jr., who coordinates the group 'Neoliberalism and Social Classes'. In a special way, I thank my colleagues Leonardo Granato, Caio Bugiato, Danilo Martuscelli and Mariana Davi for their constant readings and dialogues. I also thank the members of the group 'Foreign Policy and Social Classes' (CNPq) and the colleagues from the Brazilian Foreign Policy and International Insertion Observatory (opeb.org) of the Federal University of the ABC.

I thank my friends and family for their encouragement and for understanding my absences.

This book would not be possible without the generosity and friendship of Prof. Alfredo Saad-Filho, who accepted me to be a Visiting Scholar at SOAS in 2016 and encouraged me to take this step. An earlier version of Chapters 1, 2, 3 and 5 and Armando Boito's Foreword in this volume appeared in my 2015 Portuguese publication, *A burguesia brasileira e a política externa nos governos FHC e Lula* Curitiba, Editora Appris.

Finally, I thank FAPESP (Fundacão de Amparo À Pesquisa Do Estado de São Paulo) for the resources that ensured the payment of the translation of this book into English by Martin Charles Nicholl through grant #2021/00290-5.

# Figures and Tables

### Figures

1. Power blocs and international relations   32
2. Direct investment flows 1995 to 2010 in US millions   84
3. Brazilian balance of trade 1998–2010   85
4. Brazilian exports to imperialist countries (IC) and dependent countries (DC) by destinations and by values – in billions of dollars   122
5. Latin America and the Caribbean: Outward foreign direct investment, 1992–2011 (in millions of dollars)   137
6. Brazilian balance of trade 2010–2022   211

### Tables

1. Hegemonic fraction and political stance of the state in each historical conjuncture   30
2. Latin America and the Caribbean: Foreign direct investment inflows by receiving country or territory 2000–2011 (millions of dollars and relative difference in percentages)   135
3. Latin America and the Caribbean: Foreign direct investment outflows by country 2000–2011 (millions of dollars and relative difference in percentages)   136
4. API project details   141

# Abbreviations and Acronyms

| | |
|---|---|
| ALBA | *Aliança Bolivariana para os Povos de Nossa América* (Bolivarian Alliance for the Peoples of Our America) |
| BM | Banco Mundial (World Bank-WB) |
| BNDES | Banco Nacional de Desenvolvimento Econômico e Social (Social and Economic Development Bank) |
| CAMEX | Câmara de Comércio Exterior (Chamber of Foreign Trade) |
| CDS | Conselho de Defesa Sul-americano (South American Defense Council) |
| CEB | Coalizão Empresarial Brasileira (Brazilian Business Coalition) |
| CELAC | Comunidade dos Estados latino-americanos e caribenhos (Community of Latin American and Caribbean States) |
| CNA | Confederação Nacional da Agricultura (National Confederation of Agriculture) |
| CNI | Confederação Nacional da Indústria (National Confederation of Industry) |
| CONTAG | Confederação Nacional dos Trabalhadores na Agricultura (National Confederation Workers in Agriculture) |
| COSIPLAN | Conselho Sul-americano de Infraestrutura e Planejamento (South America Infrastructure and Planning Council) |
| CUT | Central Único dos Trabalhadores (Unified Workers Central) |
| DEM | Democratas ('Democratas' political party) |
| FCES | Fórum Consultivo Econômico e Social do Mercosul (MERCOSUR Social and Economic Consultative Forum) |
| FIESP | Federação das Indústrias do Estado de São Paulo (Federation of Industries of the State of São Paulo) |
| FMI | Fundo Monetário Internacional (International Monetary Fund-IMF) |
| FOCEM | Fundo de Correção das Assimetrias (Fund for the Correction of Assymetries) |
| FTAA | Área de Livre Comércio das Américas- ALCA (Free Trade Area of the Americas) |
| IDE | Investimento Externo Direto (Direct Foreign Inverstment-DFI) |
| MDA | Ministério do Desenvolvimento Agrário (Ministry of Agrarian Development) |
| MDIC | Ministério do Desenvolvimento, da Indústria e do Comércio Exterior (Ministry of Development, Industry and Foreign Trade) |
| MERCOSUR | Mercado Comum do Sul (Southern Common Market) |
| MST | Movimento dos Trabalhadores Rurais Sem Terra (Landless Rural Workers Movement) |
| NAFTA | Tratado Norte-Americano de Livre-Comércio (North American Free Trade Area) |

| | |
|---|---|
| OCDE | Organização para Cooperação e Desenvolvimento Econômico (Organization for Economic Cooperation and Development-OECD) |
| OMC | Organização Mundial do Comércio (World Trade Organization – WTO) |
| ONU | Organização das Nações Unidas (United Nations Organization-UNO) |
| PSDB | Partido da Social Democracia Brasileira (Brazilian Social Democracy Party) |
| PSOL | Partido Socialismo e Liberdade (Socialism and Liberty Party) |
| PSTU | Partido Socialista dos Trabalhadores Unificado (United Workers Socialist Party) |
| PT | Partido dos Trabalhadores (Workers Party) |
| SACU | União Aduaneira da África Austral (Southern African Customs Union-SACU) |
| TEC | Tarifa Externa Comum (Common External Tariff) |
| UE | União Europeia (European Union-EU) |
| UNASUR | União das Nações Sul-americanas (Union of South American Nations) |

# Introduction

> The foreign policy of Luiz Inácio Lula da Silva, reflects, at least in part, the traditional positions that the Workers Party (PT) accumulated after the late 1970s.
> VIGEVANI & CEPALUNI, 2011, p.273

∴

> due to his excessive protagonist participation, the irrefutable success of presidential diplomacy was inseparably bound to the charisma of President Lula and became unduly personalistic and untransferable.
> RICUPERO, 2010, p.38

∴

> There is a certain ambivalence in our foreign policy because, on the horizon there is an old idea … on the horizon is the idea of the North against the South. That is a mistake.
> CARDOSO, 2009

∴

> Brazil, with its legitimate aspiration to take on a role in global leadership cannot dispense with being able to count on a strong industry.
> SKAF, HENRIQUE & SILVA, 2011

∴

The above quotations illustrate part of the debate on Brazilian foreign policy during the Lula administrations. The Brazilian State's performance was notably outstanding during the Fernando Henrique Cardoso (hereafter referred to as FHC) and Lula presidencies. The interpretations are very different. To some the Brazilian State had become an imperialist one (Fontes, 2010) while to others foreign policy after the year 2003 represented the ideals of the PT and for that reason it was the most successful area of the Lula presidential administrations.

There were even those who declared that Brazil had become a power (Lima, 2006) or that Brazilian diplomacy had committed great blunders and harmed the national interest. Those comparisons and the plurality of interpretations of the two foreign policies justify interest in the research object of this book.

What characteristics did Brazilian foreign policy acquire in the 1990s and how did it become modified in the years 2000? Were there any changes made to it between the FHC and Lula governments? Those are the questions this book has endeavored to answer. As part of the collective research of the 'Neoliberalism and social classes' (CNPq) group, the book sets out to identify the class interests that determined the Brazilian State's position in the international power structure during the FHC and Lula administrations.

The thesis being defended is that there was an inflection in the foreign policy of the Brazilian State during the transition from the FHC administration to the Lula administration and that it was linked to the new configuration of the Power Bloc, namely, the ascending trajectory of the internal bourgeoisie within the Power Block itself. To Poulantzas (1978) the internal bourgeoisie would be that class fraction occupying an intermediate position between the purchasing bourgeoisie and the national bourgeoisie. It does not perform as a mere chain of transmission for imperialist interests, as the purchasing bourgeoisie does, nor can it be characterized as a national bourgeoisie capable of involving itself in an anti-imperialist struggle. It is a fraction whose behavior not only reflects the dependence on external capital that it maintains but is also linked to the fact that, for it to survive, the State needs to limit the presence of external capital in the heart of the national social formation and that leads it to assume conflicts with imperialism, however sporadic they might be.

The Brazilian internal bourgeoisie is made up of the big national capital, state-run corporations and occasionally, multinational companies. It is a heterogeneous fraction embracing various sectors, including the manufacturing industry, construction companies, agribusiness corporations, state-run corporations, mining companies and others. In the course of the Lula administrations, that heterogenous fraction gained strength, benefitting from the government's social and economic policies. This research focusses on foreign policy and the thesis is that the internal bourgeoisie united around a set of common interests which basically were: (I) the conquest of new markets for the exportation of its products; (II) direct investment overseas; (III) prioritization of its products and services in State and State corporation purchasing; (IV) greater protection for the domestic market.

Supposedly that bourgeois fraction would have called on the State for multifaceted support to insert itself in the world markets and to protect the domestic market in some way. It was precisely for this reason that, unlike the FHC governments in which the hegemony of national and international financial capital led the state to adopt a stance of passive subordination to imperialism, in the Lula governments, the main focus of the State's international actions was on: emphasizing South-South relations; setting priority on South America; creating South-South coalitions such as the India, Brazil and South Africa (IBSA) Forum, the G-20 Trade group and the BRICS group made up of Brazil, India, China and South Africa, as well as various other groups.

The intention of the text unfolding in these pages is to demonstrate what the Brazilian State's main actions in the international scenario have been and how, in a strategic way, it has coherently linked the overall orientation of its foreign policy to the interests of the internal Brazilian bourgeoisie. To that end, the research has sought out, and drawn on not only secondary sources (books, articles, theses and dissertations) but also primary ones (the notes, manifestations and declarations of class entities) which have helped in the identification of the demands and positions of the classes of the various segments that integrate the internal bourgeoisie, in regard to the Brazilian State's international performance.

There are very few studies that endeavor to identify the extant relationship of the interests of class entities such as the São Paulo Federation of Industries (*Federação das Indústrias de São Paulo* – FIESP), the National Confederation of Industry (*Confederação Nacional da Indústria* – CNI), and the Overseas Trade Chamber of the National Confederation of Agriculture (*Confederação Nacional da Agricultura, Câmara de Comércio Exterior* – CNA) with foreign policy. The studies of Ardissone (1999), Oliveira (2003), Carvalho (2003), Cruz and Silva (2011), Bonomo (2006) and, Bezerra (2008) basically concentrate on a given international negotiation or on a specific theme or entity. They do not address the overall set of the Brazilian State's actions in the international scenario. Furthermore, their analyses are based on other theoretical reference frameworks, especially the two-level game theory as proposed by Robert Putnam (1988). To those extant foreign policy analyses, our thesis sought to introduce a Marxist analysis inspired on the Power Bloc concept that Nicos Poulantzas developed.

The book is divided into six chapters. The first chapter presents the theoretical framework used and dialogues with the international relations studies and with foreign policy analyses. The proposed analysis considers the relations of a hegemonically weak fraction in the heart of the power bloc with the external capital, to gain an understanding of the State's political position in the international structure in a given historical conjuncture.

The second and third chapters address the power bloc's relations with foreign policy in FHC's and Lulas governments. First, there is a description of how the relations among the class fractions in the interior of the bloc became configured and then the text seeks to establish the relationship between the State's political position in the international power structure and the interests of the hegemonic fraction. Thus, Chapter 2 defines what neoliberalism is taken to mean in this context and describes how that model came to be implemented in heart of the Brazilian social formation. It shows how the classes and class fractions organized and manifested themselves to address the main policies that the Brazilian state adopted. Then comes an analysis of the relationship between the hegemony of national and international financial capital and the foreign policies of the FHC administrations. Attention is also concentrated on investigating how the internal bourgeoisie agglutinated in order to weather the impacts of the trade opening process and especially in connection with the negotiations for the Free Trade Area of the Americas (FTAA). Chapter 3 offers a lengthier explanation of what neo-developmentalism is understood to be and establishes the relationship between that program and the Brazilian State's political position in the international power structure during the Lula administrations and, more specifically, between the interests of the internal bourgeoisie and the South-South foreign policy. Chapter 4 addresses Brazil's relations with South America. It is divided into two sections: the role of the State and the corporations in the regional integration processes, and the role of the grassroots social movements and trade unionism in regional integration. The first section is designed to contribute to the political left's debate on imperialism and Brazilian sub-imperialism whereas, in the second, the interest is in pondering on the limitations and advances of south American regionalism during the PT administrations, for the Brazilian grassroots and the trade unions.

Chapter 5 summarizes the years under FHC and Lula.

Lastly Chapter 6 addresses the years from 2010 to 2021, with a systematization of the relations between the Power Bloc and the foreign policy of the Dilma governments in an endeavor to identify elements that can enable an understanding of the political crisis and the 2016 Coup as well as the changes that have occurred in Brazilian State's international insertion in the years that followed it.

CHAPTER 1

# Power Bloc: Brazilian Theory and Policy

This chapter is based on Nicos Poulantzas's theoretical contribution, especially his Power Bloc concept and its ramifications. The chapter is divided into two sections. The first is a dialogue with the international relations studies, aiming to demonstrate the differences and proximities of realism and Marxism by making a comparison between the concepts of the State of realist Hans Morgenthau and Marxist Nicos Poulantzas. The second section addresses the challenge of thinking how the theoretical categories that Poulantzas proposed could be of use to foreign policy analyses. It also debates the main foreign policy analysis theories, namely, Robert Putnam's two-level game theory, Charles Hermann's foreign policy change model and Graham Allison's bureaucratic politics models. The focus is on demonstrating the relationship between the Power Bloc and the State's political stance in a given historical conjuncture.

## 1      Theory: The Power Bloc and International Relations

Beginning with the relations between realism and Marxism in the extant international relations studies, it is well known that Marxism has not occupied an important place in the academic debate on international relations. Generally, the realists have sought to limit the application of Marxism, treating it as an ideology merely and exclusively interested in constructing socialism, or they have addressed it as a limited interpretation of reality due to the fact that it only deals with economic considerations. That is readily apparent in the following texts from Hans Morgenthau's (1948) book *Politics among Nations*:

> Marxist theory rests on the conviction, which serves as the foundation for all Marxist thinking, that all political problems are a reflection of economic forces (p.103).
>
> To Marx and his fellows, Capitalism is at the root of international discord and war. They declare that international socialism will end the struggle for power on the international scene and usher in permanent peace (p.61).

Along the same lines, jurist and political scientist Norberto Bobbio (1988) raised the following questions: is there a Marxist theory of international relations? What is that? In a similar way to his treatment of the Marxist theory of the State (Bobbio, 1979), that author gave negative answers to those questions and made two accusations against Marxism: (I) the object of Marx and Engels' reflections was not war, but revolution; and (II) the Leninist theory of imperialism is reductionist insofar as it is based on the primacy of economic aspects over political ones.

Regarding Bobbio's first criticism, it would be no exaggeration to state that, like Morgenthau, he reduces Marxism to a revolutionary ideology. That aspect is indeed present in historical materialism but not it alone. Historical materialism is actually a theory of history and, in the aspect of greater interest to us, a theory of society and politics which articulates, within a complex whole, social productive forces and production relations, economic interests, class struggles around the distribution of power and resources, relations of domination, etc. In that open instrumentation, Marxism conjugates the economic analysis with the analyses of juridical-political structure and the active ideologies. That junction makes it possible to think through not only the reproduction of social relations in their various spheres (economic, political and ideological) spheres but also the ways the actions of the agents, the social classes and their political organizations overcome those structures (Althusser, 1999).

Marx's basic presupposition was that, in order to transform a concrete reality, it was necessary to be profoundly knowledgeable about it. That is the task he set himself in his works: a meticulous, in-depth study of the forms of organization and reproduction of capitalist society. In the view of French philosopher Louis Althusser (1999), Marx and Engels' contribution to the social sciences was just as profound and revolutionary as the contribution of Thales to mathematics or of Galileo to physics. They inaugurated a veritable science of history, a new scientific continent.

In the specific field of International Relations, we consider Marxism to be capable of explaining not only wars but all the subjacent relations leading up to such extreme episodes. Without due study of the political social and economic relations among the States and of how those relationships between what is produced in the heart of a given social formation and how they are reflected in the international scenario. Then it is the theory of international relations itself which is restricted and limited. For there to be any understanding of diplomatic traditions, the institutional framework, and changes in foreign policy, they must be situated in the relations among the different social classes in both the domestic and the international ambits.

Fred Halliday (1994), an important thinker in the area of international relations, states that Marxism is widely acknowledged as having developed analytically fertile work in sociology, history and other social sciences and there is enormous potential waiting to be exploited for its use in international relations studies. Although very few Marxists have dedicated themselves to a systematic study of wars, it could be said that the debate between Vladimir I. Lenin (1999) and Karl Kautsky (2008) on Imperialism and Wars preceded the later debate of idealists versus realists after the first World War.[1]

In fact, that earlier debate, which took place in the heart of the international socialist movement, is very close to the discussions that had their origins in the international relations studies at the beginning of the 20th century. We can safely say that, despite the differences among the arguments that the academics mobilized, Lenin was very close to the position defended by the realists, whereas Kautsky ended by getting closer to the idealists.

That is why, in the face of Bobbio's accusation regarding Lenin's economic reductionism, we identify five presuppositions in Lenin's work 'Imperialism: the highest form of Capitalism' (1999). They indicate the classic nature of the work, whose contribution has by no means been exhausted by historical changes or the passing of time. Furthermore, they show that Marxism was not reduced to being a mere economic analysis when reflecting on international relations. Lenin's presuppositions when analyzing international relations were as follows:

1) There is unequal development among the nations, related to the Imperialist States' domination of the colonies and/or the dependent States.
2) There is a dispute among Imperialist States for the dominance of markets, raw materials, and for the control of territories and the natural resources of colonies and dependent States.
3) There is no possibility of peace as long as society is split into social classes.
4) The real class nature of a war cannot be found in its diplomatic history, but in the analysis of the objective situation of the ruling classes of all the belligerent powers
5) There is a relationship of mutual influence between civil wars and imperialism. It means that a State's domestic policy and foreign policy are intertwined.

It is also worth stating that, to Lenin, imperialism was not just the actual stage of capitalism, as the following text shows.

> Colonial policy and imperialism existed before the latest stage of capitalism, and even before capitalism. Rome, founded on slavery, pursued a colonial policy and practiced imperialism. But "general" disquisitions

---

[1] Kautsky's text 'Imperialism and War' was written in 1914 and Lenin's 'Imperialism: the highest form of capitalism', in 1917.

on imperialism, which ignore, or put into the background, the fundamental difference between socio-economic systems, inevitably turn into the most vapid banality or bragging, like the comparison: "Greater Imperialism, the Highest Stage of Capitalism, Rome and Greater Britain". Even the capitalist colonial policy of previous stages of capitalism is essentially different from the colonial policy of finance capital.

LENIN, 1999, p.86–87

While it is true that his main concern was to identify the specificities of imperialism under the hegemony of financial capitalism, nevertheless, the text is full of elements that go far beyond a simple conjunctural analysis. Arguing against Kautsky's (2008) 'super-imperialism' idea, whereby the monopolies could lead to the constitution of a 'Holy Alliance' of the imperialist States so that the arms race would then come to an end, Lenin said that:

The question has only to be presented clearly for any other than a negative answer to be impossible. This is because the only conceivable basis under capitalism for the division of spheres of influence, interests, colonies, etc., is a calculation of the strength of those participating in the division, their general economic, financial, military strength, etc. And the strength of these participants in the division does not change to an equal degree, for the even development of different undertakings, trusts, branches of industry, or countries is impossible under capitalism. ...

Therefore, in the realities of the capitalist system, and not in the banal philistine fantasies of English parsons, or of the German "Marxist", Kautsky, "inter-imperialist" or "ultra-imperialist" alliances, no matter what form they may assume, whether of one imperialist coalition against another, or of a general alliance embracing all the imperialist powers, are inevitably nothing more than a "truce" in periods between wars. Peaceful alliances prepare the ground for wars, and in their turn grow out of wars; the one conditions the other, producing alternating forms of peaceful and non-peaceful struggle on one and the same basis of imperialist connections and relations within world economics and world politics.

LENIN, 1999, p.116

Those arguments roughly indicate Lenin's proximity to the realist approach to international relations. E. Carr (2001), author of 'The Twenty Years' Crisis', recognized that convergence of realism and Marxism and was responsible for introducing the debate between realism and idealism into the studies of international relations at the beginning of the 20th century. According to that author, Marxism and realism address politics as it really is, conflictive. That is why they are both in opposition to the idealism of Kant.

Waever (1996) follows the same line as Carr (2001) and describes in detail what he called the 'inter-paradigmatic' debate among realism, liberalism and Marxism that occurred in the 1970s and 1980s. Regardless of those aspects of proximity, it is important to underscore that Marxists understand the origin of conflicts among States to lie in their classist natures. So that, despite the points of contact between realism and Marxism, one should not lose sight of the fact that they are quite different theoretical currents.

Realism was to become one of the most-used theoretical frameworks in international relations studies. The authors of that current based themselves on classic political theory and especially on Machiavelli and Hobbes in their thinking on international policy. The main points they assert are: (I) the centrality of the State; and (II) the permanent presence of conflicts in the international environment. Actually, the State is just as much the central category in international relations for realists as it is for Marxists. However, as Halliday (1994) has pointed out, the two conceptions are quite distant from one another.

Those currents that criticized realism, especially neo-liberalism (Keohane and Nye, 1973), supported their arguments for the reduction of the State's role in the 'neoliberal globalization' context on the emergence of supposed 'new actors' in international relations, namely, the transnational corporations, NGOs, international organizations, social movements, international migrations and so on. They did so without bothering to proffer a definition of the concept of 'the State'. What distinguishes our position in this work from those critics is that our objective is not that of discussing the weight of the State in international relations, insofar as we even have a divergent opinion on its centrality, rather, our objective has been to present the theoretical instrumentation that Nicos Poulantzas systematized as an alternative for the study of international relations and for foreign policy analyses.

It must be said that even though the State is the fundamental analytical category of realist theories of international relations,[2] we have been unable to find, among the works of realist authors, any clear, precise definition regarding the State. It seems that the adepts of the realist current presume that the reader knows what is meant by it, for the State only appears in the term

---

2   We would underscore that in the renewed version of realism, neorealism, the State is maintained as an analytical category, and the leading author of the neorealist approach, Waltz (1979), likens the international scenario to the metaphorical model of a billiard table where the States are the balls, solid and undividable, colliding with one another in their quest for security.

'practical State', that is, in the form of an empirical category. According to Fred Halliday (1994, p.78):

> It is indeed paradoxical that a concept so central to the whole discipline should escape explication as this one has. One can find many discussions of war, sovereignty, institutions, and so forth but one can search in vain in the textbooks for comparable discussion of the State. International relations theorists assume we know what it is: e.g. Bull, that it is a political community. Waltz, that it is in practice coextensive with the nation. The reason is that International Relations as a whole takes as given one specific definition: what one may term the national-territorial totality. Thus the State (e.g. Britain, Russia, America etc.) comprises in conceptual form what is denoted visually on a political map – viz. the country as a whole and all within it: territory, government, people, society.

One of the reasons for choosing Poulantzas was the fact that his theory of the State gives a straight answer to the realists' criticisms of Marxism. Poulantzas does not consider that politics is a reflection of the economic forces as the realists presume. The study object in his work *Political Power and Social Classes* is 'politics' in its aspects as a complex of structures, institutions and practices distinctive of the capitalist mode of production. While in his explanation Poulantzas maintains the primacy of economic determination, he simultaneously attributes weight to the political ideological and conjunctural determinations. Furthermore, his analysis is not centered on the transition to socialism. Many of his peers accused him of having centered his studies only on understanding the reproduction of the capitalist mode of production, leaving aside questions regarding the socialist transition process.

Two important defenders of realism, the aforementioned Noberto Bobbio (1988) and Stephan Krasner, identified the possibility of using Poulantzas's instrumentation for international relations studies. Both considered that if the concept of the State's relative autonomy that Poulantzas put forward were used in international relations studies, it could indeed contribute greater explanatory power than the instrumentalist vison of the State that many Marxists defended.[3] The relative autonomy idea opens up the possibility of deeper analysis of the relationship between the State and the dominant (or ruling) classes. It is worth mentioning that Rosenberg (2001), Linklater (2001b) and Callinicos (2007) also made comparisons between the realist and Marxist concepts of the

---

3  For example, Ralph Miliband (1972).

State. However, they based themselves on concepts of the State different from the one we use here.

Poulantzas's theoretical systematization enables the extraction of elements for the characterization of various types of State – slavery-based, feudalist and capitalist. In general, the State is an institution that organizes the domination of a set of social classes over others, having as its main function, the reproduction of the social totality (Saes, 1985a). To Poulantzas, the capitalist State is different from the other types of State because the class-based political domination is not readily apparent in its institutions. Thus, the State presents itself as a National State of the people, concealing the class contradictions present inside the social formation that it organizes and represents. It organizes its institutions around the principles of freedom and equality of the citizens, the bases for the sovereignty and legitimacy of that State. "The modern capitalist state thus presents itself as embodying the general interest of the whole of society, i.e. as substantiating the will of that "body politic"-which is the "nation" (Poulantzas, 1975, p.123)".

In the pre-capitalist States, the institutions were monopolies of the members of the dominant class and the law did not conceal the exploiting nature of the relations of production. It was an essentially unequal law. The slavery-based States denied the slave a legal personality insofar as he was determined to be the property of the master. In feudalism, society's division into Estates and Orders of the Realm corresponded to an inequality in legal status between the lords and the serfs. The courts were all composed of nobles and clergy. Posts of command in the armed forces and in the State were occupied according to estate-based criteria or they were sold as family titles. There was therefore no servile class participation in the State apparat. "Feudal juridical ideology made no effort to conceal the exploitation, rather it presented it as being necessary" (Boito, 2007, p.71).

According to Poulantzas (1975), the capitalist State seems to represent the political unity of the people-nation; it is both able to and does' present itself' as a "neutral body embodying the general-interest"; and its political functioning vis-à-vis the classes is thus systematically masked. The relationship between territory and national community is what architects the nation ideologically and conceals the contradictions present in the capitalist relations of production.

The State is the official representative of society, "the place where the unity of a [social] formation is deciphered" (Poulantzas, 1975, p.47). The social formation, to Poulantzas, is a concrete combination of various 'pure' modes of production with the dominance of one mode over the others. That domination is a complex reality marked by unequal development. Just as various nationalities may live together consubstantiated in the national ideology so various forms of production may co-exist in a given social formation, pre-capitalist forms, forms typical of patrimonialism, or forms associated to capitalist relations, but always with the predominance of one. It is precisely on the social formation that Marxism develops its analysis of the concrete reality. Thus, the State and the mode of production are formal-abstract concepts that embrace ideological and political relations and relations of production. The modes of production, however, can only exist and reproduce themselves in historically determined social formations.

The capitalist State's juridical-political structure is formed by capitalist law and bureaucratism. The relations of production depend on those structures which in turn have a doubly isolating effect, namely, the constitution of juridically atomized individuals and the representation of unity through the creation of the 'people-nation' political entity. Through it the State exercises the function of disorganizing the dominated classes while organizing the dominant ones.

Morgenthau (1948) considers that the 'Nation-State' is introduced in the discussion merely to illustrate the difference between domestic policy and international relations. In other words, the description of the national environment has been used as a standard of comparison to define international relations. On the one hand there is a society governed by laws and an accompanying coercive apparat in which social peace and order exist. On the other, there is an anarchic society, that is, one without a central power. Accordingly, what characterizes the international system is the permanence of the Hobbesian-type State (the struggle of all against all).

To that realist the nation-State is a compulsory organization of society. It is an institution that enables the legal continuity of the nation and that possesses the necessary institutional bodies for the implementation of laws and social changes. The State apparat concerns itself with maintaining the *status quo* to which it owes its very existence. Accordingly, it uses power and force to constrain any eventual disturbance of the order that may arise in the heart of society (Morgenthau, 1948).

Morgenthau (1948) states that:

> Peace among social groups within the State reposes upon a dual foundation: the disinclination of the members of society to break the peace and their inability to break the peace if they should be so inclined. Individuals will be unable to break the peace if overwhelming power makes an attempt to break it a hopeless undertaking. They will be disinclined to break the peace under two conditions. On the one hand they must feel

loyalties to the society as a whole which surpass their loyalties to any part of it. On the other hand, they must be able to expect from society at least an approximation to justice through the at least partial satisfaction of their demands. The presence of these three conditions – overwhelming force, supra-sectional loyalties, expectation of justice – makes peace possible within states. The absence of these conditions on the international scene evokes the danger of war.

For the realists, even though a national community is made up of various interest groups, it is unified nationally. The nation is an abstract entity of individuals who share symbologies such as language, customs, history, hero figures, etc. Those symbologies, in turn, construct a collective imagery which comes to be the national identity. Morgenthau uses a concept of the State that he declares to be different from that of Marxism and from that of the 19th century liberal doctrine. Liberal doctrine held that society's organized violence was completely neutral whereas for Marxism, it is a tool that the dominant or ruling class uses to maintain its dominance over the classes it exploits. Morgenthau's position is that the State's use of force is not entirely neutral, as the State is in fact at the service of maintaining the *status quo* which gave rise to it (Morgenthau, 1948).

That maintenance of social cohesion is therefore a point of contact between realism and Marxism. However, unlike Marxism and more like pluralism in political science, Morgenthau sees the dominance, not of a class, but of various interest groups such as ethnic, cultural, religious groups as well as economic groups.

For Marxism, even though free and equal individuals do appear in regimes of exchange, in the production structure, the agents occupy contradictory positions defined by the social division of labor in which there is private appropriation of labor, and the direct producers are subjected to a collective production process. That is to say, relations of domination and exploitation crosscut the most important moments in all social and individual lives, namely the moments of social production. At the same time that all integrate the same national community, they acquire economic interests, forms of awareness and political projects that are contradictory and, in some circumstances, even antagonistic.

Thus 'nation' corresponds to the ideological effect of representing the unity of the 'people-nation' which alludes to the reality of individuals atomized within a given territory. The capitalists, experiencing the competition of the market, find it difficult to organize themselves as a distinct social class. Thus, it is up to the State to organize the Power Bloc – that contradictory unity of bourgeois classes and fractions of classes.

In short, for both Marxism and realism the State's social function is to unify the national society. The difference lies in the fact that for Morgenthau that unity occurs around the national interest, around the State's power in the international scenario, whereas for Poulantzas, the unity of the 'people-nation' occurs around the interests of the dominant classes.

From the Marxist point of view, Morgenthau's definition of the State is superficial and misleading as it addresses the State to appears to be not as it really is. The legitimate monopolization of the use of force and the guaranteed protection of the security of the national territory are not the only functions the State performs. Actually, the State uses those arguments to legitimize itself and, in that way, it conceals the class domination and the nature of government policies. Using the discourse of guarantor of the Democratic Legal State and defender of national sovereignty the State uses force to repress and neutralize collective activities or, in other words, it isolates the social classes deeming them to be 'free and equal' individuals, citizens of the same nation.

Morgenthau (1948) considers that the State's institutional aspect is comprised by the civil and military bureaucracies. Those employees represent the State in the international arena and act according to legal and rational rules. Evincing his affiliation to the theories of the elites, the realist Morgenthau argues that, in the international scenario, only certain individuals are qualified to represent the State. Because the masses are irrational and cannot cast their thoughts beyond the good versus evil disjuncture, it is up to the Statesmen/women to make foreign policy decisions. The people or rather, the amorphous masses are incapable of policy thinking and formulation and accordingly only participate in politics via elections when they decide on and choose the rulers. Against that theoretical background, society is not divided into dominant and dominated classes with relations between them mediated by political representations but, instead, indiscriminately into those who govern and those who are governed.[4]

Poulantzas (1975) also considers that the civil and military bureaucracies make up the State's institutional aspect but that the parliament too may

---

4 Contradictorily, as has been shown, in domestic politics society, is formed by a diversity of groups with expectations of justice that will enable them to present their demands to the democratic control mechanisms: elections, public opinion, parliaments etc. We therefor infer that Morgenthau makes use of incompatible theoretical currents like the theory of elites and pluralism.

eventually be part[5] and furthermore, the State's apparatus entails a strictly hierarchical functioning by the delegation of power and of sectors of functions, a particular internal form of distributing authority and 'legitimation from above', a perpetual referring of responsibilities to the upper echelons. So, to Poulantzas, within the framework of that legitimacy, the State seems to represent the political unity of the people nation presenting itself as a 'neutral body' embodying the general interest and its political functioning vis-à-vis the classes is systematically masked.

To Marxism the capitalist mode of production divides society into producers and non-producers (working class and bourgeoisie) and not into governors and governed or interest groups. The relations between the working class and the bourgeoisie are relations of domination in which there is appropriation of the producer's surplus-labor by the owner of the means of production. The State is responsible for maintaining the relations of production (the political interest of the dominant classes) without any need to interfere directly in production.

According to the Marxist Poulantzas, the State apparat consists of a social category, the bureaucracy. The power of the State itself is in the hands of the dominant class or fraction of a class in the Power Bloc. The civil and military bureaucracy conform a specific social category[6] that serves the interests of the dominant class not because of its class origin but because it carries out the objective role of that State. The role corresponds to the political interests of the dominant class which is to maintain the structure of the relations of production and the organization of a bloc of classes in power. Within the bloc the interests of its component classes or class fractions are served according to an internal hierarchy (Poulantzas, 1975, p.21). Poulantzas went so far as to say that:

The capitalist State best serves the interests of the capitalist class only when the members of this class do not participate directly in the State apparatus, that is to say, when the ruling class is not the politically governing class. In fact, that hegemonic class or fraction which finally holds the political power of a

---

5 Parliament appears as eventually being included because, to Poulantzas, the regime and form of government are subject to the class struggle within the national social formation. The bourgeois State may be democratic or dictatorial, parliamentary or monarchic, biparty and so on. However slight the political liberties that are tolerated may be, the right to property, mercantile circulation, and wage labor are invariably preserved.

6 Marxism distinguishes social classes from social categories, strata and class fractions. It takes into account the economic differentiations and the particular role that the political and ideological relations of each one performs without abandoning its state of class-belonging. Depending on the concrete conjuncture, those categories, strata and fractions may become social forces and be influential in changing the reality.

capitalist formation autonomous from the economic and political struggles, can dominate effectively only if it sets up its economic interests as political interests. "In holding state power, it can. perpetuate existing social relations only through a whole series of compromises which maintain the unstable equilibrium of the classes present, and through a whole range of political organization and particular ideological functioning, by which it manages to present itself as the representative of the general interest of the people and the embodiment of the unity of the nation" (Poulantzas, 1969, p.73).

Poulantzas adopts Gramsci's concept of hegemony and uses it to interpret the struggles and political practices of the ruling classes and affirms that the capitalist State is a State run by a hegemonic class directorate (Poulantzas, 1975). The concept of hegemony indicates the constitution of the political interests of the ruling class by means of the State. Among the classes and fractions of classes within the Power Bloc, one exercises the hegemonic domination when its interests receive priority treatment in the social and economic policy of the State. The policy, however, is presented as if it represented the general interests of the people-nation as a whole, at a given historical juncture.

> The hegemonic class is the one which concentrates "in itself", at the political level, the double function of representing: the general interest of the people/nation and of maintaining a specific dominance among the dominant-classes and fractions. It-does this through its particular relation to the capitalist state.
> POULANTZAS, 1975, p.137

That is why the researcher's task is, on the one hand, to descry, within the State's social and economic policies, the relations among the different measures and stances adopted by the political representatives and the agents of the bureaucracy. On the other, it is to descry the hierarchy within the power bloc and its constant tension with the dominated classes. That must be done at every conjuncture, and, obviously, in relation to foreign policy as well.

Effectively the relations of the State with the set of dominated classes are also understood in the light of that relative autonomy. Poulantzas (1975) argues that the capitalist State constantly addresses the economic interests of the dominated classes but provided it is only up to a certain level or below a certain limit. The overriding objective of the State is to ensure the upkeep of the ruling class's political interests or, rather, the maintenance of the capitalist mode of production. It is worth quoting Poulantzas here:

"Thus, the capitalist state's particular characteristic feature of representing the general interest of a national-popular ensemble is not simply a mendacious mystification, because within these limits it can effectively satisfy some of the economic interests of certain dominated classes. Furthermore, it can do this without however allowing its political power to be affected" (Poulantzas, 1975, p.192).

In that sense the State organizes the ruling classes while maintaining the dominated classes disorganized. However, the dominated classes are not irrational and illuded as Morgenthau would have it. The dominant ideology, in Poulantzas's view, refers to a reality that a society lives in, not necessarily just an abstraction or a misleading illusion.

In turn, the definition of national identity corresponds to what Poulantzas follower Lucio Flávio de Almeida (1995) calls 'nationism'. According to the latter, it would be the dominant ideology that seeks to legitimize the State's role and conceal the class domination that exists within the social formation. The nation is an ideology with the function of maintaining social order inside the State territory. Almeida (1995) states that nationism is the expression of a feeling of belonging to a national community: it is the ideological effect that stems from the representation of the unity of the juridical-political structure of the capitalist mode of production, which is susceptible to class struggle.

The national ideology depends on the hegemonic fraction or class being able to take on different configurations, according to the political conjuncture and the social forces in play.[7] The Nation is therefore an expression typical of the capitalist mode of production. By means of its juridical-political structure, the capitalist State constructs the idea of nation, often supported on a broad set of symbols (language, culture, ethnicity) that contribute towards the representation of unity. In the words of Almeida (1995, p.48):

> The capitalist State functions in a national manner. Its structures and the ideology they articulate with produce the nation. However, the relation seems to be inverted as the State appears as if it were a consequence of the nation, as if it were the final, polished result of a national being which, only then, through the intermediation of the State becomes self-determining and expresses its sovereignty.

To Poulantzas, the dominant ideology does not consist of a mere false awareness in the light of which the bourgeois discourse fools the worker, quite the contrary; the ideology alludes to the reality that the citizens effectively experience and produces an illusion whereby the individuals come to think of themselves as equal members of the society. As Almeida (1995, p.50) puts it:

---

7  It should be remembered that, in many cases, the socialist revolution may be of a national nature.

> Let us remember that in many cases the socialist revolution may be of a nationalist nature. [The national ideology] as we have seen, harks back to capitalism's fundamental ideological relations, for it is strongly bound up with the legitimacy of the bourgeois-type State. In that sense it can be said that in any capitalist social formation, there must have been, in normal times, some kind of 'nationism', that is to say, reproduction of the national ideology. It is a range of practices that express and reproduce the feeling that all the agents of the respective social formation constitute, in some dimension or other, a singular collectivity of essentially equal individuals.

Morgenthau (1948) stated that modern nationalism emerged from the Napoleonic wars; that is to say, after the bourgeois revolutions. Nevertheless, that author fails to acknowledge relations among State, nation and capitalism. It should be remembered that the bourgeois revolutions of the 18th and 19th centuries, among them the Napoleonic wars, were determinant for the formation of the Bourgeois State. Morgenthau fails to consider that kind of State as being related to the capitalist mode of production.

States have the function of maintaining the cohesion of the social formations which are divided up into antagonistic classes. Based on that conception, what is relevant to international relations theory is that belonging to a State, being a Brazilian, French or Indian citizen, does not merely refer to the territory of residence or the language spoken there. It has to do with the economic, political and ideological determinants of that social formation.

For the realist school, the objective of foreign policy is power, construed as being 'the national interest'. The relations among States are of a strictly political nature, that is to say, the only thing they seek is power. In that sense, foreign policy is defined on the basis of three strategies that are designed to increase, conserve and demonstrate power. Those strategies are, respectively:

(I) Imperialism. Altering the power relations of the worldwide system;
(II) *status quo*. Conserving or reacquiring the formerly occupied position in the distribution of power among the nations;
(III) Prestige policy. Demonstrating power by means of diplomatic ceremonies, troop parades, arsenal displays, etc.

Marxism, however, holds that the State actually defends the interests of the Power Bloc but veils that defense with its deceitful 'national interest' discourse. In turn, the realists argue that the States struggle for power and the foreign policies correspond to the national interests of each State, as if that power were indeed real. We therefore infer that Morgenthau entirely ignores the contradictory social bases on which the State is founded and conceives the State as being a homogeneous entity.

The idea of the 'national interest' that Morgenthau defends fails to disclose the interests and causes of conflict or the nature of the diplomatic, trading and war-related activities. According to Marxism the decision-making does not correspond to the interests of all the social classes so, as a general rule, the nation is divided when an external dispute arises. Foreign policy appears to represent the general interest of the nation but, in actual fact, it corresponds to the interests of the Power Bloc. In the words of Oswald Amaral (2007, p.130):

> When it describes the State as a rational agent that always pursues the 'National interest' the realist theory, albeit indirectly, treats the State as being the incarnation of the general will of all the free, isolated individuals thereby contributing to ensure that the agents of production fail to perceive the class relations present in their economic struggles [...] That characteristic of the realist theory is all the more apparent when it emphasizes the international system and refuses to observe the internal factors that actually determine the 'national interest' that the State defends, thereby definitively concealing its class nature.

Based on Poulantzas's contribution, we hold that foreign policy should be analyzed in the perspective of the Power Bloc. That demystifies the idea of the representation of a society's 'general interest' in the international scenario: the State does not represent the interests of the people-nation but instead, those of the ruling classes; that is to say, the Power Bloc. Therefore, foreign policy is not an autonomous State policy as regards the social classes and the governments; the hegemonic fraction of the Power Bloc determines it, and it is permeated by contradictions among classes and fractions of classes. Obviously, the bureaucracy, the diplomatic tradition and their objectives influence that process. However, it is necessary to capture those determinants in the larger sphere of the class conflicts within the social formations and among the classes of the ruling formations in regard to the dependent formations. That will be examined in greater detail in the next item.

## 2   Theory: Power Bloc and Foreign Policy Analysis

Foreign policy analyses (FPA) generally endeavor to understand how foreign policies are formulated and the decision process are taken. They differ from the realists' approach insofar as they introduce an internal scrutiny rather than one external to the State, to ponder on the decision-making processes in this field. To that end they establish a dialogue between the international relations studies and all the other areas of the human sciences such as psychology, political science, geography and others.

The first analytical foreign policy studies date back to the 1960s, but it was in the 1990s, with the end of the cold war, that the different approaches began to gain greater academic space and importance. James Rosenau is considered to be the first author of a foreign policy analysis. Strongly influenced by behaviorism and making use of a broad database, he endeavored to construct typologies of States' behaviors in international politics. Using data on populations, territories, arms, industrialization and other aspects, Rosenau intended to explain why the great powers get involved in conflicts and wars. Critics of Rosenau's work allege that with a database like the one he used, it would not be possible to foresee political crises and so it could be of little use for gaining an understanding of the reaction of a State facing a conflict with another State insofar as the political and social ambit in which the decision-making takes place is highly influential (Hudson & Vore, 1995).

Authors like Laswell, Holsti and Margareth Hermann studied the subjective characteristics of leaders (their beliefs, motivations, decision making styles and so on). Those authors considered that the personalities of heads of State had a strong influence on foreign policy. They too were severely criticized and accused of being reductionists. According to Monica Herz, their studies switched the focus from the State to the individual thereby maintaining the methodological individualism that is present in the realist theory of international relations (Herz, 1994).

At a later stage, foreign policy analyses began to incorporate new variables like the role of State bureaucracies (Allison), the pressure stemming from domestic groups, (Robert Dahl), the political culture (Almond and Verba), the relation between the political regime and foreign policy (Russet), and the role of the legislative branch and other elements (Hudson & Vore, 1995).

Two points characterize the foreign policy analyses that we agree with, namely: 1) the criticism of the conception of the State and national interest that the realists use in their theories of international relations; and 2) the thesis whereby there is an imbrication of States' foreign policies and domestic policies contrary to the suppositions made in realism-inspired studies. We choose to dialogue with three of the many extant foreign policy analyses: the bureaucratic policy studies of Allison (1990), the two-level game theory of Robert Putnam (1988) and the model proposed by Hermann (1990).

After a brief presentation of each of those approaches to clarify our differences in regard to them, we will develop the main theoretical concepts for a Marxist analysis of foreign policies – still a rare approach in the respective studies. It must be remembered that our theoretical instrumentation rests on Nicos Poulantzas's contributions in his works *Political Power and Social Classes*, and *Classes in Contemporary Capitalism*.

Graham Allison (1990) considers that the foreign policy decision-making process can be explained on the basis of the interaction among the various bureaucracies; that is to say, the State is not necessarily a homogeneous entity as the realist theoreticians would have it. Instead, it is an agglomeration of institutions each with its own rules and interests and, in the face of a decision on international performance, they may cooperate with it or oppose it. In that sense, there are three theoretical models for the occurrence of that process: the classical model, the organizational model and the bureaucratic model. Examining them one by one we have:

1) In the classical model a single rational actor such as the head of the State administration makes the decision. In this case the decision is consensual and guided by considerations of 'the national interest of the State', namely, security and defense. The policy choice seeks to maximize the gains in the international scenario.

2) The organizational model is based on the idea that the State is made up of a set of organizations with different rules and logics and their own ways of functioning. Each one of them retains specific knowledge regarding its area of activities. For that reason, a foreign policy decision is based on a coordination among the State's various bureaucracies assisting in the decision-making process. In other words, the decision is the result of an interaction of bureaucracies that takes place prior to the respective international action.

3) In the bureaucratic model there is the appearance of a competitive dispute among the various State actors. It is a hierarchic dispute among the upper echelons of the bureaucracies. For example, it may be between the heads of the Department of defense and the State Department and the Office of the President or between the head of the armed forces and the Executive branch. The head of each State institution is imbued with a different perception of the political conflict so each institution's representative lobbies for the conduct it wishes the State to adopt. Thus, they negotiate the decision politically and the wish of a political coalition or of an individual State institution will eventually prevail.

In turn, the theoretical scheme that Putnam (1988) developed, the two-level game theory, considers that the conflict among the different interest groups of the domestic society to be a determinant factor in the decision of the State representative in the international scenario. According to that author, international negotiations correspond to a two-level game with level I the international level and level II, the domestic one. In that perspective the intersection of those two spheres would determine foreign policy. The challenge facing the negotiator is to maximize the gains in the international sphere while at the same time guaranteeing an equilibrium or forming a coalition among the domestic society's different interest groups. Putnam explains that:

> It can be useful to conceive the political struggles of the various international negotiations as if they were a two-level game. At the national level the domestic groups pursue their interests pressuring the government to adopt policies that favor them, and the politicians seek power by constituting coalitions among those groups. At the international level, the national governments strive to maximize their skill at satisfying the domestic pressures while minimizing the adverse consequences of the external evolutions Decision makers cannot ignore either of the two games.
> PUTNAM, 1988, p.151

In other words, for an international negotiation to obtain the greatest possible 'win set', it must harmonize, as much as possible, the internal demands and conflicts of the different domestic societies involved. The political actions and the conflicts among the domestic groups (Level II) vary according to the degree to which the issue at stake has been politicized, affecting the difficulty of the negotiator's task. That is why when negotiators participate in an international negotiation, they need to bear in mind the needs and demands intrinsic to their domestic societies.

The model that Charles Hermann (1990) proposed also considers foreign policy to be based on the interaction between the international and domestic ambits. That author considers that just as an international crisis can influence the reorientation of a foreign policy so can an electoral change or a change of governmental regime. He too considers that foreign policy changes are gradual and are the result of a governmental decision-making process, that is, of the correlation of forces and external constraints to which the respective Statesmen and Stateswomen are submitted. The primary agents of change are: leaders, bureaucracy, domestic restructuring and external shocks. Thus, any change of head of government, of the Foreign Affairs minister of the Secretaries of State or Defense, or the passage from an agrarian economy to an industrial one may, together or separately, be the causes of changes in the State's foreign policy. The changes that arise are gradual and may vary, including adjustments, programs, or change of objective and a new international orientation.

The adjustments are quantitative changes such as an increase in the amounts destined for humanitarian assistance to a given country, a reduction in the numbers of embassies and consulates in a given region, and so on. The program corresponds to an alteration in the instrument used in foreign policy such as abandoning the use of diplomacy as a substitute for an armed intervention. The change of objective is linked to the foreign policy's strategic objective and may result, for example, in the decision to put an end to an intervention replacing the former offensive stance with a more defensive one. International reorientation, the highest degree of change, means an alteration to the State's role in the international system and it might mean transformation of a weak State into a powerful one or vice versa.

In the Marxist theoretical perspective, foreign policy and domestic policy are indeed imbricated but the State's international performance depends on the interests of the Power Bloc and not exclusively on the head of State, or the government team or on the interactions among the bureaucracies. We argue that the theory of the State that Marxist Nicos Poulantzas (1975) elaborated presents elements that enable an analysis of foreign policy based on political and economic conflicts among classes and fractions of classes inside a social formation or, rather, based on the Power Bloc concept. We believe that by using the theoretical elements presented by that author we can analyze foreign policies in the same way that we analyze social and economic ones. We consider that there is an inter-relation between internal and external policy in addition to the relations that exist among the different Power Blocs and that both determine the configuration of the interests of the Power Bloc ensconced within a social formation.

Poulantzas states that the general function of the capitalist State is to maintain the cohesion of a social formation, the unity of the different modes of production under the domination of one, while at the same time, organizing the hegemony of a ruling class or fraction of class and disorganizing the dominated classes. The State's juridical-political structure, the law and the bureaucratism, are responsible for maintaining and reproducing the capitalist mode of production, for they produce a representation of unity and the isolation of the social classes. The State portrays itself as representing the general interests of society when in reality it organizes the Power Bloc and suffocates and represses the revolutionary organizations of the dominated classes.

Although Poulantzas (1978) did analyze the State's role in the face of the emergence of supra-national organizations and the internationalization of production in the current stage of capitalism's development, he did not devote attention to thinking about the relations among the Power Blocs nor did he concern himself with analyzing the relation between foreign policy and the Power Bloc. This last is the objective of our work here.

Poulantzas elaborated the Power Bloc concept to indicate the relation that existed between dominant classes and fractions of classes and the State. He considered that the division of capital into various fractions makes the bourgeoisie a prisoner of its own immediate economic interests. The various fractions engage in fratricidal struggles that divert them from, and make incapable of political self-organization. The bourgeoisie hardly ever deliberately organizes itself into political parties; it is up to the State to organize the political interests of the ruling classes and to unify them.

The Power Bloc presupposes a contradictory unification of the different fractions of the dominant classes. That unity corresponds to mutual sacrifices among the class fractions with a view to constructing a relative unity at all levels of the class struggle. It is a political, ideological and economic unity directed against the working class. The State, through its policies, articulates the interests of distinct classes and fractions of classes of the dominant class: it is not a case of an explicit formal agreement but instead of a political unity around the maintenance of social order guaranteed by the apparatus of the State. There is a tendency in that articulation of the Power Bloc to form a hegemonic fraction. It is a fraction capable of ensuring priority for itself in obtaining the benefits of the State's foreign, economic and social policies. However, it is not always the fraction that obtains the highest profits. The hegemonic fraction controls, influences and benefits from the government's policies and acts by incarnating the general interests of the people-nation and in so doing conditions a specific acceptance of its dominance on the part of the dominated classes (Poulantzas, 1975).

The configuration of the Power Bloc, the specific mode of articulation among the classes and fractions of classes and the hegemony of one fraction over the others, defines the stage of a determined social formation: the form and political regime of the State. The form refers to the relations between the political and economic spheres, whether the State is interventionist/developmentalist or liberal. The political regime consists of the arrangement between the social classes and the political parties or political representatives, and the elections. It could be democracy, dictatorship, presidentialism, monarchy, pluripartidism, bipartidism or others.

According to Poulantzas, the social classes are not defined exclusively by the position they occupy in the production process, that is, their economic level (Bukharin), nor do they only exist only insofar as they are historical subjects deliberately organized into distinct parties that struggle for power in the State (Lukács). In reality, the social classes are the effect of the set of structures and their relations, in the case in point, in the economic ideological and political levels.[8] The existence of a class or fraction of a class as a social force or distinct class depends on, but is not exclusively determined by the economic level, by its place in the process of capital production and circulation; it depends on all the other levels, especially the political and ideological ones. Poulantzas (1975) States that the social classes cannot be conceived of at all other than in terms of class practices.

Thus, there are two levels of class struggle: the political struggle for the power of the State and the conflict around the distribution of wealth, that is, the sharing out of the total surplus value. Here we are interested, above all, in the last level in which the social classes are not just divided into capitalists and workers but there are various fractions, strata and categories linked to the different combinations and interrelations present within the social formation. That is because in a real social formation, unlike the situation in an abstract 'pure' mode of production, various modes of production coexist despite the fact that one of them, the capitalist mode, is dominant. Furthermore, there is conflict among the capitalist sub-groups. In that light, according to Décio Saes (2001, p.50):

> The reproduction of capitalist social formations does not preclude the conflict of economic interests specific to the different dominant classes (landowning class, capitalist class) and to the different fractions of the same dominant class (capitalist subgroups that can be distinguished from one another because they perform different functions –production, trade, banking – in the capitalist economic process, or by the different dimensions of their capital – big capital, medium capital).

A fraction of a class does not necessarily correspond to an economic sector or to one of the different dominant classes or to the capitalist sub-groups. Poulantzas actually devoted little thought to what it is that unites a fraction of a class. Décio Saes (2001) and Francisco Farias (2010) consider that interests in common may be what make different economic sectors unite to support or reject a given State policy such as: exchange rate policy, interest rate policy, financing policy and tax/tariff policy. "State policy would be the agglutinating factor of a fractioning system" (Farias, 2010, p.16).

Thus, the fractioning is linked to the economic, political or ideological level. The fraction unites or dissipates according to the pertinent effects produced

---

8  As Marx and Engels stated in their political works: *The Eighteenth Brumaire of Louis Napoleon, The Civil War in France* and *The Class Struggles in France*.

by the current economic and political conjuncture. Pertinent effects can be understood as being just as much the State policy as the actions and positions of the social classes on the political scene. So, it is not only the State policy that can produce pertinent effects but also the action of the class or class fraction itself and the dynamics of the world economy: the configurations of the Power Blocs the imperialist States, the economic crises, the political conflicts, the wars, demographic growth and the increase or decrease of international demand.

In fact, there is a temporal succession of fractions and a crossing of paths among them: the emergence and disappearance, the crossing over of fractions can vary circumstantially. The political position of class depends on the interests of the classes and fractions of classes in the face of State policy and the extant social relations and conflicts. Agglutination may occur as a function of a political crisis, of the support or opposition to a given government, in regard to a specific political agenda, or associated to a broader political project – industrialization, imperialist expansion etc. The main conflict among the bourgeoisies is the division between the interests of the industrial Bourgeoisie and those of the banking and trading Bourgeoisies. In other words, the contradiction between the production process and the circulation of capital in those societies whose capitalism has developed to an advanced stage.

There may also be situations of discrepant lags between the structural determination of class – origin – and the position of class, as was the case with the role of the peasant smallholders in the Bonapartism of the State in France. There is also the possibility for a dissociation of political hegemony and ideological hegemony because, generally speaking, the banking Bourgeoisie and the trading Bourgeoisie find it difficult to exercise ideological domination because they have no insertion in the production sphere, and so they are accused of being parasitic. The industrial Bourgeoisie, however, manages to have more active presence on the political scene because if its association to the production of wealth and creation of employment in the national territory. That being so there can be situations in which the banking Bourgeoisie may be the hegemonic fraction but not exercise the ideological domination.[9]

In the case of financial capital, an interpenetration of banking capital and industrial capital, a differentiated economic fraction may form whose interests could enter into conflict with both the exclusively industrial Bourgeoisie and the exclusively banking Bourgeoisie. However, even in a multifunctional group

---

9  According to Décio Saes (2001), as we will see below, that occurred during the military dictatorship in Brazil (1964–1984).

or economic conglomerate active in various different spheres, banking, industry and trading, sector-orientated interests may prevail. The corporations tend not to have a shared position in regard to State policies. Their posture is usually referenced by the dominant function within the group, but it may oscillate depending on the issue at stake. As an example, the Itaú group in Brazil, despite its industrial investments (Itautec), generally positions itself considering the interests of the banking sector which is its main source of profit. That is to say, it is a group which, in spite of its diversified investments, mainly behaves as a banking Bourgeoisie on the political and ideological planes.

As regards international relations, the political fractions of a dominant social formation can unite or divide in relation to: 1) expansionist or isolationist policies; 2) opening up or protecting internal markets; and 3) priority political coalitions and alliances with other States, etc. In the dependent social formations, the dominant class splits in different ways according to the relations it establishes with imperialist capital and the dominated classes, not those referring to the division according to the production process. Poulantzas States that there are three different types of bourgeoisies in the dependent States: the purchasing Bourgeoisie, the national Bourgeoisie and the internal Bourgeoisie.

The purchasing Bourgeoisie is that fraction which has no base of accumulation of its own and performs as an agent of imperialist capital, so its interests are subordinate to imperialism (Poulantzas, 1978). It is a fraction mainly composed by the oligarchy of big landowners and the financial, banking and trading sectors. The national Bourgeoisie, in turn, is the autochthone fraction which does possess a base of accumulation of its own within the national social formation and accordingly evinces a degree of political and ideological autonomy in the face of imperialist capital. In certain conjunctures this fraction may take an anti-imperialist stance, form an alliance with the dominated classes, and/or involve itself in a struggle for national liberation (Poulantzas, 1978).

The internal Bourgeoisie[10] occupies an intermediate position between the purchasing and national Bourgeoisies. It is a fraction that has complex relations with imperialist capital as it has its own base of accumulation but at the same time it is dependent on foreign capital. That is why, to a certain extent, it endeavors to limit the presence of foreign capital in the domestic market to ensure its survival, but it shows no intention of breaking off its ties with imperialist capital. There is dissolution of political and ideological autonomy

---

10   The development of this new, mainly industrial fraction of the bourgeoisie was largely due to the new stage of imperialism associated to the dependent industrialization process of the peripheral countries (Poulantzas, 1975, p.34–35).

in the internal Bourgeoisie so it has no desire to construct alliances with the dominated classes, that is, to become a national one (Poulantzas, 1978).

It is a fraction constituted by sectors of the consumer goods industry (household appliances, textiles, mechanical, chemicals and metallurgy), the construction industry and other sectors that depend on the industrialization process (transportation, distribution) or services, which can even include tourism. It is:

> interested in State intervention which can ensure certain domains for it in the country and also make it more competitive in the face of foreign capital. It wishes for the expansion and development of the internal market to be achieved by a slight increase in the purchasing and consuming power of the masses which would provide it with more outlets; and lastly it expects assistance from the State that would enable it to develop exportation.
> 
> POULANTZAS, 1976, p. 36–37

We argue that the political position (stance) of a State in the international power structure is linked to the relations between that State, and its Power Bloc and their relations with the all the other Power Blocs and especially with the imperialist States. For that reason, the relation between the hegemonic fraction and the external capital determines the State's position in the international scenario in any given historical conjuncture.

Albeit we consider that there is indeed an imbrication of domestic policy and foreign policy and that often it may be difficult to define the limits between one and the other, we consider, for systematization purposes, that the foreign policy encompasses three spheres: 1) the State's actions vis-à-vis other States (agreements, treaties, regional blocs, alliances, supports and conflicts); 2) the State's performance in the international forums and organizations; and 3) the State's economic and foreign trade policies (currency exchange rate, importation and exportation tariffs, financing policies, contract fulfillment, foreign debt payment, roles of foreign and national capital, etc.). For foreign policy analysis purposes, we consider both the decision-making process and the policy's action and result.

The presupposition is that the States intend to obtain the maximization of their Power Blocs' interests in the international political sphere and that leads them to establish alliances and coalitions to enhance their projection in the scenario. The State must insert itself in the international policy game seeking out allies and partners, investing in diplomatic ceremonies, arbitrating conflicts, heading humanitarian missions, or even going to war. Its incumbency is to construct an international image that reflects the political and economic interests of the hegemonic fraction in its Power Bloc.

It must be underscored that the State's actions in the international scenario do not mechanically reflect the direct interests of the bourgeoisie. As an example, closer alignment with another State or involvement in a political conflict do not exactly serve an immediate economic objective such as the signing of a trade agreement or obtaining access to another country's market or the installation of a company in that country's territory would. It must be understood that policy is the synthesis of multiple determinations.

There is nothing simple about interpreting the relations between social classes and the political scene; all the more so when the political representation of a class is not declared, when there is no party that openly presents itself as being of a certain fraction of a dominant class. Likewise, in foreign policy, the conflicts among parties, political groups and social movements that organize themselves within the society and within the State apparat are not necessarily openly declared as such. That is because, on the political scene, the class position tends to be concealed. The scholars and the analysts' task is to discern any existing relations between class interests and foreign policy decisions.

Generally, in any given historical conjuncture, the hegemonic fraction of the Power Bloc determines the State's position. Thus, the political stance of an imperialist State at a given historical conjuncture may oscillate between expansionism and isolationism depending on the prioritized destination of its production. If its production is preferentially destined for the domestic market, the State's political stance will tend towards isolationism. However, if it is destined for other markets, then it is likely that State policy will be expansionist. In turn the political stances of the dependent States may vary from passive subordination to conflictive subordination or even be anti-imperialist. When the hegemonic fraction is the purchasing Bourgeoisie, then the political stance will be one of passive submission to imperialism. When the hegemonic fraction is the internal Bourgeoisie then the political stance in regard to the imperialist States will tend to be conflictive insofar as the State will be obliged to obtain a wider margin for maneuver in the face of imperialism. However, if a composition of anti-imperialist forces should arise, that is, the formation of an alliance between the national Bourgeoisie and the class of the masses, then the State could go so far as to break off relations with the imperialist States. Table 1 schematizes all the above.

Situations may arise in which there is apparently no interface between the interests of the hegemonic fraction and the foreign policy. There are cases in which the State is led to act in a strategically coherent manner with the interests of the hegemonic fraction even if at first sight, that initiative might

TABLE 1  Hegemonic fraction and political stance of the state in each historical conjuncture

| State stance in the international power structure | Hegemonic fraction in the power bloc | Political stance of the State in a given historical conjuncture |
|---|---|---|
| Imperialist State | Bourgeoisie with production destined for foreign market | Expansionist |
| Imperialist State | Bourgeoisie with production preferentially destine for domestic market | Isolationist |
| Dependent State | Purchasing Bourgeoisie | Passive subordination |
| Dependent State | National Bourgeoisie | Anti-imperialist |
| Dependent State | Internal Bourgeoisie | Conflictive subordination |

jeopardize the businesses of the bourgeoisie. That kind of situation is covered by the expression 'unstable equilibrium of compromises'.

Similarly, an apparent incompatibility may arise between foreign and domestic policies or by means of them the State may endeavor to seek the said 'unstable equilibrium of compromises' among classes and fractions of classes regardless of whether they are dominant or dominated. It means that in certain situations, the domestic policy favors the interests of a certain fraction, and the foreign policy then serves as a counterweight to represent the interests of the other fraction and vice versa; it may even be that the foreign policy actually serves the interests of the dominated classes. That situation generally occurs during political transition processes or during hegemony crises inside the Power Bloc.

It can therefore be argued that one must take into account the interests of the middle classes, the petit bourgeoisie, as well as those of the working class. Foreign policy is not generally influenced by the interests of the dominated classes but like all State policies it is subject to the relations between the dominant classes and fractions of classes and the dominated classes.

The active presence of those dominated classes on the political scene in the form of social movements, political parties or spontaneous demonstrations can lead the State to meet the respective demands of the ordinary people in the name of the aforementioned 'unstable equilibrium of compromises'. In other words, in the name of maintaining the extant social order, the State accedes to some of the subaltern class's demands and may even go so far as to orchestrate a reduction in the dominant classes' short or medium-term gains.

Grassroots movements and demonstrations against international policies can be seen when there are mobilizations protesting against wars, free-trade agreements, overseas debt payment or migration policies, among others. It was not by chance that during the late 1990s and early years 2000, anti-globalization movements like the World Social Forum, the Continental Campaign against the FTAA and others were strongly present on the international political scene and together with other political practices of the dominated classes and some sectors of the dominant classes, influenced the electoral defeats of many parties that had implanted orthodox neoliberalism in Latin America.

Foreign policies may address workers' interests when the policy is being adopted to protect the domestic market because the resultant strengthening of the industrial Bourgeoisie will be reflected in the form of more jobs and wage and consumption increases. So, by adopting policies that strengthen the national or internal Bourgeoisies, the State may also manage to meet some of the demands of the dominated classes who, in turn, may become supportive, forming part of the support base of the respective government.

In such cases there may be political processes leading to an alliance among the dominated classes or the formation of a political front. When an alliance is formed, the dominated classes may become a supporting class and, in so doing, boost an anti-imperialist struggle or a national liberation struggle. It is a case in which the relations among the classes are established deliberately in the construction of a common political program. In the case of a political front the relations among the classes involved are more fluid and the alignments may occur without any deliberate intention of the parts. Accordingly, this latter form of relations among different classes has less political force and, in the international conjuncture, the dependent State will tend to adopt a posture of conflictive subordination and only manifest sporadic divergences with imperialism.

The so-called 'national interest' actually corresponds to the interests of the hegemonic fraction and not those of general interest as the State purports.[11] It is determined by the way in which the State organizes the interests of the

---

11   If, at a moment of crisis or instability, there is no hegemony of a class fraction inside the Power Bloc then the State bureaucracy may step in and take over the political direction of the State becoming a social force in itself. It may favor certain interests of the dominant class or class fraction and enjoy the support of the dominated classes as for example in Bonapartism in France or populism in Latin America.

power bloc and the dominated classes and in that sense, it could correspond to the interests of alliances or political fronts formed among the classes and class fractions, depending on the political conjuncture. In the case of a political front or alliance between ruling classes and the lower class sectors the national interest will be of a developmentalist, national democratic or 'people's nature', that is, anti-imperialist, depending on the correlation of internal forces and the relations with external capital.

We propose that international relations can be thought of as mutual influence relations among the internal power blocs of the various States involved (Figure 1). "Actually, at the present stage of imperialism there is no such thing as factors acting purely from the 'exterior' on the one hand and on other factors that are 'internal', 'isolated' in their own particular space" (Poulantzas, 1976). The induced reproduction of capital in the different social formations establishes a bond among the endogenous fractions of capital and the external capital which has direct repercussions on the configuration of forces in the power bloc. The dependent countries' Power Blocs articulate around the relations that the fractions of their endogenous capital establish with the imperialist capital and in this case, the inter-imperialist contradictions may influence new power configurations not only in the hearts of the Power Blocs of the dependent countries but in those of the imperialist countries as well. Thus, international relations are relations that develop among classes and class fractions of the imperialist and dependent countries simultaneously. As can be seen in the figure below, the Power Blocs of the imperialist States are in the center and those of the dependent States are intertwined with, and orbit around the imperialist blocs.

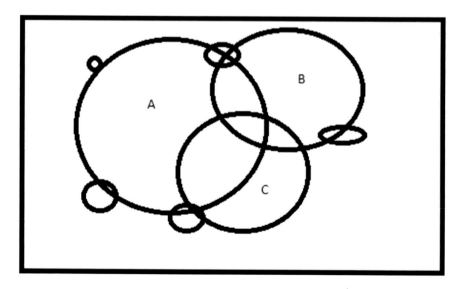

FIGURE 1  Power blocs and international relations

International relations should be thought of in terms of an imbrication of power blocs. There are situations in which a bourgeois fraction of a given country is interested in drawing closer to another State or of establishing a trade agreement with it that would benefit the interested State by enabling the exportation of its products or the importation of raw material, for example. That interest may clash with the interests of a different fraction of the same country or of a fraction in the other State or even with those of a fraction in a third country which has the same interest. Thus, the disputes among fractions in the internal and external ambits articulate with and shock with one another at the same time; that is what makes international economic negotiations or political coalition negotiations so complex. They depend on; a) the relations among the States-part; and b) the relations among each State and the classes and class fractions within and outside of the national social formation. That makes them closely consistent with Putnam's two-level game theory.

We agree with Gramsci when he States that the "internal relations of a nation-State are intertwined with the international relations, creating new, original and historically concrete combinations" (Gramsci, 2000, p.42). In that sense, a change in the Power Bloc could affect foreign policy and State policy as a whole. As an example, a country exporter of agricultural products with a dominant agrarian Purchasing bourgeoisie would probably have strong links with imperialist countries. However, if the industrial Bourgeoisie were to become stronger inside the Power Bloc, then the alliance with imperialist States might become less of a priority and lead the respective State to diversify its international partnerships and insertion strategies. In that case the hegemonic bourgeoisie would not depend exclusively on access to imperialist countries' markets and would demand access for the exportation of its products or demand protection for the internal market.

As we have seen, foreign policy in the dependent social formations is determined by the hegemonic class fraction and the relations that it establishes with imperialist capital. Bourgeois fractions may also enter into conflict over the devaluation of the local currency, the removal of trade barriers. free trade agreements or strategic partners and allies, among other aspects. If the dominant fraction is the purchasing Bourgeoisie, then foreign policy will be subservient to the interests of the imperialist States. If, however, it is a national Bourgeoisie then it will confront the dominant countries and may even break off formal ties with them. An internal Bourgeoisie would probably merely limit itself to competing with imperialism, without breaking its ties or completely drawing away from the world powers.

In the case of an Imperialist State, the capital linked to the big multinational corporations could pressure the State for an expansionist foreign policy, whereas the fraction whose production is based on accumulation and sales to the domestic market would prefer an isolationist policy (Poulantzas, 1976, p.31).

In that sense we believe, as Allison does, that it is also important to consider the dynamics within the State apparat, the cooperation or conflict that may exist among the various bureaucracies, the weight and importance of each Ministry and the political groups inside the State institutions themselves such as the Departments and the Ministries of Foreign Affairs. Again, we would argue and underscore, as Hermann does, the importance of analyzing the impact on the State's foreign policy of the so-called external shocks: change in the political regime, an economic crisis or a war. However, the relations among the different bureaucracies, the influence of a new government or change in the political regime are determined by the Power Bloc.

CHAPTER 2

# The FHC Governments

*Neoliberalism, Power Bloc and Foreign Policy*

To understand the changes that occurred in the configuration of the power bloc and in foreign policy in the 1990s, we will first present a short definition of neoliberalism and of the classes and class fractions that it benefits. Then follows a description of how the implantation and consolidation of neoliberalism took place in Brazil. The presentation and description will be referenced and supported by the studies of Armando Boito Jr., Décio Saes, Eli Diniz, Sebastião Velasco e Cruz. The object is to identify the trajectory of the different classes and class fractions and their relations with the neoliberal policies of the 1990s. After that there will be a presentation of the points of conflict among the various class fractions in regard to specific neoliberal policies that were intensified in the course of that decade. The last section of the chapter addresses the specific object of analysis; the relations between the Power Bloc and foreign policy during the FHC administrations (1995–2002).

## 1    Neoliberalism

Neoliberalism is a political and economic ideology first formulated in the 1940s by Austrian economist Friederich Hayek in his work 'The Road to Serfdom'. Albeit based on traditional, economic liberalism, neoliberalism took on a new guise more adapted to 20th century reality (Fine & Saad, 2017).

Duménil and Lévy (2004) describe how, after the economic crisis of 1970, neoliberalism became a common policy and paved the way for global capitalism's new stage of development. It symbolized the victory of financial capital over the dominant class fractions and intensified the monopolization of the economy. From the ideological point of view, neoliberal discourse argued that 'globalization' was a new historical moment, boosted by technological and communication transformations and the supposed dilution of territorial frontiers; one that would unify and homogenize the various social formations. State policy then directed itself towards guaranteeing that new hegemony in the international system. To that end the social policies for the dominated classes were suppressed and labor rights achieved through decades of struggles and demands of the subaltern sectors were reduced. According to Boito Jr. (1999, p.27):

> A superficial examination of the neoliberal discourse gives the impression that neoliberals would always be in favor of replacing State production, regulation and intervention with the freedom of action of the market's economic agents. It would also be reasonable to suppose that they were against monopolies in general and not merely against public monopolies. That however is not what happens in practice. The principles of neoliberal ideology do not coherently correspond to the political proposals and practices that they inspire. The defense of the market is limited to what is most convenient for the big monopolies and imperialism, in the age of monopolist capitalism and financial speculation.

In other words, neoliberalism has intensified the tendency to concentration and centralization of production and wealth. That is why neoliberal policies favor the actions and interests of the great transnational corporations and financial capital. It is well known that the neoliberal reforms were aimed at opening up trade, financial deregulation, privatization, weakening labor legislation and reducing the public services offer, especially in the fields of health, education and social insurance (Fine & Saad, 2017). Actually, the defense of a reduction in customs tariffs spearheaded by the neoliberal ideology and coordinated by the World Trade Organization, instead of creating a homogeneous world, fostered the expansion of the multinational corporations based in the imperialist countries into the peripheral social formations.[1]

Nevertheless, despite that growth of big corporations, the role of the nation-State was not supplanted. What actually occurred was a reorientation, a reformulation of its role. The State became the reorganizer of the world economy's new dynamics – new relations among the Power Blocs under the hegemony of financial capital. According to Cruz (1999, p.241):

> the liberalization of goods and services, the global production chains, and the instantaneous financial flows are phenomena that do not emerge spontaneously as simple properties of the capitalist economy; they are largely the result of State policy decisions.

---

1  Regarding the criticism of theses purporting the existence of a 'global bourgeoisie' or a 'transnational class', see Martuscelli (2010).

In that new arrangement among distinct classes and class fractions, the dominated classes experienced an obvious debasement of their living conditions, restriction of liberties, increased unemployment, lower wages and de-indexing. Notoriously, the criminalization of strikes and people's movements and mobilizations has been present in almost all the neoliberal governments. In other areas, however, especially in exchange rate and interest rate policies, State intervention has become even more marked as Duménil and Lévy (2004, p. 13) explain:

> In many domains the power of the state has been reinforced. That is especially the case with monetary policies which, ... almost exclusively, seek price stability despite the unemployment they generate. Everywhere the States have been the vectors for the establishment of neoliberalism in both the national and international planes. The levers in the hands of the promotors of the neoliberal order at the company level are, principally, high interest rates and the macroeconomic policies.

Neoliberalism has also altered the form of organization and international division of labor and, above all, inaugurated a new stage of economic and political dependence for Latin American countries. It is in a fact a new stage of imperialism and of the international division of States into imperialist states and peripheral ones. Foreign Direct Investment (FDI) and portfolio investment has become the current pathway for imperialism's exportation of capitals and economic dominance. The pursuit of lower labor and environmental costs and greater consumer markets is the contemporary form of the dispute among the large corporations and their respective host-States. There is a similar pursuit of higher interest rates and fewer constraints on financial investors (Duménil & Lévy, 2004).

From the political standpoint, the geopolitical disputes, especially for access to strategic natural resources like oil, have been maintained. Furthermore, the imperialist states and the international financial organizations have pressured the peripheral states to execute neoliberal policies. Those orientations have led to what José Luis Fiori (1995) Samir Amin (2002) and Décio Saes (2007) call 'extremely new dependency[2]'. Before we examine what those authors mean

---

2 "But what does this extremely new dependency consist of? The First World financial capital and monopolist industrial capital along with governments, such as that of the USA and the entities that represent them, like the International Monetary Fund (IMF), the World Trade organization (WTO) and the World Bank no longer wish to make new investments in the reproductive apparatus designed to advance associated industrialization in the peripheral

by extremely new dependency, we will briefly reconstitute the periodization of Latin American dependency over the centuries to gain an understanding of the differences among the stages: the colonial stage, the new stage and the extremely new stage.

In the first phase of dependence, the colonial phase, the role that the international division of labor imposed on the peripheral social formations was that of supplier of raw materials and agricultural products to the central economies, while the latter exported manufactured goods. Between 1950 and 1970, the 'new dependence' achieved by means of the 'associated development'[3] model, fostered foreign capital investment in the production sector of the peripheral social formations. The foreign capital, associated to the local bourgeoisies, commanded the durable goods sectors – automobiles and household appliances and the national industrial sector supplied inputs and non-utilitarian consumer goods. The State, in turn, guaranteed the physical infrastructure and power supply necessary for those two sectors. There was a progressist element present in that model that pleased the dominated classes to some extent, which was the creation of jobs and urbanization.

The 'extremely new dependence' entirely undermined the positive effects of the earlier model and expanded the financial exploitation of the region. The priority goal became monetary stabilization, to the detriment of growth and the distribution of income; the nationalization of the foreign debt ensured the security of foreign investors and the high interest rates and overvalued exchange rates ensured high returns for both the national and international financial capital. In other words, what occurred, to the detriment of foreign investment in the production sector, was a huge increase in indirect investment in investment portfolios. The most immediate consequence was increased unemployment, a drop in industry's participation in the Gross Domestic Product (GDP) and the alienation of the national patrimony.

In short, neoliberalism undermined the political autonomy of the peripheral states thereby increasing the external vulnerability of their economies and tightening the bonds of imperialist subordination.

---

countries but, instead, to obtain easy gains by taking over all the existing economic sectors that are capable of providing immediate, real gains" (Saes, 2007, p.159).

3  On that aspect, see Cardoso and Faletto (1981).

## 2  Neoliberalism and the Power Bloc in Brazil

Brazil was one of the last Latin American countries to implant neoliberalism. That was largely due to the powerful movement of strikes towards the end of the 1970s and in the early 1980s, and the resistance on the part of the State and some sectors of the internal Brazilian bourgeoisie that benefitted from the extant developmentalist model. Let us examine that in detail.

The development that the military government unfolded depended excessively on borrowing foreign money. With that the increase in the portion of federal resources destined for interest payments and debt servicing and rescheduling became exorbitant. From 1973 on, the Brazilian economy was quickly affected by the first oil price shock and the period of great economic growth, which propaganda referred to as the 'economic miracle', came to an end. Against that background emerged the first contestations of the developmentalist model the military had implemented, marked especially by the industrial bourgeoisie's opposition to the nationalization of the economy during the Geisel administration. Those rumors of discontent intensified in 1979 with the second oil price shock and became even more intense during the 1980s (Cruz, 1997).

With the higher interest rates on their foreign debts the United States imposed on its dependent countries in 1982, the Brazilian economy entered on a period of economic crisis whose most evident aspects were hyperinflation and economic stagnation. It was also a period of mobilizations of ordinary people in Brazil – workers strikes, women's movements, peasant movements, etc. – which culminated in the *Diretas Já* (Direct elections for President) that put an end to the military dictatorship imposed by the *Coup d'état* of 1964.

As regards the classes of the grassroots movements , it must be remembered that the early 1980s were the years when the Worker's Party (*Partido dos Trabalhadores*-PT), the Landless Rural Worker's Movement (*Movimento dos Trabalhadores Rurais Sem Terra*-MST) and the Unified Workers Central (*Central Única dos Trabalhadores*-CUT) were created. Those organizations played an important role in the resistance to neoliberalism up until 1989, when they were defeated in electoral terms and formed the opposition to neoliberal governments that followed.

Bianchi (2010, p.167), states that "among the corporate businessmen, the sudden drop in the GDP in 1981 had the impact of a historical trauma". As the situation gradually grew worse and worse so the government increasingly lost the support of the industrial bourgeoisie. The efforts to revert the situation in the form of the *Planos Cruzado* (I and II) actually intensified the opposition of sectors of the industrial bourgeoisie to the state policies, especially the price and wage-freezing policy. The great concern was to achieve monetary stabilization, but little by little, the Brazilian industrial bourgeoisie turned to what it thought was the only possible alternative, neoliberalism (Bianchi, 2010).

According to Boschi and Diniz (1992), the economic crisis of the 1980s contributed towards fostering the propagation of theses and ideas regarding the exhaustion of the 'industrialization by replacement of imports' model and arguing in favor of neoliberal policies. The ideological neoliberal propaganda campaign was vociferated by intellectuals, bureaucrats and representatives of the Brazilian and international bourgeoisies. Neoliberalism's defenders argued that the time of the model of industrialization by replacing importation was over. It was therefore necessary, they proposed, to adapt to, and integrate a new global political economy via opening markets, reducing production costs by reducing taxes and payroll costs and reducing State spending. Boschi and Diniz (1992, p.5) considered that:

> As regards the perception of the redefinition of the direction the country's economic development should take, there is an observable basic consensus that the model of industrialization via the replacement of imports under the aegis of the State is exhausted. However trivial that might seem, it is useful to remember that until recently there was still some controversy about the possible survival of that model and particularly about the definition of the limits of State interventionism. There is a relatively uniform view that the nationalist, statist, autarchic model of the past has been surpassed. It needs to be rejected because of the distortions it generated such as 'cartorialismo',[4] excessive regulation, low levels of competitiveness and productivity, technological backwardness and aversion to risk. In contrast, the new model, associated to the recovery of the role of the private company and of the market, would enable a recuperation of the aspects of efficiency needed to overcome the extant predicaments.

It is well-known that the debates associated to the Constituent Assembly contributed considerably to fostering the dominant classes' adherence to neoliberalism. The PT, supported by the grassroots movements and in its struggle for increased democratization of access to land and distribution of income in Brazil, also participated vigorously in those debates. So much so that the

---

4  'Cartorialismo' is a type of clientelism whereby persons in public service take the opportunity to ensure advantages or employment for determined persons or groups.

second round of the highly polarized 1989 presidential elections was a run-off between Fernando Collor de Melo and Luiz Inácio Lula da Silva (PT), in which the PT's democratic people's project opposed Collor's neoliberal project. It is worth remembering that the President of the Federation of Industries of São Paulo (FIESP) threatened that there would be an exodus of Brazilian businessmen if Lula were to win the elections. According to Cruz (2001, p.142–143):

> in 1989, the political center was momentarily disaggregated, with the country divided into two camps separated by strong feelings of antagonism. The fundamental issue for both sides was the role d the State, a central element in any development strategy. Right to Left: for the first the solution for the national problems was to remove state-imposed restrictions on the functioning of the market, privatize public corporations, attract foreign capital, and expose the national production system to international competition; for the second, the solution was to de-privatize the State and break away from the logic of feudalization by those holding political and social power, in order to place the State at the service of a development model based on de-concentration of wealth and income and the country's affirmation as an autonomous actor in the international scenario.

It must be underscored that even among the bourgeoisies there was divergence regarding whether to adhere to the neoliberal program or not. The lack of consensus is illustrated by the creation of two entities by Brazilian companies in the 1980s, with a view to fostering a new industrial project for Brazil. They were the National Thinking of the Corporate Bases (*Pensamento Nacional das Bases Empresariais* – PNBE) and the Industrial Development Studies Institute (*Instituto de Estudos para o Desenvolvimento Industrial*-IEDI).

Nevertheless, the neoliberal policy did unify, to some extent, the different classes and fractions within the power bloc in Brazil. All the fractions of the Brazilian bourgeoisie could see advantages stemming from the implantation and consolidation of neoliberalism, especially in the aspect of making the labor laws more flexible and reducing expenditure on social policies. Both the external imperialist capital and the Brazilian bourgeoisie saw, in those policies, the possibility of enhancing their revenues. It was a case of the unification of the dominant classes and fractions of the dominant classes against the dominated classes (Boito Jr., 1999).

In general, the middle classes and part of the Brazilian working class also adhered to the neoliberal program. According to Décio Saes (2001, p.84–85), a conservative political front was formed. The front was unified by, and rallied around the flag of economic stability. That is what explains the support for the Plano Real and the election and re-election to the presidency of Fernando Henrique Cardoso (PSDB)[5] to whom the authorship of the monetary stabilization plan was attributed.

Nevertheless, the driving force behind that political front was the imperialist capital, that is, national and international financial capital; the fraction that benefitted from the high interest rates and opening up of the markets, from privatizations, financial deregulation and the weakening of labor rights. The behavior of that fraction of the bourgeoisie is compatible with what Poulantzas (1978) defines as the '*comprador*' or purchasing bourgeoisie, the intermediary of external interests inside the national social formation. For that reason, foreign policy and domestic policies were at the service of the stabilization plan and the interests of the imperialist States and international financial capital. This will be examined in greater detail later in the chapter.

The privilege granted to financial capital, from the macro-economic point of view, was afforded by the tripod: high interest rates, fixed exchange rate (up until 1999) and the primary surplus. It was a monetary policy designed to achieve economic stability. What the monetary policies really guaranteed was the high profitability of investments for international financial capital (shares and investment portfolios). Reduction of State spending was to assure financial capital that the foreign debt would be serviced, and the interest duly paid. Financial deregulation associated to interest rate and monetary stability policies conferred considerable benefits on the banking sector insofar as, to compensate for the losses incurred through the reduction of the inflation rate, concentration of the banking sector was stimulated by means of the Financial System Restructuring and Strengthening Program (*Programa de Reestruturação e Fortalecimento do Sistema Financeiro*-PROER) and through the privatization of the Brazilian states banks.

As mentioned above, the banner of economic stability and cuts in government spending and labor costs unified different classes and class fractions. However, in regard to the other neoliberal reforms, the privatizations, the

---

5   The presence of the working classes in that political process was not only due to the Plano Real but, above all, in the case of Collor, to the mention of the '*descamisados*' (people in rags) and all the personalist discourse the president used. We could say that the ordinary people were ideologically illuded by the paternalistic discourse of those politicians, supported by the anti-inflation policies and the idea of sanitizing the State. According to Décio Saes "perhaps the more profound historical reason for that success was the 'socially perverse effect' of the State interventions that had typified the preceding stage of the development of capitalism" (Saes, 2001, p.79).

opening up of markets and financial deregulation, there were conflicts inside the power bloc that intensified as the years went by. According to Eli Diniz (2010, p.106):

> From the ideological point of view, there was an observable articulation for consensus among the businessmen around the neoliberal posture and a questioning of the economic model consecrated in the preceding decades. Above all they questioned the Statist content of the developmentalist strategy. A broad disagreement persisted, however, regarding more specific aspects of the new market-based model, especially in regard to the form and rhythm of implementation of items on the new agenda such as privatization and the liberalization of trading.

Boito Jr. (1999) argues that there was a split in the power bloc separating orthodox neoliberals and moderate ones. In the course of the 1990s that split became wider. Martuscelli (2012) considers that the Brazilian internal bourgeoisie offered selective resistance to the Collor government's (1990–1992) economic policy especially to the rhythm of the liberalization of trading. That would have been the reason why it was the fraction that headed the movement to impeach Collor in 1992. Nevertheless, it was the middle-class students that actually took on the role as agents of the process, replacing the leading fraction because the internal bourgeoisie was being harassed by international pressures and the strikes movements of the 1980s.

The Itamar Franco government (1992–1994) endeavored, to some extent, to contain the advance of neoliberalism in Brazil and calm down the political crisis that had led Itamar to become President of the Republic. Once the crisis was over and the Plano Real in force, the FHC governments took on the task of consolidating neoliberalism in Brazil.

Regarding the privatizations, the only beneficiaries of selling off the State corporations were the financial capital and the monopolist capital. In the bidding process, the groups that bought the companies at sub-estimated prices and paid for them with 'rotten currency' and furthermore were able to count on financing from the National Social and Economic Development Bank (*Banco Nacional de Desenvolvimento Econômico e Social-*BNDES) were mainly concentrated in the banking, industrial and construction sectors. Foreign capital, especially European capital participated in the privatization of telephone companies and state banks and as partners of the large national corporations in the acquisition of steelworks, mining and fertilizer companies. Some sectors of the Brazilian bourgeoisie, especially small and medium capital, the transformation industry and sectors connected to State-run corporations, were not so optimistic about the privatizations because they did not benefit those sectors directly. Furthermore, the small and medium-sized capital demanded the right to participate in the purchasing of shares of those corporations which was only possible after 1997 when legal measures were taken that allowed small shareholders to purchase such shares (Boito Jr., 1999).

The privatization of the state-owned telephone, mining, railroads, energy, gas and bank corporations (*Telebrás, Companhia Vale do Rio do Doce, Usiminas, Companhia Paulista de Força e Luz* – CPFL –, *Rede Ferroviária Nacional* the local state banks *Banespa, Banco Meridional, Banco do Estado de Goiás, Banco do Amazona* and the *Companhia de Gás de São Paulo* – Comgás) added to the alteration to the regulatory statute of the Petrobras that enabled the concession of oil well exploration rights to foreign companies via tendering and bidding processes, all together, as a set, represent the denationalization of the economy and the passage of the control of national assets and resources to international capital. Furthermore, the privatization of state-provided services like health, education and social insurance led to the formation of a new 'services bourgeoisie' especially connected to the banking sector.

A combination of the liberalization of trading via the reduction of customs duties and importation tax rates and the overvalued exchange rate was responsible for the increase in importation, the heightened concentration of wealth and property, and the deindustrialization and denationalization of the Brazilian economy. Importation was specifically greatest in the machinery and equipment, electronic materials and apparatus, and communication materials segments of the capital goods sector. The Brazilian balance of trade began to show ever increasing deficits.

Furthermore, the increased rate of importation of components of production chains transformed several industries into mere assemblers or *maquiladoras* as they were called in Mexico. That process was highly regionalized in Brazil and its greatest concentration was in the Manaus Free Trade Zone. Automotive, IT and electronic products sectors were the ones most affected. The most notable change in the field of production, however, was the denationalization of the industrial sector which, in many cases, was accompanied by deindustrialization. That occurred not only through the privatization of state corporations but also through the mergers and acquisitions of Brazilian plants by international groups, increasing the participation of foreign companies in the national company

> the participation of foreign companies, in the group of the five hundred biggest Brazilian companies, which was already considerable, increased as the years went by, especially in the case of sales and importations. In

the year 2000, 46% of the five hundred biggest companies in Brazil were foreign (in 1989 the foreign companies were only 30%). The participation of the foreign companies in the group was significant: 56% of the turnover, 49% of the importations and 67.2% of the exportations.

SARTI & LAPLANE, 2003, p.21

Brazil was one of the world's main recipients of Foreign Direct Investment (FDI) from 1995 to 2000 (Sarti & Laplane, 2003, p.15). Despite the increase in foreign direct investment, there was no proportional investment in modernization or expanding production capacity as part of the money was destined for the acquisition of existing assets, in the privatizations, for example, and the services, financial and telecommunications sectors were the ones most intensely targeted. That FDI boom intensified the degree of internationalization of the Brazilian economy increasing its external vulnerability even more.

Regarding the liberalization of trading and financial deregulation, the most outstanding resistance was that shown by the industrial bourgeoisie and the Brazilian national banks. Their resistance stemmed from their perception that indiscriminate opening up to free trading would result in the destruction of Brazil's installed industrial capacity and that financial deregulation would destroy the national banks. "The liberalization of trading and the interest rate policy are the reasons for the more or less efficient protests and pressures organized by the FIESP and the CNI at various moments of the 1990s" (Boito Jr., 1999, p. 61). Two important episodes associated to industry's criticism of the liberalization of trading and the interest rate policy were the industrialists' demonstrations in Brasília in 1996 and the Reforms Forum that FIESP organized in 1997. After the demonstration in Brasília:

> Without altering the general orientation of its policy, the government was obliged to make concessions to the industrialists. Even though it had reaffirmed and maintained the trading liberalization policy, the government took advantage of the WTO legislation on safeguard institutions, compensatory rights and the prohibition of dumping, and created tariff and non-tariff barriers to the importation of textiles and clothing from China, South Korea and Formosa and also against the importation of toys.
>
> BOITO JR., 1999, p.63

During FHC's second mandate, the impact of the economic crises in Asia revealed the fragility and unsustainable nature of the orthodox neoliberal policies. In order to put off a serious economic crisis, the FHC governments had recourse to the International Monetary Fund (IMF) thereby increasing Brazil's external debt. On January 1st, 1999, at the outset of the second mandate, an exchange rate crisis erupted and increased the dissatisfaction of fractions of the Brazilian bourgeoisie with orthodox neoliberalism. According to Diniz (2010, p.110):

> The later years of the 1990s revealed some changes ... from the point of view of the configuration of the political forces; strong signs appeared of a rupture of the consensus that had sustained President Fernando Henrique Cardoso's first mandate, based on setting absolute priority on economic stability and fiscal discipline.

"In the corporate milieu, an important split in that class's support for government policies is observed. The IEDI, by means of a widely publicized document, Agenda for an Industrial Development Project (*Agenda para um Projeto de Desenvolvimento Industrial*) and the FIESP, the latter already headed by a new president, Horácio Lafer Piva, adopt a critical posture in regard to the reforms agenda. Above all they question the form that the economic opening had taken on, the privileged treatment afforded to foreign companies, the closure of the decision-making process and the absence of an industrial policy."

Thus, we can safely state that a part of the Brazilian bourgeoisie agglutinated as a fraction that came to acquire the role of a veritable internal bourgeoisie. That can be observed in the growing participation in, and opposition to the international economic negotiations that sought to intensify even further the opening up of trading and the set of neoliberal policies. Furthermore, increased unemployment, loss of rights, reduction of social policies and the increase in social problems generated great dissatisfaction among the ordinary people. Both the sectors in favor of a moderate form of neoliberalism (the industrial bourgeoisie and the banks) and the social and trade union movements began to mobilize against the economic policy resulting from the implantation of orthodox neoliberalism. That is why Lula's electoral victory in 2002, as we will see later, can be seen as a rejection of orthodox neoliberal policies by both the big internal Brazilian bourgeoisie and the dominated classes, contributing to the formation of the neo-developmentalist front.

## 3   Foreign Policy in the FHC Governments

Foreign policy was one of the main elements of the consolidation of orthodox neoliberalism in Brazil. In addition to adopting policies of open markets, privatization, reduction of State expenditure, deregulation of labor and of finance, the Collor (1990–1992) and FHC (1995–2002) governments were notable for the return of the special alliance with the United States in foreign affairs. It was a considerable change in comparison with the preceding decades in which, even though the country was under a military regime, it had strong disagreements with the USA. That was true, above all, in regard to negating the treaties that perpetuate and ratify inequalities among the different social formations, especially in the aspect of access to technology, as was shown by the rejection of the Nuclear Non-proliferation Treaty (NPT) since 1967, the Brazil-Germany Nuclear Agreement of 1974 and the Law designed to protect the domestic IT market.

Actually, according to Lima (1994), the Geisel government (1974–1979) implemented a policy of diversifying partners and sought for autonomy by distancing itself from the United States; a policy that San Tiago Dantas had previously formulated in the early 1960s. The Independent Foreign Policy (*Política Externa Independente*-PEI) of the Jânio and Jango governments (1961–1964) inaugurated a new Brazilian foreign policy paradigm: globalism. With its origins back in the Getúlio Vargas government, which had adopted a policy of bargaining between Germany and the United States, and afterwards, through the Pan-American Operation that Juscelino Kubitscheck proposed, the PEI had marked a rupture and conflict with the Americanist paradigm of Barão do Rio Branco (1902–1912). As the globalism paradigm diversified the Brazilian State's international relations, it therefor guaranteed it a greater margin for maneuver in the international scenario.

During the 1980s, both Figueiredo and Sarney persisted in an alliance with the dependent states, especially in the activities to combat the liberalization of services foreseen in the General Agreement on Tariffs and Trade (GATT) and in the struggle to renegotiate the foreign debt. However, Casarões (2011) states that the United States began to exert great pressure on the Brazilian State for it to adopt neoliberalism. The pressure was for the Brazilian bourgeoisie and diplomacy to accept the idea of changing their stances .

In the 1980s, the main point of conflict between the Brazilian State and the United States was the foreign debt. Given the serious economic crisis and the increase in the interest rate for the debt that the United States implemented after the oil price shocks, the Brazilian State found it difficult to afford the interest payments and so endeavored, through its activities in the GATT and the formation of the Grupo da Contadora,[6] to renegotiate the dependent states'

---

6  Group formed by Argentina, Colombia, Mexico, Panama, Peru, Uruguay and Venezuela.

debts. In turn as a bargaining counterpart for the concession of new loans and a review of the payment of the amounts accumulated over the preceding decades, especially during the military dictatorship, the United States stipulated the liberalization of the IT, pharmaceutical and services sectors (Cervo 2008; Casarões, 2011).

In 1983 and 1984 the Brazilian State presented several letters of intent to the IMF in which it committed itself to reducing the public debt by means of a stabilization plan and structural adjustments in exchange for new loans. However, in 1987, unable to afford the interest payments, the Brazilian State declared a six-month moratorium on the foreign debt payments. The United States reacted negatively and that provoked a reaction in various Brazilian sectors fearful that they would suffer retaliations directed at their exports or that there would be a further increase in the interest payable on the debt. So, in a short space of time the debt payments were resumed (Casarões, 2011).

Even so, the United States decided to retaliate against Brazilian exports as a way of pressuring for an end to the protection of the IT sector market (equipment and software). That measure had such strong repercussions on the Brazilian bourgeoisie that:

> A little less than a week after the announcement of economic sanctions on Brazil, the Brazilian government thought it better to draw back and review its decision on the MS-DOS. The actions and positions of the FIESP allied to national companies interested in using that software contributed to that change of government position.
> CASARÕES, 2011, p. 98

Cruz (2010, p.36) relates how, against that background:

> even before he took office, Fernando Collor de Mello made it clear that the solution for the severe contention that was poisoning Brazil-United States relations would be one of his government's priorities. That intention, as is now known, translated as: opening trade, a change of attitude in the negotiations of the Uruguay round of the GATT, new positions on 'sensitive' issues such as ecology, human rights and nuclear proliferation.

Casarões (2011) considers that the Collor government endeavored to draw closer to the United States and renegotiate the foreign debt on other planes. According to Lima (1994, p.41), "the paradigm of a special alliance with the United States (implemented by the Collor government) had 'modernization via internationalization' as its foundation". The reasons for that change of direction in the Brazilian State's international performance were based, according to Przeworski (apud Lima, 1994), on an acceptance, albeit partial, of subordination of national sovereignty in the political, economic and social spheres, given that the new direction presupposed the adoption of neoliberal policies and the Brazilian Armed Forces loss of control over its martial and technological capacity (Lima, 1994).

Sallum Jr. (2011) argues that the Collor government's liberalizing reforms and foreign policy (and those of its successors) were orientated by two distinct ideologies: neoliberalism and 'competitive integration'. The latter became stronger towards the end of the 1980s supported by technical personnel of the BNDES and industrialists associated to the Industrial Development Studies Institute (*Instituto de Estudos do Desenvolvimento Industrial*-IEDI).

> The central idea of that 'competitive integration' project was to transfer the center of the driving force for Brazilian development to private enterprise, reducing the State's corporate functions, and international 'opening' of the Brazilian economy.
> SALLUM JR., 2011, p.264

According to the author, that ideology would correspond to a kind of non-defensive nationalism and its main ramification came to be MERCOSUR. Thus, the Collor government's foreign policy would seem to have headed in two directions. On the one side it endeavored to reduce the tension with the imperialist states and, on the other, to expand its international sphere of action by drawing attention to the so-called 'new themes' in international policies, human rights and the environment and constructing MERCOSUR (Sallum Jr., 2011, p.269).

It is well-known that the Collor government was short-lived, and the presidency passed to Itamar Franco. He faced the task of containing the political crisis left by his predecessor and so there were no great changes in foreign policy. The only notable ones were the emphasis placed on gaining a seat on the UN security council (Hirst & Pinheiro, 1995) and the more political nature that Minister Celso Amorim impressed on the MERCOSUR negotiations and the South American Free Trade Area proposal (Menezes, 2006, p.79).

Saraiva (2011) considers that the Collor governments realignment of foreign policy exacerbated the split inside Itamaraty (the Ministry of Foreign Affairs and Diplomacy) leading to the formation of two political groups which he called the 'pragmatic institutionalists' and the 'autonomists'. The author states that the opposition of those two groups intensified and became consolidated in the course of the 1990s. The former group became stronger during the FHC governments and in political party terms it has its reflection in the PSDB and the DEM (Democrats Party). The other group performed an oppositionist role during the FHC governments and only became stronger when Lula ascended to the presidency.[7]

We would argue that the Collor and FHC governments' foreign policies broke away from the Brazilian State's former position of drawing closer to the dependent States and criticizing the international division of labor in the aspects of access to technology, as defended by the military governments. It attempted to review the foreign debt in the 1990s. That break away meant the abandonment of the developmentalist policies that had been present in Brazilian politics between 1930 and 1980. Hirst and Pinheiro (1995, p.6) underscore that:

> Just as they raised expectations in the internal sphere that Brazil would set in motion a speedy modernization process and would overcome the obstacles created by the old economic order, so the idea arose that the government elected at the end of 1989 would modify the country's international profile. To that end, priorities were established which were designed to achieve three goals, namely: 1) update the country's international agenda with the new international issues and new international momentum; 2) construct a positive agenda with the United States; and 3) deconstruct the third world country characteristics of Brazil's profile.

In that sense, to ensure the loan concessions, attract foreign investment and address the aspirations of national and international finance, it was not enough merely to implement the IMF and World Bank's directives; it was also necessary to demonstrate proximity with, and subordination to the imperialist powers. It was against that background that the closer alignment with the United States and Europe and the adherence to the main international disarmament treaties took place. As we shall see, those treaties embrace the renunciation of the use of nuclear technology and nuclear weapons. There were also observable actions during the FHC governments (1995 to 2002) in which the Brazilian State demonstrated explicit subordination to United States policy, permitting intervention in, and monitoring of Brazilian territory by foreign agents. The principal actions confirming the Brazilian State's posture of subordination to the United States were as follows:

1) The consented presence of United States agents inside the Federal Police on the pretext of combatting drug trafficking and foreseen in the

---

[7] The autonomists, historically, have largely been identified by their defense of developmentalist policies whereas the pragmatic institutionalists defend the liberalization of the economy.

terms of the Brazil-United States Mutual Cooperation Agreement for the Reduction of Demand, Prevention of Illicit Use, and Combatting the Production and Trafficking of Illicit Drugs. According to Bandeira (2004), their presence made spying activities and monitoring the Amazon feasible.

2) Adherence to the Missile Technology Control Regime (MTCR)
3) The 'choice', later questioned by a Parliamentary Committee of Inquiry, of the United States company Raytheon to execute the Amazon Surveillance System (*Sistema de Vigilância da Amazônia* – SIVAM) (Menezes, 2006, p.101).
4) The ratification of the Treaty on the Non-Proliferation of Nuclear Arms (TNP) on September 18, 1998, 29 years after the Brazilian State had refused to accept a discriminatory agreement that accentuated the inequality of power among the states. The actual signing of the treaty was associated to two episodes: it occurred some time after the 1997 round of the FTAA negotiations in which Brazil's position had clashed with that of the United States (Bandeira, 2004) and it was shortly before Brazil obtained a loan from the IMF.
5) The signing of an agreement (Protocol 505) on April 18, 2000, whereby low-cost defense equipment would be transferred to Brazil and as a counterpart, complete control of the Alcântara Base in Maranhão would pass to the United States. The Brazilian state was impeded from using the base and from inspecting the importation of equipment (spaceships, vehicles etc.) that the United States would bring in to store or launch.
6) The non-opposition to the dismissal of Maurício Bustani from the presidency of the Organization for the Prohibition of Chemical Weapons, (OPCW).
7) Minister Celso Lafer's signs of approval regarding the United States reaction to the attack on the Twin Towers in September 2001.
8) The Efforts to Reactivate the InterAmerican Treaty for Reciprocal Assistance (ITRA)
9) The episode in which Lafer took off his shoes like an ordinary person during American airport security checks, which was considered to be offensive and unrespectful to the Brazilian State and an infraction of the laws of diplomatic immunity on the part of the United States.

In addition to the above, the foreign trade policy was at the service of a stabilization plan (Bezerra, 2008, p.39) which was itself "a positively appreciated objective in Washington" (Vigevani & Cepaluni, 2011, p.107).

Two agreements were signed with the IMF during the FHC governments, one in 1998 and the other in 2002. The 1998 agreement, of a preventive nature, was signed at a Fund meeting in November, just after the eruption of the financial crises in Asia. It was to the amount of 41 billion US dollars which was to be disbursed over a three-year period but most of it in the first twelve months. Finance Minister Pedro Malan had the following to say about it in a formal communication to President FHC:

> That understanding with the International Monetary Fund represents an important signal to the international financial community in regard to the solidity of the Brazilian economic policy and constitutes an important factor for boosting confidence in the country, keeping the flows of direct investments high and enabling the international capitals market to be gradually reopened in the interest of, above all, financing investments in the expansion and modernization of the private sector.
> MALAN, 1998

The 2002 agreement reaffirmed the Brazilian State's commitment to maintaining a primary surplus and to achieving monetary stability. "The Central Bank also commits itself to informally explaining the reasons that govern their monetary policy decisions to the IMF technical staff" (Ministério da Fazenda, 2002). The agreement foresaw disbursements for 2002 and 2003 with the amount for 2003 being greater than for 2002.

Other notable events were the approval of Constitutional Amendment nº6/95 and the signing of at least six International Investments Promotion and Protection Agreements (*Acordos de Proteção e Promoção de Investimentos Internacionais*-APPIIs). The constitutional amendment eliminated the concept of 'Brazilian company with foreign capital' thus transforming all such companies installed in Brazil into Brazilian companies and thereby guaranteeing the Brazilian constitutional benefits and security to foreign capital. Those APPIIs were agreements under the aegis of the WTO which referred to them as Treaties Related to Investment Measures (TRIMs) and they addressed aspects like reducing political risks for foreign investments in dependent social formations. The Brazilian State signed six bilateral agreements in the period 1994 to 1999 with France, Great Britain, Switzerland, Germany, Portugal, Chile and with MERCOSUR, which were forwarded to the Brazilian Congress via Presidential message, but they were not approved (Azevedo, 2001).

The reasons for that rejection were clauses in the agreements that specified: a broad definition of investment that did not distinguish between investments in assets and investments in productive capital; the express prohibition of nationalizing or expropriating investments via obligatory state compensation should any eventual breach of contract occur within a period of less than ten years; and the possibility of the investor's choosing the legal forum (national or international) for the solution of any controversy that might arise around investments; in other words the Brazilian State and the foreign investor would be on a juridically equal footing (Pimenta, 2010). That is yet another demonstration of how the foreign policy was entirely at the service of international financial capital as Brazilian independence would have sunk to an even lower level if those agreements had been ratified.

On this topic, it is also worth remembering the acknowledgement of the intellectual property agreement signed at the Uruguay round of the GATT and sanctioned by the Brazilian Congress in 1996, considerably earlier than the time limit established for compliance, 2005. Those measures restricted the State's sovereignty and favored the interests of the big corporations (Cruz, 2010). On the other hand, there were notable multilateral actions seeking to acquire greater international projection for the Brazilian State. They were the recognition of the InterAmerican Human Rights Court (1997) and the International Penal Court, adherence to the Kyoto Protocol (1997), participation in the humanitarian missions in East Timor (from 1999 on) and the efforts, albeit timid, to obtain a seat for Brazil on the UN Security Council. As a set, those multilateral actions sought the recognition of Brazil as player on the international political scene; in other words, as a State that participated in the centers with decision-making powers. It is important to clarify that those actions did not confront the position of the imperialist states either; quite the contrary, they were actually a:

> movement carried out by the medium-sized powers processing a displacement from a stance directly antagonistic to the international order, to one in attunement with the system's general principles, its regimes and its procedures (Sennes, 2003). That movement meant abandoning the third-world discourse and international comprehension based on the North-South conflict.
> SILVA, 2012, p.30

According to Pinheiro (2000), adherence to the international regimes was in the interests of obtaining financing and technology, the support base of the neoliberal project. The human rights and trading regulations facilitated the quest for participation in the international system and boosted the autonomy of the State's action.

Another salient feature was the drawing closer to African and Asian countries, especially with the creation of the Community of Portuguese-speaking Countries and the relations with China, India and Russia. Those relations were mainly orientated by the trading partners' interests in economic diversification which, along with MERCOSUR,[8] reveals the interests of the industrial bourgeoisie in the power bloc, albeit on a lower plane.

The main divergences between the Brazilian State and the United States only surfaced in the WTO, especially in regard to breaking the patents of AIDS medicines, the opening of the Cotton Panel in 2001 and the formal complaints that Japan and the United States lodged in 1996 and 1997 respectively, against the Brazilian State's 1995 automobile agreement. However, as will be shown below, over the years the regional policy, and MERCOSUR and the FTAA negotiations in particular, became a more serious point of conflict between the two States. It was specifically in response to greater presser applied by the organized internal Brazilian bourgeoisie that those conflicts intensified, and the Brazilian State was led to refuse to accept the terms of the FTAA agreement with the United States and to intensify the regional integration process and the search for new international partners, albeit to the apparent displeasure of the FHC government.

### 3.1   FTAA, MERCOSUR and the Internal Bourgeoisie

Between 1995 and 1998, MERCOSUR came into force and lived its years of glory. The bloc had been conceived as an initiative of 'open regionalism' (CEPAL, 2000), of integration marked by the opening of markets and increased competitive pressure which would thus be an instrument complementing the neoliberal policies implanted in the region. The adoption of a common external tariff was to have been an instrument of open regionalism as it drastically reduced the extra-bloc importation taxes. MERCOSUR became a huge opportunity for expansion of the markets of foreign company subsidiaries that were installed or would be installed in national territory. According to Bastos:

> one of the impacts of that trading opening on regional integration was that it reinforced the orientation of the subsidiaries of foreign companies

---

8  As we will see later, in our view, MERCOSUR played a hybrid role insofar as it served, not only to amplify the opening up of trade but also to guarantee an increase in the exportation of products manufactured by Brazilian industries. The political aspect which conferred on MERCOSUR the role of giving the Brazilian State a greater margin for maneuver in the face of imperialism, only came to be effective once the FTAA negotiations were underway, that is, starting in 1996.

installed in Brazil to export in the direction of the South American market, especially in those branches more intensive in technology and scale.
BASTOS, 2012a, p.35

However, during that period, the Brazilian industrial bourgeoisie also benefited from the process because the reduction in intra-bloc customs tariffs led to an expressive increase in trading exchanges among the member-countries. That increase in trading exchanges among the Member-States was intended to compensate for the losses incurred with the increase in importation from other countries. According to Sabbatini (2003), Brazilian exports to MERCOSUR countries increased by roughly 15% from 1989 to 2000 while in other regions around the globe the increase was only around 4.5%. Manufactured goods, machinery, transportation equipment and chemical products accounted for 80% of the products exported to MERCOSUR.

Even so, the Brazilian balance of trade was one of deficits up until the years 2000. The adoption of the Common External Tariff coupled with the tariff reduction and the reduction of the importation taxes contributed to the increase of Brazilian importation. Even the trading between Brazil and Argentina registered deficits due to Brazil's oil and wheat purchases.

To sum up, the bloc benefited the multinational companies installed in the territories of the region and also served to capture highly important exportation markets for the Brazilian industrial bourgeoisie. Furthermore, over the years, as will be shown below, MERCOSUR performed the important role of increasing the Brazilian State's bargaining power in the FTAA and the MERCOSUR-European Union negotiations (Pinheiro, 2000).

Sallum Jr. (2011) states that:

> [by means of MERCOSUR] it was intended to expand Brazil's economic space, and not only for national companies; the greater economic space was expected to attract the multinational companies and with that, obtain a relatively greater proportion of the world productive system.
> SALLUM JR., 2011, p.272

In the analysis of Mello (2000), the regional policy of the 1990s can be interpreted from two points of view. The first is the idea that it was subproduct of the neoliberal policies seeking to intensify the liberalization of trading. The second argues that the implementation of the CET brought to the bloc the possibility that it could become a common market and not just a Free Trade Area agreement like the North American Free Trade Agreement (NAFTA). A common market would make it possible for the Member-States to act jointly in the extra-bloc negotiations and that would enhance the Brazilian State's bargaining power.

In the same direction, the Brazilian State made every effort to consolidate MERCOSUR and expand it, that is, to aggregate other South American States that were part of the Latin American Integration Association (*Associação Latino-americana de Integração*-ALADI), and to stimulate the formation of the South American Free Trade Area (*Área de Livre Comércio Sul-americano*-ALCA).

The Brazilian industrial bourgeoisie then began to mobilize to establish relations with the industrial bourgeoisies of the other member countries and sought, above all, to instruct and encourage Brazilian businessmen in regard to that new internationalization process. According to Ardissone (1999, p.54):

> MERCOSUR is also going to provoke transformations in the dynamics of corporate action, ... MERCOSUR performs an important role in regard to the national businessmen ... it is a way of encouraging the Brazilian businessmen to seek out new market opportunities, forming partnerships for their businesses and diversifying their investments.

In the view of Oliveira (2003) and Carvalho (2003), the Brazilian bourgeoisie only had a slight participation in the formation of MERCOSUR. According to those authors "it was only in 1993 that the first organizational movements of the corporate sector took place; that was when it began to realize that much had already been negotiated without any private sector participation (Oliveira, 2003, p.24)". Contradicting what those authors state, we would argue that ever since the beginning of the MERCOSUR creation process, the Brazilian industrial bourgeoisie had perceived the importance of the bloc and sought for ways of participating in the negotiations. It is worth examining the respective FIESP document (Viana, 1991, p.25):

> Itamaraty was still headed by chancellor Abreu Sodré, thus, it was in the time of the Sarney government, when the FIESP/CIESP spoke out against the government's tendency, on various occasions, to keep corporate leaders away from the negotiations for Latin American integration. Perhaps the situation has not been entirely reverted but one plea that the entities made was acceded to: generally speaking, the negotiations are no longer initiated without there being official documents that precede them informing what is going to be negotiated.

It is also important to underscore the participation of the National Confederation of Industry (*Confederação Nacional da Indústria*-CNI) in the

MERCOSUR Industrial Council since 1994 and the creation of the Economic and Social Consultative Forum (*Fórum Consultivo Econômico e Social*-FCES) in 1996, both spaces favoring the articulation of Southern Cone bourgeoisies. Among the various state Federations of Industry, FIESP was the one that showed the most enthusiasm for MERCOSUR as can be seen in the excerpt below:

> In a document published in April 1994, the FIESP industrial businessmen highlighted the strategic value of MERCOSUR, seen as part of the implementation of a new model of the region's countries in the international market and a means of strengthening the position of the member countries in the face of other regional groupings.
> ARDISSONE, 1999, p.61

Actually, it was when the external negotiations for the FTAA and the MERCOSUR-European Union began that MERCOSUR enjoyed the strongest support of the Brazilian industrial bourgeoisie. It began to defend the continuity of the bloc as a priority. By means of its performance in the MERCOSUR Economic and Social Consultative Forum (*Fórum Consultivo Econômico e Social*-FCES) that fraction sought to strengthen its position of resistance to orthodox neoliberalism in Brazil and in the region.

Unquestionably, the FTAA represented an intensification of neoliberalism and United States hegemony in Latin America. The agreement not only foresaw the liberalization of trade but also the imposition of WTO regulations known as the WTO-plus. They covered the liberalization of services (education, health, sanitation, transportation, etc.), access to government purchasing, protection for investments, guarantees for intellectual property rights etc. If all those directives were to come into force, then new environmental and labor rights would be necessary, drastically reducing the conquests achieved by the workers' historical struggles. Furthermore, they would have a destructive effect on the national industrial park, increasing unemployment, denationalizing the economy, agriculture, trade and services all of which would pass into the hands of the big United States corporations. It would form the world's largest economic bloc with 34 countries. The great beneficiary would be the United States as there would be no counterpart sacrifice on its part such as reducing agricultural subsidies for example (Jakobsen & Martins, 2004).

The FTAA proposal first appeared in 1990 in the Bush administration's launching of the Initiative for the Americas. In principle, the proposal foresaw bilateral agreements and sought, above all, to contain the advance of regional integration without the presence of the United States. In 1994, when the Clinton government relaunched the proposal at the First Summit of the

Americas in Miami, it had already incorporated the WTO-plus themes. The United States argued that the internationalization of the corporations would build transnational production chains. They alleged that protectionism could impede the benefits that foreign investments would generate, above all, by contributing to overcoming trading deficits. However, as mentioned above, the increase in direct foreign investment in Brazil actually led to a high rate of denationalization of the economy and brought with it no reversal of the balance of trade deficit, quite the contrary. In reality the direct foreign investment was mainly directed at company mergers and acquisitions and not at the installation of new production plants. The perception that the results were not so positive as had been expected became increasingly clear to the Brazilian industrial bourgeoisie after 1996 and so it began to mobilize to curb the progress of that process.

In 1996, the Brazilian industrial bourgeoisie carried out a big mobilization in Brasilia in which it clamored for an increase in importation taxes for the toys, textiles, footwear, electronics and capital goods sectors and made a point of underscoring that their demands did not mean a return to the old Brazilian development model. They stressed the need for Brazilian industry to have conditions to compete on an equal footing with products coming from the United States and China. According to the FIESP (1996b, p.6):

> It has become evident that Brazil reduced its trade barriers very rapidly and it is understood that the time has come to consolidate the position already achieved before trying out any new advances. That spurt has already caused serious impacts in the reduction of costs and prices inside the country, but it has also affected industrial sectors that were still in the process of adapting to the new reality.

The year 1996 was also notable in the international sphere with big events affecting the interests of the Brazilian industrial bourgeoisie. The first was the negotiation of the protocol for the defense of competition in the ambit of MERCOSUR. The second was the adherence of Bolivia and Chile as members associated to the bloc. The third was the complaint, formally filed in the WTO by Japan, against the Brazilian automotive agreement.[9] Lastly there were

---

9  Provisional Measure 1,024 of June 1995 was scheduled to remain in force until the end of 1999 and was designed to enhance protection for the automotive industry installed in Brazil by means of importation taxes and tariffs and the requirement of a certain minimum percentage of nationalization of parts/auto-parts. Those measures sought to curb the surge in car imports in Brazil and stimulate the formation of new industrial plants.

the rounds of the FTAA negotiations, especially the Business Forum of the Americas in Cartagena.

During the negotiation of the protocol for the defense of competition in the ambit of MERCOSUR, FIESP organized a seminar on the topic jointly with the Administrative Council for Economic Defense (*Conselho Administrativo de Defesa Econômica*-CADE) linked to the Ministry of Justice and that was the theme for the cover and editorial of the Industry Journal (*Revista da Industria*) (1996a). A reading of the editorial reveals the weight that the Brazilian industrial bourgeoisie attributed to the bloc. The editorial stated that:

> The creation of MERCOSUR faced all of us with fascinating, complex challenges. After all we live under different fiscal, labor and social security systems. We have discordant policies in sensitive areas such as interest and exchange rates, and there are peculiarities in the field of economic law that require a great effort of conciliation to make the living together of those who produce under different regimes possible [...].

"Competition is the determinant condition for the efficacy of the integration project. We will only manage to make MERCOSUR an instrument favoring the region's countries and consumers if we have liberty for entrepreneurs and equal conditions in the dispute for the market" (FIESP, 1996a). The Federation began to call for an increase in BNDES financing for exportation as way of increasing overseas sales and it closely accompanied the conflicts between the Brazilian State and the Japanese State, pressing for the defense of the industry installed in Brazil.

Considering all that has been set out above we would argue that the set of events in 1996 are a sign of the negative impact the opening of trading had and of the reaction of that fraction we refer to as the internal bourgeoisie. That fraction began to organize itself and to take a more active part on the national and international political scenes which culminated, in the year 2002, with the rejection of the FTAA proposal as it was then being presented on the negotiating table. As we will see below, the Brazilian industrial and agrarian bourgeoisies, led by the National Confederation of Industry, organized the Brazilian Business Coalition (*Coalizão Empresarial Brasileira*-CEB) in order to closely accompany the international negotiations that the Brazilian State was involved in and which could drastically affect the national industrial park.

The CEB was created after some Brazilian businessmen had participated in the 2nd Business Forum of the Americas in 1996 in Cartagena; it was a meeting of Latin American bourgeoisies to negotiate the FTAA proposal. At that meeting, which was one of a series of FTAA negotiating meetings, the Brazilian bourgeoisie was surprised by the degree of preparation of the United States businessmen and felt themselves threatened by their technical knowledge and their capacity to influence the positions of the United States government in international negotiations. Coincidentally or not, it was agreed that the next forum would take place in Belo Horizonte, in Brazil. The National Confederation of Industry realized the need to expand its influence and offered to organize the Forum itself (Oliveira, 2003).

During the organization process, the CNI managed to bring together broad sectors of the Brazilian bourgeoisie around the need to participate in the formulation, negotiation and decisions of the international negotiations. The objective of the CEB was to centralize the businessmen's demands in regard to the FTAA negotiations and transform them into the community's requirements to be presented to Itamaraty and to guide the businessmen's participation in the meetings of the Business Forum of the Americas. It was the Brazilian bourgeoisie's first national multi-sector organization. According to the *Revista da Industria* (Hamilton, 1996, p.21):

> Brazilian businessmen who accompanied the meeting state that, in the formation of the FTAA it is important to avoid the mistakes made at the time of the creation of MERCOSUR. In that case the Brazilian private sector had been left out of the most important deliberations. "The intention now is to avoid having the economic opening process leading the Latin American countries to face competitive difficulties concentrating its exportation portfolio in raw products", says Douat.

In the ambit of the FTAA, at the Belo Horizonte meeting in 1997, the adopted strategy was to guarantee that the negotiation should be conducted on the basis of building blocs, especially between MERCOSUR and NAFTA. Also, the commitments should be ratified in a single undertaking: "Nothing is agreed until everything has been agreed on". Furthermore, the FTAA agreements needed to be compatible with the WTO rules. According to the *Revista da Industria* editorial 'Integration without Subordination' one week after the meeting:

> Government people, economic authorities, diplomats, businessmen, trade unionists and politicians, in unison, as if orchestrated by a sensible conductor, reacted with thoughtfulness and rationality to that attempt to reedit the anachronistic big stick policy of the northern hemisphere power. And instead of a defensive attitude, what one saw was the formulation of a firm and integrated policy of the MERCOSUR countries.
> 
>   FIESP, 1997

Oliveira (2003) reports that the CEB's position varied from one of engaged support (demanding) to one of engaged opposition. In regard to market access, non-tariff barriers, antidumping, subsidies, competition policies and controversy solution the demanding support position prevailed. In regard to intellectual property rights, investments, services and government purchases, the posture was to call for a more restrictive agreement in regard to the WTO rules. However, the CEB did not fail to demand progress in the negotiations of the so-called 'new themes'. The Brazilian bourgeoisie in general saw, in the FTAA, an opportunity to address the issue of the so called 'Brazil cost'. In that sense, the support for the new themes was predominantly related to reducing State expenditure by privatizing public services.

Actually, there were also contradictions within the industrial bourgeoisie in regard to the FTAA proposal. The most intense activism was that of the protectionist sectors, especially big and medium-sized companies in the Brazilian south and southeast whose manufactured products (paper, cellulose, electro-electronics, chemicals, food products and capital goods) were directed at the internal and Latin American markets. Those sectors expressed their opposition to the FTAA proposal right from the beginning of the negotiations. Sectors orientated towards foreign markets, especially agribusiness, steel mills, footwear and textiles, had a positive view of the project. In the case of services (financial, telecommunications, transportation and trade), sectors that integrate the trading bourgeoisie, they were under-represented and hardly took a stance. According to Oliveira (2003, p.60): "among the national big businessmen three clusters of main visions coexist: unconditional rejection of the FTAA (protectionists), unconditional support (internationalists) and conditional support (cautious internationalists)".

The sectors that most strongly supported the FTAA proposal were the textile and agriculture sectors. The textile sector's stance was due to the fact that it was a competitive sector that had been benefited by productive restructuring in the 1990s decade and as a result had managed to conquer the Latin American and North American markets. At the same time the sector was fearful of Asian international competition, not only in the internal market but in the hemisphere market as a whole, and so it saw the FTAA as an opportunity to obtain greater competitive advantages. The agricultural sector wished to see a reduction in North American non-tariff barriers and gain access to that market (Oliveira, 2003).

Sectors like the automotive and automotive parts sectors were worried about the risks and opportunities of hemisphere-wide integration. They were benefited by the competitive advantages of MERCOSUR and therefore feared the unequal competition that would arise with the installation of United

States and Mexican corporations. Other sectors that were equally concerned were the steel manufacture and footwear sectors because of the high surtaxes (anti-dumping measures) enforced by the United States. The most resistant sectors were: paper and cellulose, chemicals, electro-electronics, and capital goods. According to Oliveira (2003, p.39):

> the asymmetry of sector participation led to a tendency to form a coalition of a defensive nature. Although the institutional structure sought to stimulate a balanced participation of the various sectors and class entities, there was an observable unbalance leaning towards the greater participation of clearly defensive associations, as was the case with Abimaq, Abinee, Abiquim, and Eletros.[10] According to the CNI representative (2000, interview), those sectors tend to be more organizationally structured to exert influence and be more vociferous insofar as they more clearly identify the potential risk they run in the case of an intensification of opening and liberalization via continental integration. On the other hand, those sectors with a positive interest in integration tend to be less active.

In the early years of the negotiations, agribusiness's performance was parallel to that of the CEB. The National Confederation of Agriculture (*Confederação Nacional da Agricultura*-CNA) enthusiastically welcomed the creation of the Free Trade Area of the Americas, expressing great interest in the American proposal. According to Santana (2001, p.182–183):

> That stance was due to the fact that it was a sector that had not suffered the negative impact of the economic liberalization of the 1990s. Furthermore, the difficulties at the GATT negotiations experienced to reduce the agricultural subsidies and the American and European Union importation taxes fostered that sector's expectation that via the FTAA, it would be possible to ensure access to the United States market.

---

10   ABIMAQ-*Associação Brasileira da Indústria de Máquinas e Equipamentos* [Brazilian Machinery and Equipment Industry Association], ABINEE – *Associação Brasileira da Indústria Elétrica e Eletrônica* [Brazilian Electrical and Electronics Industry Association], ABOQUIM – *Associação Brasileira da Industria Química* [Brazilian Chemical Industry Association], Eletros, *Associação Nacional de Fabricante de Produtos* Eletroeletrônicos [National Association of Electrical-Electronic Products Manufacturers].

Clashes between agribusiness and the industrial bourgeoisie continued up until the 1999 WTO meeting in Seattle. In February of that year, the National Confederation of Agriculture and the Brazilian Agribusiness Association (*Associação Brasileira de Agrobusiness*-Abag) and the Brazilian Cooperatives Organization (*Organização das Cooperativas Brasileira* – OCB), all agriculture sector organizations, went so far as to create the Permanent Forum of International Agricultural Negotiations (*Fórum Permanente das Negociações Agrícolas Internacionais*), a body specifically intended to defend agribusiness interests. Even so:

> there was no significant divergence presented by the CEB or the Forum for the Seattle meeting.
> CARVALHO, 2003, p.373 *apud* CNI, 1999 and FÓRUM, 1999

"The business sector proposed a broad agenda for negotiation in which there was a demanding posture in regard to agriculture, antidumping measures, subsidies and compensatory measures and defensive attitudes in regard to industrial goods and services. In relation to the so-called 'new themes' (investment, competition, intellectual property and government purchasing), the position was one of caution. According to the CEB, Brazil could negotiate those themes according to the extent the demanding interests were met" (Carvalho, 2003, p.373–374).

In other words, in the course of the FTAA negotiations, the contradictions between the agribusiness and industry gradually lost their importance. That was connected with the fact that the United States adamantly refused to relinquish their protectionist agricultural policies. Thus, Brazilian agribusiness had no good reason to pressure the Brazilian State to sign the free trade agreement and ended up joining the ranks of the anti-FTAA sectors.

"According to the head of the CNA's foreign trade department, Antônio Donizete Beraldo, agriculture is one of the most sensitive and problematic issues in the FTAA negotiations, mainly due to the subsidies that the USA provides for its agriculture" (DG ABC, March 30, 2001). Furthermore, the disputes around tariff and non-tariff barriers and the lack of consensus on the social, labor and environmental clauses of the agreement, became increasingly apparent, contributing towards the unfruitful outcome of the negotiations. In other words, the Brazilian industrial bourgeoisie and agribusiness eventually agglutinated in the same political fraction whose demand was the non-acceptance of the unequal rules of those international trade agreements.

> the exporting sectors which could have taken the stance of exerting a strong pro-FTAA force did not do so for different reasons. The most important was its perception that the North American non-tariff barriers, production subsidies and anti-dumping measures impacted most blatantly on those sectors in which Brazil had comparatively more advantages in the context of hemisphere integration. Accordingly, those sectors began to demand more access to the North American market and in the absence of any substantial concessions, began to support a more defensive position on the part of the Coalition and the Brazilian government.
>
> OLIVEIRA, 2003, p.65

The Brazilian State, according to Thorstensen (2001), found itself facing a triple challenge in the ambit of the international economic negotiations. The FTAA, MERCOSUR EU and WTO negotiations intertwined and made it possible for the Brazilian State to perform strategically on the international scene. The WTO and MERCOSUR-EU negotiations served as a counterweight to the FTAA negotiations. As a way of obtaining advantages and gaining time in the FTAA negotiations, the Brazilian State made a question of displaying a positive attitude in relation to the negotiations with the European Union and the WTO. It is important to state that from the Brazilian point of view, those three negotiations represented asymmetrical relations between imperialist states and dependent ones, a threat to Brazilian industry and the expectation of a reduction in agricultural protectionisms.

In its aspect as an international actor, MERCOSUR became a hindrance to the progress of the FTAA negotiations especially because of the stance adopted by the Brazilian government. Fernando Henrique declared that favoring trade links with the United States to the detriment of a stronger MERCOSUR and the trade links with the European Union "would be an "impoverishing option" (*apud* Bandeira, 2004, p.129). When it saw that the Brazilian State was more resistant to intensifying the FTAA negotiations than the other states, the United States began to propose bilateral agreements with Argentina, Uruguay, Paraguay and with the Central American states. According to Bandeira (2004, p.120):

> the creation of the FTAA was based on an ideological premise, Pan Americanism, which in other words meant America for the Americans and it sheltered a political objective insofar as it intended, on the one hand to repel the competition of the European Union and, on the other, to prevent the formation of the MERCOSUR bloc (MERCOSUR T. B) in the Southern Cone headed by Brazil.

In the face of that scenario Brazil adopted two strategies: 1) participate in the negotiations as it feared that MERCOSUR would become isolated and weakened if the bilateral agreements between the United States and the other MERCOSUR member states were to be ratified; 2) take advantage of the negotiations between MERCOSUR and the European Union and the Doha Round of the WTO to unfold a policy of bargaining with the United States.

The Brazilian Business Coalition in turn, became a reference standard for all the other international economic negotiations in course at the time, especially the Doha Round of the WTO and the MERCOSUR-European Union negotiations. In addition, in contrast to Itamaraty's insular nature, the FTAA negotiations represented gains in terms of the institutionalization of the relations between the Ministry of Foreign Affairs and the Brazilian bourgeoisie. Special sections for consultation and debate on the international economic negotiations were created. The first was the FTAA Special Section (SENALCA) and the second was the Europe Special Section (SENEUROPA), and lastly, the Permanent Business Committee (*Comitê Empresarial Permanente*-CEP) was created (Figueira, 2010).

In regard to the MERCOSUR-European Union negotiations, which began in 1999 during the 1st Latin American and Caribbean Summit, it can be said that there were three great objectives orientating the Brazilian State's position: 1) the possibility of increasing exports of agricultural and agro-industrial products. 2) increasing European investments in Brazil; and 3) strengthening MERCOSUR as an international actor and regional bloc (Bezerra, 2008).

In 2001 the bloc's negotiations accelerated and that contributed towards the internal Brazilian bourgeoisie's rejection of the European Union's initial proposal given that what was excluded from the tariff reduction universe were precisely the agricultural, agro-industrial and fishing industry products (Bezerra, 2008, p.64).

"According to an assessment that the CEB/CNI publicized in a release there was asymmetry in the treatment of the various sectors compared with that for industrial goods, a sector in which the Europeans are more competitive and for which the offer covered almost the entire tariff universe in addition to foreseeing the total or almost total elimination of customs rights by predefined dates. In the offer for the agricultural and agro-industrial goods in which the MERCOSUR countries are more competitive, however, the proposal was limited to reducing *ad valorem* tariffs which are merely a secondary barrier to Brazilian exports. Basically, the fact that the European market for industrial products is already considerably open reinforces the concentration of European protectionism in the agricultural sector. Thus, dissatisfaction with the European proposal is not limited to the industrial sector alone, threatened as it is by the competition of European products, because the interests of MERCOSUR exporters of the agricultural sector were not considered either. Domestic discontent with the European proposal seems to have drawn together sectors of industry and that of agribusiness due to the strong disequilibrium in the European proposal."

### 3.2   Regional Politics between 1998 and 2000: The MERCOSUR Crisis and the Launching of the IIRSA

In regard to regional politics, despite the dubious position of Alberto Fujimori in Peru in the year 2000, there was a notable growth in the Brazilian State's role as regional arbitrator, starting with the frontier conflict between Peru and Ecuador in 1996 and the defense of democracy in Paraguay in 1996, 1999 and 2001. In 1998 MERCOSUR, driven by the political crisis in Paraguay in 1996, adopted the Democratic Clause by means of the Ushuaia Agreement. With that the bloc acquired a more political profile.

On the other hand, again in 1998, the trading conflicts among the member States began. Little by little it became apparent that the TEC fulfilled its political objective in the external negotiations, boosting the bargaining power of MERCOSUR in the face of the United States and Europe but, in regard to economic aspects, the innumerable exceptions that had been conceded in the course of the preceding ten years made that an unfulfilled commitment. The first conflict arose when the Brazilian Ministry of Health and the Ministry of Agriculture issued a preliminary License for the importation of chemical, pharmaceutical and agricultural and livestock related products. That measure led the Argentinean Chamber of Exporters to set in motion the MERCOSUR mechanism for resolving controversies.

"In retaliation for the Preliminary Licensing requirement, Argentina announced the signing of a bilateral Free Trade Agreement with Mexico by the end of 2001, going against the Brazilian proposal to negotiate in the 4+1 mode (MERCOSUR + Mexico). Since then, the trading controversies between the two major MERCOSUR partners have only grown. Brazil threatened to appeal to the arbitration courts against Argentina for its discrimination of Brazilian sugar which, at the time, was being penalized with a 23% tariff for it to gain access to the Argentine market. In the same way, Brazil threatened to activate the controversy solution mechanism against the anti-dumping action that Argentina had moved against Brazilian steel and which according to the Brazilian exporters was harming Brazilian sales of hot-binding steel to the neighboring market. In the dairy products sector, Brazilian producers threatened to file an anti-dumping action in the ambit of the MERCOSUR, accusing Argentina of the practice of dumping" (Ardissone, 1999, p.113).

However, the issue that most gave rise to disagreements in 1998 was the automotive agreement. The Brazilian and Argentinean States disagreed about the nationalization criterion for automobiles. The Nacional Association of Automobile Manufacturers (*Associação Nacional de Fabricantes de Veículos Automotores*-Anfavea) clamored for parts production to be regional while Argentina wanted to protect its own industry. The Argentine State went so far as to try to apply Common External Tariffs to those Brazilian products that enjoyed local state benefits such as the Manaus Free Trade Zone.

In December 1998, the automotive regime was debated at the 32nd Meeting of the Ministers and at the Summit Meeting of MERCOSUR presidents in January 1999, an agreement was signed that foresaw the establishment of 60% nationalization index for automotive parts produced in member countries and a 35% common tariff on imports from third countries. There was to be a transition period for the agreement, and it would enter into force on January 1st, 2000. At that meeting, an agreement was also reached on reducing the sugar tariff (Ardissone, 1999).

The scenario seemed to have improved but the currency exchange crisis in Brazil exacerbated the internal conflicts and MERCOSUR experienced its first big crisis (Onuki, 2006). The devaluation of the real against the dollar affected Argentina's sales to Brazil and brought about a trade unbalance between the two economies. That led Argentina to adopt a series of unilateral measures that put the very existence of the bloc in check. Among the more outstanding measures were: a reduction on the tariff charges on imports from outside MERCOSUR covering electronic products, agricultural machinery, and capital goods in general; a prior consultation for importations worth more than US800; and state incentives and increased safeguards for exportation. Trade exchanges between Brazil and Argentina dropped by 25% in the first quarter of 1999 (Mathias, 2011, p.193 and p.194). The trading disagreements worsened with the outbreak of the political and economic crises in Argentina in 2000 and 2001.

The Brazilian industrial bourgeoise, anxious to preserve the flow of trade in the bloc, "took the road of direct negotiations with its partners in the neighboring country seeking for agreements that might 'calm down' the market" (Mathias, 2011, 194 195). A considerable part of the Brazilian industrial bourgeoisie began to self-limit its exportation to Argentina most notably in the paper and cellulose sector. Meat and poultry exporters also adopted a regime of quotas for the supply of their products to the neighboring country (Ardissone, 1999, p.121).

Thus, the crises in the bloc's two main countries revealed MERCOSUR's institutional fragility and the need for more profound integration especially urgent measures to reduce the asymmetry among the countries. The MERCOSUR Industrial Council, which brought together the Brazil's National Confederation of Industry, the Argentina Industrial Union, Uruguay's Chamber of Industry, and Paraguay's Industrial Union, published a communiqué in March 2000 proposing greater progress for the macro-economic and sector-based coordination as part of the 'MERCOSUR Relaunching'. That very year the bilateral automotive agreement came into force (Mathias, 2011, p.198–199). According to Ardissone (1999, p.112):

> Despite the drop in MERCOSUR trading exchanges, there was a readily apparent flexible stance on the part of the Brazilian business sector in its quest for formulas to re-compose matters with its partners in the other countries. The aim was to avoid the imposition of any new trade barriers against their products which had been abruptly favored in the intra-regional trading.

Clearly the Brazilian industrial bourgeoisie saw MERCOSUR as a favored space for a possible reversal of the economic slowdown. For that reason, the Brazilian State sought to expand and intensify South American integration to ensure the perpetuation and expansion of the bloc and in that way guarantee greater gains for the Brazilian industrial bourgeoisie which was increasingly displaying its dissatisfaction with the set of economic policies and with the foreign policy.

Against that background, the Brazilian State convened a meeting of twelve South American presidents in August 2000 in Brasília. At that meeting the Initiative for South American Regional Integration in Infrastructure (*Integração em Infraestrutura Regional Sul-americana*-IIRSA) was launched and the discussion of the fusion of MERCOSUR and the Andean Community of Nations (*Comunidade Andina das Nações*-CAN) was invigorated. The launching of the IIRSA was to inaugurate the expansion of the regional integration project which previously had been based exclusively on economic and trade aspects but then began to incorporate the question of infrastructure.[11]

However, the projects presented at that time were designed primarily to create regional corridors for exportation to other regions of the world and

---

11   The reference here is not just to MERCOSUR but also to the ALALC and ALADI integration initiatives in the 1960s and 1980s respectively.

were not expected to exclusively address local interests and necessities. As we will see in greater depth in the coming chapters, the meeting in Brasília is considered to be a milestone for the new regional integration process and especially for the creation of the Union of South American Nations (UNASUL). Nevertheless, according to Honório (2013, p.29):

> One could consider that although the 2000 meeting did represent a change in regard to the themes that had guided regionalism since the 1990s decade (tariff measures, facilitating trade among the countries and other trade-related issues), the objectives to be achieved by the new strategies proposed at the Brasília meeting still aimed for results of open regionalism with greater regional economic insertion in world markets.

It must also be said that the expansion of the natural gas purchase and sale agreement between the YFPB and Petrobras in 1998 and the entry into operation of the Brazil-Bolivia gasoduct in 1999 were the first strategies representing progress in integration in infrastructure and energy carried out by the FHC governments (Fuser, 2011). The FIESP gave strong support to both projects, as can be seen from the excerpt below:

> The participation of corporate businessmen is of fundamental importance to avoid shortages in energy supply to industry; the thermoelectric plants fired by natural gas could be one of the solutions for the achievement of cheap energy, according to Luis Gonzaga Bertelli, director of FIESP/CIESP's Industrial Infrastructure Department (*Departamento de Infra-Estrutura Industrial*-Deinfra). "For that to happen, the long hoped for gasoduct from Bolivia has yet to be made feasible".
> 
> FIESP, 1996a, p.20

The 1993 agreement between the Brazilian and Bolivian States had been aligned with the recommendations of the World Bank and the IMF not only in the aspect of privatization of the electricity sector in the two countries, but also in the diversification of their power supply matrices. The initial contract provided for the construction of the Brazil-Bolivia Gasoduct (Gasbol) and the purchase of 8 million cubic meters of gas a day, to be gradually increased until it reached 16 million. The new contract increased the supply to 30 million cubic meters a day. The Hydrocarbons law of 1996 benefited the Petrobras, and it took control of the main Bolivian gas reserves (*Margarita, Itau, San Alberto abd San Antonio*) and became the biggest corporation installed in Bolivian territory. It was regulated by a concession contract whereby Petrobras paid the Bolivian government a mere 18% of royalties (Fuser, 2011).

> The introduction of the figure of 'new' hydrocarbon fields governed by a fiscal regime highly favorable to foreign companies, was obviously intended to make investment in Bolivian gas a more attractive proposition with a view to its exportation, especially to the Brazilian market (Villegas, 2004, p.83). However, there was a considerable lack of transparency associated to all the measures the Bolivian government adopted to favor the multinational corporations. As a result, Petrobras's debut in the exploration, production and trading, transportation and distribution of Bolivian gas occurred under a cloud of suspicion and denouncements many of which have yet to be clarified and which would later fuel the nationalist campaign against the privatization of hydrocarbons.
> 
> FUSER, 2011, p.138–139

In the year 2000 with the electricity crisis in Brazil and the notorious 'Blackout' (*Apagão*) the consumption of Bolivian natural gas increased. At the same time, the impacts of the neoliberal policies led to the reactivation of the Bolivian movements for the nationalization of gas. As is well known, those movements led to the election of Evo Morales and a new contract between Petrobras and the Bolivian State in 2006. That will be further explored in the next chapter.

It is important to remember that in 2000 the United States launched its Colombia Plan and installed around 20 military units and bases in South and Central America (Manta in Ecuador, three in Peru, four in Colombia, one in Bolivia, one in Guyana and the rest in Central America). They justified that as part of the combat against drug trafficking. However, as is well known, those bases and the FTAA project as well, were basically aimed at gaining access to, and control over the natural resources and energy resources available in South and Central America, among other intentions. Only the Brazilian and Venezuelan States refused to allow the concession of their territory for the installation of the bases, and they did not accede to the Colombia Plan.

Bandeira (2004) considers that the main reason for that rejection was the Brazilian military's stance. The military were highly reticent in regard to the United States' real intentions in the Amazon. They saw the Colombia Plan as an excuse for United States occupation and monitoring of that important region. In response to the proposal, they began to intensify military exercises and called for the reequipping of the Armed Forces, which had been greatly neglected in the course of the 1990s decade in obedience to the IMF and the World Bank's requirement of a reduction in State spending.

## 3.3 The Lafer Administration and the Brazilian State's Passive Subordination to Imperialism

On January 29, 2001, Celso Lafer was nominated Minister of Foreign Affairs of Brazil. In the two years that Lafer headed the Ministry many things happened, among them: attack on the twin towers on September 11, the launching of the Doha round of the WTO and the progress of the MERCOSUR-European Union negotiations. In that same year, the litigation between the Brazilian and Canadian States involving the Embraer and Bombardier companies reached its height and even spilled over to affect the meat sector.[12]

Lafer's administration was quite turbulent and that contributed to the intensification of criticism and dissatisfaction with the FHC governments' foreign policy. We differ from Cervo (2008), Silva (2012) and Vigevani and Cepaluni (2011) and do not consider that in the years 2000 there was a change in foreign policy which, later, the Lula administrations would merely deepen. We argue that, on the contrary, during the FHC governments, the Brazilian State's subordination to the United States became ever more explicit.

Minister Lafer's most emblematic actions confirm that affirmation. They were: the declaration that Brazil would support the United States in a war against those responsible for the attack on the World Trade Center towers; the attempt to reactivate the InterAmerican Treaty for Reciprocal Assistance (ITRA) as a continental defense instrument; the affirmation that Bush's going to the UN general assembly to try to justify the invasion of Iraq was a positive thing (according to Lafer, it was demonstration of multilateralism); the episode where he, the Brazilian Chancellor, agreed to take off his shoes for security checks on entering and leaving the Miami and New York airports; the failure to contest the deposition of ambassador José Mauricio Bustani from the post of Director General of the Organization for the Prohibition of Chemical Weapons when the United States unjustly accused him of corruption. Actually, the position Bustani took created difficulties for the invasion of Iraq (Bandeira, 2004).

All those attitudes showed that the FHC government, in the figure of its Minister of Foreign Affairs, adopted every stance possible to avoid creating any kind of friction with the United States (Bandeira, 2004). Another notable fact marking Lafer's time in office was the instauration of what came to be called the 'Gag Law'. "The notorious and polemical Gag law (*Lei da Mordaça*) was actually an internal circular of recommendation referring to diplomats expressing their opinions in regard to foreign policy" (Mesquita, 2013, p.124). Mesquita informs

---

12   The litigation between the Brazilian and Canadian States began in 1996 and was only settled in 2002.

us that the circular was designed to curb any manifestation, on the part of diplomats, of opposition to the neoliberal political project. Based on that circular, Minister Lafer dismissed ambassador Samuel Pinheiro Guimarães from the presidency of Itamaraty's Institute of International Relations Studies (*Instituto de Pesquisa de Relações Internacionais*-IPRI).

The ambassador's dismissal came after he had participated in a meeting of the Brazilian Equipment and Machinery Association (*Associação Brasileira de Máquinas e Equipamentos*-ABIMAQ). Samuel had been highly critical of the FTAA and had published several interviews and documents declaring his positions. In his view the Brazilian State should abandon the FTAA negotiations insofar as it was a United States project for political and military annexation. The ambassador's dismissal provoked the immediate reaction of ABIMAQ president Luis Carlos Delben Leite who sent a letter to Celso Lafer:

> declaring that if the 'last straw' for Samuel Guimarães's dismissal had been his manifestation regarding the FTAA during the debate organized by the ABIMAQ, then "it would be profoundly regrettable, given the propriety and seriousness of his arguments".
> BANDEIRA, 2004, p.209

The Abimaq president's reaction demonstrates even more clearly the extent of the declared opposition that a part of the Brazilian bourgeoisie had begun to express in regard to the FTAA and to the set of financial deregulation and trade opening policies. From 2001 on after the election of George W. Bush in the United States, the FTAA negotiations became more intense and that boosted the agglutination of the big Brazilian internal bourgeoisie.

We believe that the FTAA negotiations were the framework for the agglutination of the Brazilian industrial bourgeoisie and agribusiness as a class fraction with the political behavior of an internal bourgeoisie. In reality, seduced by the neoliberal ideology, the Brazilian bourgeoisie defended the government's participation in the FTAA negotiations in spite of the disequilibrium and the risks the agreement presented. The reason was that it intended to preserve the bonds with the United States and prevent a possible exodus of capital. It is worth remembering that in its aspect as an internal bourgeoisie, it maintained its ties of dependency and its political-ideological dissolution. That is why, in spite of wishing to protect its own internal market, that fraction did not intend to break off relations with imperialism which is what led it to delay so long before explicitly rejecting the United States proposal. Furthermore, as we have seen in the position of textile industry, the internal bourgeoisie did not only desire the protection of the internal market, but it also intended to internationalize, conquer markets and install plants in other territories. Chapter 3 will show how it was precisely those three aspects that the Lula government's foreign policy would address more profoundly.

### 3.4 The 2002 Elections

We do not intend to make an in-depth analysis of the 2002 elections as that lies beyond the scope of this work. Nevertheless, it is worth retrieving from them three important elements that are related to the object of this work. The first is the FTAA's role and the opposition of the Brazilian internal bourgeoisie, the grassroots social movements and the trade unions. After that comes a presentation of a brief analysis of the documents that the CNI and the FIESP published in 2002 focusing on foreign policy-related issues. Similarly, we will delineate the trajectory that led to the PT's political program in 2002. The idea is to demonstrate how the actions and positions of the PT, the internal bourgeoisie and the social movements converged, however unintentionally, in the 2002 elections.

#### 3.4.1 The FTAA and the 2002 Elections

The FTAA was actually one of the main issues in the electoral dispute of 2002. It mobilized a considerable part of Brazilian society: the bourgeoisie, the diplomats, the trade union federations, social movements, the progressive wing of the Catholic church and the left-wing political parties. The positions in regard to the FTAA surfaced in the dispute between the PSDB and the PT. In 2001, a year before the election, the FHC government had begun to display a more assertive position in regard to the agreement negotiations whereas the PT declared its complete opposition to it. Lula and the PT declared that the FTAA was more of a project for the annexation of Latin American economies to the United States than a project of regional integration (Oliveira, 2003).

Prior to the 2002 Summit of the Americas in Quito, the CEB published a document of recommendations in which it stated that the FTAA should: 1) respect existing regional agreements (meaning MERCOSUR); 2) eliminate internal subsidies for agricultural production; and 3) take structural asymmetries and regional development into account (CEB, 2002). The Quito meeting was marked by the disagreement between the Brazilian State and the United States in regard to the FTAA. In that very year the Bush government had managed to get Congress to approve the Fast Trade Promotion Agreement, the equivalent of creating a fast track, but as a counterpart it had also passed the Farm Bill, an agricultural law that ensured 160 billion dollars in agricultural subsidies over the next ten years. Furthermore, it imposed safeguards on steel.

It is safe to say that both in the aspect of the Brazilian internal bourgeoisie's opposition and the situation of the United States agricultural and steel sectors, the FTAA negotiations had reached a stalemate. No State could make such an external commitment because it would be impossible to get it ratified internally. Again in 2002, the FIESP conducted a study of the FTAA's possible impacts on the Brazilian production sector and declared that the sector's losses would amount to one billion dollars. Furthermore:

> "The FTAA would be fatal for any who were not duly prepared" declared the entity's president, Horácio Lafer Piva. Apparently, Brazil as a whole is not prepared. The meshwork of FIESP numbers reveals, for example, that the country has the lowest average schooling index, the highest interest rate, and the second worst infrastructure index among the six countries that represent 93% of the Bloc (Brazil, Argentina, Canada, Chile, Mexico and the USA). "We come out losing the match as soon as the ball is put in play", laments Piva.
> ISTOÉ-INDEPENDENTE, 2002

Added to that was the resistance and mobilization of the classes of ordinary people throughout Latin America. 2001 was the year of the first edition of the World Social Forum (WSF) in Porto Alegre, which brought together various social movements, union federations and non-governmental organizations against neoliberalism. From that conference emerged the Continental Campaign Against the FTAA.

The grassroots movements and the Brazilian trade union federations organized themselves around the call of the National Campaign Against the FTAA, the Brazilian version of the campaign launched at the WSF. The campaign brought together 55 organizations and outstanding among them were the Unified Workers Central (*Central Única dos Trabalhadores*-CUT), the Landless Rural Workers Movement (*Movimento dos Trabalhadores Rurais Sem Terra*-MST), the social assistance organizations of the National Conference of Brazilian Bishops (*Conferência Nacional dos Bispos do Brasil*-CNBB), the Consulta Popular, the Women's World March (*Marcha Mundial das Mulheres*), the Unified Workers Socialist Party (*Partido Socialista dos Trabalhadores Unificado*-PSTU) and sectors of the Workers Party (*Partido dos Trabalhadores*-PT). Most of those organizations had come into being as part of the struggle for the re-democratization of Brazil and the fight against neoliberalism. That articulation of organizations had already conducted a people's plebiscite regarding the foreign debt, in the year 2000. The movement against the FTAA began in 1997 but the effective organization of the campaign as such only came about in 2001. The aim was to work with the non-bourgeois classes of ordinary people to raise awareness and mobilize the population to pressure the government not to sign the treaty (Silva, 2008).

It should be remembered that the anti-FTAA campaign sprang from the World Social Forum and so it had its national sections in almost all countries of the continent. Thus, the opposition to the FTAA played a fundamental role in unifying the forces of the left in various countries of the continent. That was the reason why the electoral changes that took place in the following period, but which actually began with Chaves in Venezuela in 1998, included in their discourse and their political banners, an emphasis on the reform of neoliberalism, on South American integration and the negation of the FTAA. That aspect was important in the election of Lula in Brazil in 2002, of Nestor Kirschner in Argentina in 2003, Tabaré Vasquez in Uruguay in 2004, Evo Morales in Bolivia in 2005, Rafael Correa in Ecuador in 2006 and, lastly, of Juan Manuel Santos in Colombia in 2009.

The campaign conducted a people's plebiscite in 2002 whose methodology was based on offering courses to qualify the masses in regard to the FTAA's political and economic impacts. Much teaching and instructive material was prepared for that work among the people, including, primers videos and flyers. The campaign had state committees and local ones and they held debates in schools, neighborhoods, universities, churches, and on local radio and TV channels to mobilize the population and collect signatures. The plebiscite obtained more than 10 million votes of which 95% were against Brazil's entering the FTAA. Among the plebiscite questions was one concerning the acceptance or negation of the proposed base in Alcântara.

In addition to uniting a considerable part of the Brazilian left, that articulation exerted a strong pressure on the Brazilian government's decisions, especially on the PT government whose support base had participated intensely in the mobilization. The fight against the FTAA also united large sectors of the ordinary non bourgeois classes in the struggle against the deeper penetration of neoliberalism in the region (Silva, 2008). It can be said that the fight against the FTAA contributed towards the affirmation of a neo-developmentalist platform which became clamored for as much by the working-class organizations as by representatives of the big Brazilian internal bourgeoisie each with their own particular objectives and definitions.

Lastly, the successive government spending cuts the IMF imposed increased the armed forces' dissatisfaction with the government, and they too began to express opposition to the FTAA. They feared that if the FTAA were approved there might be an exacerbation of the scenario of their debilitation by the Brazilian government (Bandeira, 2004, p.295).

### 3.4.2 The Internal Bourgeoisie and the 2002 Election

In 2002, the FIESP/CIESP and the CNI elaborated documents for a discussion with society regarding its assessment of the scenario at the time and its demands for the next government. That FIESP/CIESP document was a primer intitled 'The Brazil of all of us' (*O Brasil de todos nos*) and that of the CNI, 'Industry and Brazil: an agenda for growth' (*A indústria e o Brasil: uma agenda para o crescimento*). An analysis of those documents reveals the dissatisfaction with the foreign trade deficit, with the poor rate of economic growth and with the Brazilian economy's increased external vulnerability. All of that is readily apparent in the respective documents.

> neither the sustainability of the growth of the economy nor the relative stability of the currency exchange rates and inflation could be obtained without the rapid and incisive reduction of the high external deficit in current transactions which made the Brazilian economy highly vulnerable to external shocks.
> FIESP & CIESP, 2002, p.5

"The main reason for the low and volatile average growth of the last few years is, without a doubt, the country's macroeconomic fragility, especially, its high sensitivity to the oscillations of the financial conditions of the world economy" (CNI, 2002, p.19). The documents go on to point out the need for the renewal of economic growth with a focus on industry. The two entities recommended an effort to increase exports and curb imports.

> The solution, and it is a consensus, lies in obtaining and sustaining an expressive trade surplus in the course of the coming years and that means exports need to increase by at least 10% a year plus a detectable moderation in the expansion of importation during that stage. The reduction of the current account deficit also requires facing up to the deficits in the areas of nonfactor services, notably in freight, insurance and tourism.
> That brings into focus the indispensable need for coherent and well-articulated industrial and foreign trade policies, taking global benchmarks into account and using all the available modern instruments like the P & D review of tariff and nontariff barriers, a calibrated tax system and competitive interest rates.
> FIESP & CIESP, 2002, p.5

> Improving the foreign accounts performance is an essential condition for taking up sustained economic growth again. It requires the creation of an environment that *favors the competitiveness of national products in comparison with that of our main foreign competitors in the external and*

> *internal markets,* and that public policies should emit the right signals so that companies consider exports to be a permanent and essential component of their growth strategies. To that end, *foreign trade policy must take on an outstanding role as the axis for industrial policy and Brazil's strategy at the international trade negotiating tables must be compatible with those objectives.*
> CNI, 2002, p.33, our emphasis

However, those same documents categorically warn that the Brazilian industrial bourgeoisie had no expectation of any return of the protectionist policies unfolded in the 20th century (policies for replacing importations anchored in subsidies and control of the currency exchange rate). They reaffirmed support for the economic stability policies, that is, the primary balance of trade surplus, fiscal responsibility and reduction of State expenses and they lobbied in favor of maintaining the floating exchange rate regime and the maintenance of the private contracts. Both showed interest in increasing employment and consequently boosting the internal market. It was a case of what Boito Jr. (1999) defined as moderate neoliberalism, that is, a controlled opening of trade, reduction of State spending and the maintenance of the monetary policies.

In that sense, they argued that it would be necessary to increase Brazilian industry's competitiveness via investment in education, knowledge and infrastructure and to reduce costs with taxes, payrolls (tax reform, labor reform, and social security reform) that is, reduce the so-called Cost-Brazil. FIESP highlighted the need to reduce interest rates and the CNI emphasized the need to reduce customs bureaucracy, reduce port-related costs and international freight rates as well as increasing the credit available for exportation (CNI, 2002, p.33 and p.34). Both organizations declared that they did not recommend placing any restriction on direct foreign investment but also that it was necessary to strengthen national companies. In the terms of the FIESP document:

> Overcoming Brazil's competitive deficiencies cannot fail to count on the constitution of groups of Brazilian businessmen with global dimensions. Without them there will be no development of technological development nuclei capable of affirming brands, creating new products and generating, here, highly qualified activities and jobs.
> FIESP & CIESP, 2002, p.13

In the same line as the FIESP the CNI stated: "It is important to increasingly guide the Brazilian strategy by the links with interests in access to markets of firms in the exporting sectors and by the objective of their increasing internationalization" (CNI, 2002, p.49). In that sense, the CNI recommended proximity with the other dependent states, especially those in South America.

> Brazil must be aggressive in its quest for regional and bilateral trade agreements involving developing countries, especially in the ambit of South America. The object of the country's negotiating strategies must be the widespread removal of barriers to Brazilian exports and progress in the physical integration of the sub-continent.
>
> CNI, 2002, p.49

Given the crisis in MERCOSUR, the CNI recommended that the Brazilian State should head a bloc renovation process and above all emphasized the need to consolidate the Customs Union and eliminate the intra-bloc barriers and the re-invigoration of the common external tariff and the intensification of the bloc's institutionalization.

> MERCOSUR is strategically important to Brazil. The wear suffered by the bloc in the last few years should not be underestimated. It is essential that the country should lead the process for salvaging the strategic dimension of the MERCOSUR sub-regional integration process, launching the bases for the consolidation and deepening of the Customs Union. Once the acute stage of the Argentinean crisis has been overcome, the sub-regional project will retrieve its importance for the Brazilian partners and the country should lead the MERCOSUR revitalization process
>
> CNI, 2002, p.50

In regard to the WTO, FTAA and MERCOSUR-European Union negotiations, the two entities converged insofar as they called on the Brazilian state to act to guarantee greater equilibrium in the regional treaty agreements, and especially in the question of eliminating tariff and nontariff barriers and in the use of anti-dumping instruments. Here is an excerpt from the CNI document intended to:

> Clearly define the country's objectives in the various negotiating forums and the functionality of each one for the global strategy. In the ambit of the WTO, priority should be given to the negotiation of trading rules and discipline, while in the regional sphere (FTAA and MERCOSUR-European Union) significant gains need to be sought in terms of market access for Brazilian exports without jeopardizing those that are being sought in terms of progress in norms and discipline of interest to Brazil (anti-dumping, agricultural subsidies, etc.)
>
> CNI, 2002, p.49

In short, the industrial policy challenges in regard to foreign trade, according to the CNI were:

- Set strategic priority on exports
- Endow industrial policy with a pro-exportation bias.
- Support projects for the competitive replacement of imports
- Promote tax relief for exports
- Reduce bureaucracy in exportation operations
- Rationalize the tax/fiscal structure
- Set priority in opening markets in Brazilian international negotiation strategies
- Take on the leadership of the MERCOSUR project
- Promote social participation and legitimacy in trade negotiations

CNI, 2002, p.35

### 3.4.3  The PT and the 2002 Elections

As we have seen above, the 2002 elections took place against a background of the erosion of orthodox neoliberalism and the criticism and dissatisfaction of different classes and class fractions, especially after the currency exchange crisis in 1999 and the collapse of the electricity supply system (2000 and 2001 Blackouts). Furthermore:

> Lula's victory in 2002 dramatized yet another fragility of the political scheme in force: its socially excluding nature clearly evident in the priorities of the Fernando Henrique Cardoso government, in its conflictive relations with the organized social groups and its scant capacity to communicate with the less-favored segments of the population.
>
> CRUZ, 2013, p.18

That conjuncture opened a window for the opposition to the FHC government. The PT which up until then was the party that had played the role of parliamentary opposition to the neoliberal policies, constituted a governmental program whose proposal was the reform of neoliberalism and which, as we will explore later on, was to become the neo-developmentalist platform.

It is appropriate to underscore, at this point, that since its creation the PT had encompassed a large part of ordinary people's aspirations and at the beginning of the 1990s it had constituted itself from at least six social sectors: the new trade unionism, the progressive wing of the Catholic church, some politicians of the MDB political party, left-wing intellectuals, militants of Trotskyite organizations and militants who had taken part in the armed resistance to the military dictatorship (Secco, 2011, p.27). Therefore, even though it concentrated more on the electoral dispute, the party still enjoyed the electoral support of the unions and the social movements. What was left to do, was to conquer the confidence of the Brazilian bourgeoisie and the international investors.

To that end, in June, 2002, the PT launched its famous 'Letter to the Brazilian People' in which it stated that the "premise of that transition would naturally be to respect the country's contracts and obligations (PT, 2002a)" and it committed itself to preserving "the primary balance of trade surplus to the extent necessary to impede any increase in the internal debt and destroy confidence in the government's capacity to honor its commitments (PT, 2002a, p.4 and p.5)". Secco (2011) considers that the letter crowned a political process that had been in course since the 1990s, namely, ideological moderation. Another important element of that 2002 electoral process was the alliance with parties of the center and the choice of José Alencar as vice-president of the republic. The choice of Alencar "ratified the arc of alliances the PT program proposed, as its axis was purported to be an alliance of the workers with 'productive capital' (Secco, 2011, p.205).

It seems important to register two external elements that exerted strong pressures during the 2002 electoral dispute. They were the alarm of the international financial bourgeoisie and that of the United States extreme right wing. The Secretary of the United States Treasury, Paul O'Neill, alongside the republicans, exacerbated the climate of tension in regard to Lula's possible victory. The great fear, according to the United States neo-conservatives, was in regard to the relations among Lula, Fidel Castro and Hugo Chavez. There were even those who declared that Lula had relations with terrorist groups. That campaign, added to the concern of the international financial bourgeoisie, was directly reflected in the form of an increase in the risk index attributed to Brazil and it brought about a devaluation of the real, and of external investment shares.

To face the crisis, the president at the time, FHC, sought the help of the IMF in June of 2002. In the terms of the resulting agreement, the Brazilian State:

> had to commit itself to maintaining a primary balance of trade surplus of 3.75% of the GNP in 2003; that was an agreement in regard to which all the presidential candidates had to publicly position themselves and Lula committed himself to it.
> BANDEIRA, 2004, p.285

US president George W. Bush invited Lula to visit the United States. During the visit in June, 2002, Lula took pains to demonstrate his commitment to democracy, to economic stability and to the fulfillment of the contracts. However, he did not neglect to say that he would make the necessary changes to ensure that Brazil would resume its economic growth, intensify South American integration and guarantee its domestic interests in the international negotiations.

Another element that deserves attention is the fact that ever since its creation the PT had worried about the party's position in regard to international issues, irrespective of whether they were related to Brazilian foreign policy or to international policy itself (Mesquita, 2013, p.151). The creation of the São Paulo Forum is the main example of the PT's international actions. The forum was an initiative designed to draw together the main left-wing parties in Latin America and the Caribbean in the 1990s. In the light of the dismantling of the Soviet Union and the advance of neoliberal policies, the group proposed to think in terms of resistance and alternatives to neoliberalism. At that time the Forum could already count on the election of Hugo Chaves in Venezuela in 1998 and it also managed to elect Nestor Kirchner in Argentina in 2002.

It was not by chance that foreign policy was highlighted in the government program in 2002 and in the Letter to the People itself. Both documents declared that foreign policy would be the means to overcome economic stagnation and external vulnerability. Exhibiting a clear convergence with the documents of the Brazilian internal bourgeoisie, the government program insists on the strategic centrality of MERCOSUR, above all, in its aspect as a form of resistance to the FTAA and a way of facing up to the region's macroeconomic challenges. Thus, it suggests a convergence of the industrial, agricultural, trading, and educational policies inside the bloc. Furthermore, it emphasizes the need for the convergence of infrastructure and for solidarity with neighbors, especially Argentina (PT, 2002b, p.6).

On that point we follow Onuki and Oliveira (2007, p.145):

> Even though without the support of systematic empirical research, it is too early to state that foreign policy, whether regarding trade in the broadest sense, or a regional integration policy in a more specific way, has become a determinant of the vote, it is valid to state that the centrality these issues have acquired in the debate has no historical precedent.

Cruz (2013) considers that clash between the PT and the PSDB in the years 2002, 2006 and 2010 made the differences between the foreign policy orientations of the two political parties increasingly clear. Foreign policy was also the area in which the opposition and the media most attacked the government during the two mandates. Mesquita (2013) considers that the changes in foreign policy of the two governments were associated to the ideas of each party. According to that author, those ideas even influenced the organization of the Ministry of Foreign Affairs and the public entrance examinations for a diplomatic career. The next chapter will provide greater detail on this subject.

CHAPTER 3

# The Lula Governments

*Neo-developmentalism, Power Bloc and Foreign Policy*

Characterizing the economic, social and foreign policies of the Lula administrations has given rise to considerable controversy. Alongside other authors we argue that the State adopted a series of measures reflecting and substantially altering the correlation of forces within the Brazilian social formation. In this chapter we set out our understanding of neo-developmentalism, and its relations, as a program, with the social classes, and more specifically with the big Brazilian internal bourgeoisie. To situate this study in the face of the diversity of analyses of the Lula governments, we have constructed a succinct bibliographic review of some studies relevant for our analysis but at the same divergent from it. Following that is a description and analysis of foreign policy, examining its relations with the interests of brazilian 'bourgeoisie'.

## 1   Neo-developmentalism and Power Bloc

The State's participation in the economy intermediated by a broad policy of financing and protectionist policies, (obligatory minimum percentage of local content in government purchases and the same for companies enjoying BNDES subsidies) and through the expansion of the internal market and the social policies, justifies the choice of the term neo-developmentalist. Neodevelopmentalism is "the developmentalism feasible within the peripheral neoliberal capitalist model" (Boito Jr., 2012, p.69).

As a set, the economic, social and foreign policies contributed towards displacing big international financial capital and the purchasing bourgeoisie from their hegemony in the power bloc. State policy reorientation set priority on meeting the needs of Brazil's big internal bourgeoisie. That bourgeoisie brought together in its nucleus companies with predominantly national capital and some state companies and, in a peripheral and sporadic manner, some multinational companies already installed in Brazil. The sector distribution of those companies was: mining, construction, agribusiness, shipbuilding, transformation industry, and others (Boito Jr., 2012).

The internal bourgeoisie agglutinated, as the preceding chapter explained, based on the negative effects experiences with the implantation of neoliberalism in the 1990s. In other words, it formed because of the impacts of opening trade and deregulating finance and the denationalization and deindustrialization of the Brazilian economy. The political stance adopted by that fraction was one that Boito Jr. (1999) referred to as 'moderate neoliberalism'; greater negotiation of open trading, greater access to the privatizations for medium and small capital and a reduction in interest rates and bank spreads.

That bourgeoisie accepted State intervention because it was interested in enhanced credit, expanded investment in infrastructure, conquering new markets for exports and support for the financing and internationalization of its companies. However, it was not interested in a return to protectionism in the way it had formerly existed during the 1930s and right up until the 1980s. As an internal bourgeoisie, to some extent the fraction sought to curb and compete with imperialist capital but without going so far as break off the ties of dependence. According to Boito Jr. (2012, p.70):

> In the 1990 decade the dominant posture of industry supplying the domestic market was defensive. ... In the 2000 decade, the internal bourgeoisie abandoned that defensive position and, adjusting itself to neoliberalism, let go of the protectionism inherited from the old developmentalism and set out to conquer neighboring markets, which had also been opened.

The argument being defended is that often the Lula governments attention to the interests of the internal bourgeoisie was to the detriment of the big purchasing bourgeoisie's interests and those of international financial capital. The differences in the spheres of domestic policies (economic and social policies) and foreign policy were the result of changes that occurred inside the power bloc, namely: an ascendant trajectory of the internal bourgeoisie. The PT government's political program was one of neo-developmentalism.

The policies most obviously aligned with the neo-developmentalist program were: the Growth Acceleration program (*Programa de Aceleração do Crescimento*-PAC), the change in the oil exploration regime (from concession to sharing), the boosting of the shipbuilding industry, the requirement for minimum percentages of local products in government purchases, the creation of new state companies in the branches of infrastructure and technology, the search for export markets, the creation of the BNDESPar, a subsidiary of the BNDES to support and finance mergers and purchasing of companies, incentives for the internationalization of companies and the policy for forming 'national champions'.

The 'national champions' were companies that received finance from the BNDES and from pension funds like Previ and Petros to acquire new companies or to merge with competitors in the same line of activity, in order to become global leaders in their respective segments. Most of such companies came to monopolize the internal market of their sector and became active in other lands.

The National Economic and Social Development Bank (*Banco Nacional de Desenvolvimento Econômico e Social*-BNDES), with its lines of credit and shareholder participation helped to increment Brazilian investments in other countries. Unlike its performance in the 1990s when the bank focused on supporting the privatization of State companies and public services, in the years 2000 the focus was on financing, with subsidized interest rates, exporting companies and those that had internationalized (Bugiato, 2012). There is an expressive number of national companies operating overseas that have the BNDES subsidiary BNDESPar among their shareholders. In 2010 the BNDESPar held more than 10% of the shares of the following companies: América Latina Logística (12.21%); JBS Friboi (17.32%), Klabin (20.25%), Light (22.96%), Marfrig (13.89%), CEG (34.56%), Eletrobrás (18.50%), and Fibria (30.42%), among others (Valdez, 2011).

Figure 2 shows how the amount of Brazilian Direct Investments (BDI) in other countries in the period 2000 to 2008 was seven times greater than in the entire 1990s decade. In 2006 they reached the mark of US$32.3 billion and for the first time ever surpassed the amount of DFI in Brazil.

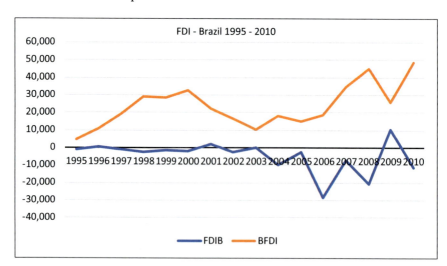

FIGURE 2   Direct investment flows 1995 to 2010 in US millions
FDIB = FOREIGN DIRECT INVESTMENT IN BRAZIL
BFID = BRAZILIAN FOREIGN DIRECT INVESTMENT
SOURCE: BANCO CENTRAL DO BRASIL; ELABORATED BY THE AUTHOR

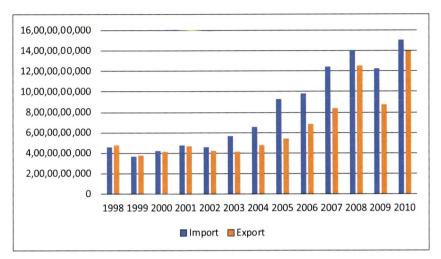

FIGURE 3    Brazilian balance of trade 1998–2010

In regard to the equity of the economic groups, although data is not available for the latter years of the Lula Governments, there was an observable expressive increase in economic groups under national and State control. The groups under state control leapt from 89.6 billion reals in 2002 to 156.3 billion 2007, and the groups with national capital evolved from 135.6 billion reals to 219.5 billion while the groups under multinational control went from 69 billion to 79.1 billion in the same period (Pinto, 2010).

The strengthening of the internal bourgeoisie is clearly apparent in the transition from deficit to surplus in the balance of trade (Figure 3).

As mentioned above, the new policies and initiatives that the PT governments implemented were designed to bring about the resumption of economic growth of Brazilian capitalism, relying on State intervention in the form of financing, protection and direct intervention in the economy. Accordingly, the political program can be considered as lying within the developmentalist spectrum. However, compared to the developmentalist period from 1930 to 1980, there are many differences, hence the prefix 'neo'. Neo-developmentalism presents several differences from the old developmentalism of the years 1930 to 1980 among which are:

1) more modest growth rates;
2) the lesser importance of the domestic market;
3) a lesser role for local industry;

4) acceptance of regressive specialization given that production was concentrated in segments with low technological density;
5) lesser distribution of income;
6) greater political-ideological fragility of the bourgeois fraction (less chance of becoming anti-imperialist);
7) the quest for increased Brazilian direct foreign investment became a strategy for the international insertion of Brazilian companies driven by the State by means of BNDES financing and the South-South foreign policy;
8) in regard to natural resources, state monopoly of oil exploration was no longer defended, and a model based on sharing was adopted
9) infrastructure works were no longer preferentially state investments but began to count on public-private partnerships

Boito Jr. (2012) reports that after 2005 and after the so-called '*Mensalão* crisis' the neo-developmentalist policies became more profound. The replacement of Antônio Palloci with Guido Mantega as Minister of Finance at the beginning of 2006 marked a change in the direction of economic policy. In 2004, Paulo Skaf's election to the presidency of the FIESP enjoyed the support of Lula and with that there was an inflection in the relations between that entity and the government. Skaf relaunched the review *Revista da Indústria* and began to criticize more emphatically the interest rate policy, the bank spread, the exchange rate, etc. FIESP was quick to recognize the replacement of Palocci with Mantega as Minister of Finance as being a positive action.

Another relevant point is that with the explosion of the financial crisis in the United States in 2008 after the collapse of Lehman Brothers, the neo-developmentalist policy was able to reap its fruits and surprised many analysts insofar as it seemed to have 'filtered' out the immediate consequences of that crisis for the Brazilian economy. The State:

> reacted to the crisis in a purposeful way, including economically, generating around 1 million jobs in 2009. The very success of that reaction to the external threat and its [potentially] devastating effects on the real economy served to legitimize those policies.
> SCHUTTE, 2012, p.24

Thus, it can be argued that after 2008 the internal bourgeoisie began to exercise hegemony within the power bloc given the intensification of the political initiatives designed to address the interests of that fraction.

Cavalcante (2012) affirms that the telecommunications sector is a good example of neo-developmentalism in the Lula governments. The fusion of Oi and BrT with the assistance of the BNDES and the return of Telebras to the National Broad Band Plan (*Plano Nacional de Banda Larga* – PNBL) were part of the policy of forming 'national champions' and the return of state corporation participation in public services.

According to Gomes (2013), the shipbuilding industry serves as an illustration of the neo-developmentalist program. According to the author it was one of the industries that the orthodox neoliberal policies had most affected. Having at one time been one of the world's biggest steel processing parks employing 40 thousand workers, the shipbuilding industry "ended the 1990 decade practically dismantled and with less than 2 thousand workers in its employment" (Gomes, 2013, p.7). The Lula government policies, particularly the one designed to form 'national champions', and the requirement for a guaranteed minimum participation of local parts, machines and equipment in the ships and platforms ordered by Petrobras, meant that the Brazilian shipbuilding industry and especially the big construction companies, obtained huge gains. The increase in the shipyard employment figures was also enormous: or the shipyards leaping from 2 thousand in the year 2000 to 60 thousand in 2010.

Furthermore, the oil exploration regime approved in 2010 was an important change from the anterior concession regime of 1977. In the latter, only 15% of the extracted oil royalties went to the Union while control over exploration and profits went to the winning bidder in the concession tendering process. With the new sharing regime, Petrobras took back decision-making control over the winning consortium, maintained 15% of the royalties for the Union and added the stipulation of at least 30% of the extracted oil to go to Petrobras. Furthermore, it created the Social Fund to administer the pre-salt resources which were earmarked directly for application in health and education.

Despite the maintenance of the public debt payments and the non-renationalization of the companies that were privatized,[1] compared to the preceding period (1995–2002), the changes were highly significant. Outstanding among them were the role conferred on the BNDES, the policy obliging the acquisition of local content in government purchases, certain protectionist measures and the new regime regulating oil exploration.

From all that has been set out above, the reader may wish to ask whether the Lula governments can be labelled as moderate neoliberal? After all, was it not

---

[1] The auctioning of the Vale do Rio Doce was questioned in various juridical spheres and it was also the object of a civil society campaign in 2007 alleging the illegality of the sale and calling for it to be cancelled.

a negotiation of a greater trade opening (rejection of unilateral opening) and a paralyzation of privatizations or at least a new form of privatization policy? Would that not have constituted moderate neoliberalism? ... The answer is No.

It does not exactly correspond to moderate neoliberalism because the State policy of the two governments did not exclusively address the wishes of the internal bourgeoisie. Actually, the strengthening of that bourgeois fraction only came about because of support from the lower classes – lower middle-class, urban working class, rural smallholders, the unemployed and the underemployed. Those sectors were contemplated by the policies to: reduce unemployment, increase the real value of the official minimum salary, increase credit availability and benefited by the expansion of social policies. We hold that a political front came into being run by the internal bourgeoisie, the main beneficiary of State policies, all of which characterize the political program as consistent with the idea of neo-developmentalism. What follows is an examination of how State policy met part of the demands of the classes of ordinary people.

First of all, economic growth brought with it an increase in the number of jobs and in the minimum salary and consequently an improvement in the workers' lives. That led to an observable shift of the pole of mobilization of the working class. In the 1990s the social movements, especially the Landless Rural Workers Movement (*Movimento dos Trabalhores Rurais Sem Terra*-MST), had played an important role in organizing the unemployed and marginalized sectors. In the years 2000, there was a renewal of the combativity of the urban workers unions (Boito Jr. & Marcelino, 2011).

In the Trades Unions field there was a double movement. On the one hand the two major national organizations, Força Sindical and CUT drew closer to the government. They represented an important part of the base that supported and sustained the PT administrations. At many moments they even took part alongside the internal bourgeoisie in the efforts to protect the internal market, to reduce interest rates and in the tripartite committees that the State set up such as the Council for Social and Economic Development (*Conselho de Desenvolvimento Econômico e Social*-CDES).

On the other hand, the unions reform and the social security reform contributed towards the merger of some of the older union confederations and the emergence of new organizations like the Conlutas and the Intersindical. Those two organizations declared their opposition to the government and were connected to the political parties PSTU and PSOL respectively (Galvão, 2012).

The social policies, especially the Family Allowance Program (*Programa Bolsa Família*) and the creation of the Zero Hunger Program (*Programa Fome Zero*) enabled thousands of families to emerge from poverty. The National

Housing program *Minha casa, minha vida* (My house/home, my life) also played an important role: it met the demands of the movements of the homeless and the unemployed. In turn, those programs ensured an expansion in the government support base which came to include residents of the peripheral areas of big cities and the interior of the Northeast region, in other words the 'marginal mass' (Kovarick, 1975 and Nun, 2001) or as Singer (2012) put it, the subproletariat.

The wage-earning rural workers and settled base of the Landless Rural Workers movement were in turn, benefitted by the financing of family agriculture and the government programs for purchasing food production. However, the poorer part, the landless rural workers, in spite of being less criminalized, were not benefitted by the State policy because the number of new settlements was very small. On the other hand, agribusiness was highly favored. That was most certainly one of the main limiting factors of the neo-developmentalist platform; it failed to incorporate structural reforms.

In regard to young people, the education policies stand out, especially the creation of new Federal Universities and more scholarships for, and places in private universities via the PROUNI Program. Both policies, especially the latter, enabled many working-class youngsters to gain access to a university education and they were mostly the first person in their families ever to do so. The middle classes, especially those with high schooling levels were strongly affected by the neoliberal policies and it would seem that they were the ones least benefitted by neo-developmentalism. Civil servants lost some of their rights with the social security reform and other sectors had almost no gains such as salary increases or reduction of expenses with education, health insurance etc.

It is apparent how the social base of the neo-developmentalist platform acted jointly at times of crisis like the so called 'mensalão' in 2005 and the 2006 and 2010 elections. On the party-political front, the PT represented the neo-developmentalist front which, in turn, opposed the conservative sectors and the PSDB. The existence of that front was of fundamental importance for the permanence of PT governments in the presidency of Brazil.

The front, however, was riddled with contradictions. One concerned the discord between the industrial bourgeoisie and agribusiness, and as is shown below, that discord was most visibly expressed in the policy of acknowledging China as a market economy. Another contradiction lay in the fact that the different classes and class fractions composing the front were agreed on the aspect of protection for the internal market and lower interest rates but disagreed in regard to labor rights, enhanced distribution of the resources stemming from economic growth and especially in regard to structural reforms. Whenever the internal bourgeoisie pressed for a reduction in labor costs (through an increase in outsourcing) and in State spending, tension between the bourgeoisie and the workers increased. The social expenses, inflation, exchange depreciation etc. could be a demonstration of the incompatibility of the government program and the interests of the internal bourgeoisie. In that lay the limits of the neo-developmentalist front.

### 1.1 A Brief Review of Some of the Analytical Literature on the Lula Governments' Social and Economic Policies

Given the great diversity of analyses, the option has been to dialogue with just some of the analyses of the Lula Governments' social and economic policies. The choice of authors and texts that will be presented was based on the importance of the respective studies and on their proximity with, or degree of divergence from the analysis adopted in this work.

First comes the analysis Brasílio Sallum Jr. (2008) made of liberal-developmentalism and populism. That is followed by a discussion of the concept of neo-developmentalism according to Bresser-Pereira (2006), whose analysis inaugurated the debate on the existence of a new political strategy in the Lula governments. To finalize, there is a description of how Bastos (2012b) interprets the strategy that Bresser-Pereira discussed, and the idea is proposed that there were two developmentalist projects there were contradictions between them. To establish the dialogue between the analysis in this work and the above-mentioned studies a position will be expressed in relation to each one.

In his analysis, Sallum Jr. (2008), considers that there were actually two schools of liberalism that influenced Brazilian policy in the 1990s and the years 2000. They were orthodox neoliberalism and liberal developmentalism. The latter, a new version of the old developmentalism, sought to implement measures designed to reduce the impact of macro-economic policies on national industry and in that way ensure the improvement of Brazil's capacity to be economically competitive in the international sphere.

According to that author, there are two points that indicate continuity between the FHC and Lula governments: both pursued the goal of monetary stability and the value of 'social protection' via social policies. He states that those policies were already present in the FHC administrations, and the Lula government merely amplified them. Furthermore, the author argues that, during the period when Lula was president, he intensified the social-liberal and democratic system of domination installed from 1995 on. That system allowed for enhanced control over adversaries and allies by means of a populist strategy.

According to Sallum Jr. (2008), the change between the two president's governments was the result of an accommodation between the stabilization policy and the old PT themes which can be briefly stated as: income distribution, protection for companies with national capital and protection for workers and the poor. Thus, maintaining stability and economic growth would have been what formed the amalgam of the government and the corporate businessmen but that did not mean there were no misunderstandings or mistrust in the light of the government's close ties with the social movements and trade unions (Sallum Jr., 2008).

In the present work we do not accept the term liberal-developmentalism, even though it does come close to what we call neo-developmentalism on some points. The main reason for the rejection is that it fails to incorporate the role of the classes of ordinary people. To address the question of the presence of those sectors, Sallum Jr. (2008) based himself on the concept of populism. That is a term that we also would not apply to characterize the Lula governments.

In turn, Bresser-Pereira (2006) argues that there has been a strategy called 'new developmentalism' in course since 2003 and that new developmentalism would be a 'third discourse' somewhere between the national developmentalism of the years 1930 to 1960 and the 'conventional orthodoxy', his term for neoliberalism. According to that economist it was the resumption of the strategy and of the ideology of national-developmentalism that had guided the policy of industrialization to replace importation in Latin America in the years 1950 to 1970. In that light it would be the result of a consensus or a national agreement among businessmen of the productive sector, workers, government technical staff and the professional middle classes stemming from the failure of the conventional orthodoxy and the dependent States' rejection of the imperialist States' pressures and proposals.

As Bresser-Pereira sees it, the new developmentalism is not protectionist and it does not count on the forced savings of the State as the old developmentalism did. There are two reasons why protectionism is not one of the pillars of the new developmentalism: 1) industry is not so incipient as it was in that former period; 2) global capitalism has transformed itself presenting other conditionalities compared to those in the United States' years of glory (1945–1975). In that sense, what the new developmentalism actually sought was to "create conditions for the national companies to be internationally competitive" (Bresser-Pereira, 2006, p.13). Unlike protectionism the new developmentalism seeks to increase exportation of (manufactured and semi-manufactured) products with greater aggregated value. The State's role in promoting the infrastructure needed by industry differs from the preceding model because the actual model does not count on State capital alone but can also count on greater private capital participation.

Bresser-Pereira (2006) considers that the current strategy, unlike orthodox neoliberalism, concerns itself more with the distribution of wealth and less with increasing foreign savings and the State pragmatically negotiates counterpart actions to the trade opening and admits the possibility of controlling exchange and capital (when necessary). The great clash between conventional orthodoxy and the new developmentalists is over the interest rate, the dispute between the rentiers and productive capital. The State's main instrument for improving the national companies' international competitiveness has to be the maintenance of a favorable exchange rate in order to combat the so-called 'Dutch disease' or in Brazil's case, premature deindustrialization. According to that author, the exchange rate tends to appreciate cyclically and only a competitive exchange rate can stimulate an increase in the exportation of manufactured goods and consequently, the longed-for increase in internal savings (Bresser-Pereira, 2012).

In his analyses, Bastos (2012b) argues that it is possible to identify two groups on the Brazilian political in the years 2000. They were: the exporting developmentalism of the private sector, and the distributive developmentalism guided by the State. "Both seek structural changes that diversify the industrial fabric, recuperate lost productive links and absorb under-employed workers through greater productivity and higher salaries" (Bastos, 2012b, p.784) The former is closer to the neoliberal policies and the latter to the old developmentalism.

Bastos (2012b) says that the exporting developmentalism, supposedly closer to the neoliberal policies, corresponds to the new developmentalism that Bresser-Pereira defends in which there is a strong belief that private capital can head the development process. He states that the group defending that project emerged from the PSDB itself and during FHC's second mandate, in the person of José Serra, expressed criticism of the macro-economic policy and became more closely aligned with the FIESP. In turn, the State-guided distributive developmentalism corresponded to 'social-liberalism'. The main axis of that project was providing incentives for the internal market, support for income distribution policies and defense of the state as a development inducing agent.

That author insists that a conflict between the two groups was liable to arise in the short term. In his words:

> One thing cannot be readily harmonized with the other: does anyone doubt that, in the short term, operations capitalizing public banks or amplifying subsidies for private investors can oppose elevations of the social expenditure? Or that the defense of a faster rhythm of exchange depreciation to stimulate investments suffers resistance from those who

want to avoid the alarm of inflation so harmful to the incomes of the very poor?

BASTOS, 2012b, p.796

We situate ourselves close to Bresser-Pereira's (2006) definition of new developmentalism in the aspects of the interest in markets for exportation, the greater weight placed on private capital, the rejection of unilateral trade opening and the acceptance of State control over exchange and interest rates. However, we would differ in regard to the idea that there was a consensus among different groups around the strategy of new developmentalism. Consensus presupposes an awareness and the existence of a pact among the different segments. The neo-developmentalist front was fluid, riddled with internal contradictions, not only within the internal bourgeoisie itself, but also between that fraction and the non-bourgeois classes of the ordinary people. The idea of a front does not presuppose the existence of a pact among the different segments that belong to it; the sectors act as a front without necessarily being aware of it.

It would seem that the project Bresser-Pereira defended corresponds more directly to the interests of the internal bourgeoisie and that which Bastos considers to be the distributive developmentalism orientated by the State or 'social liberalism' is connected to the interests of those sectors of the non-bourgeois classes that are part of the neo-developmentalist front. Although we do not agree with the idea that there are two projects, we do follow Bastos in regard to the conflicts between the internal bourgeoisie's project and the program that integrates some of the demands of the classes of ordinary people, as previously mentioned, State spending on state policies was a source of friction with the internal bourgeoisie. In this present work there is no intention to analyze the limits that existed within the front but, instead, to analyze the conflicts in regard to foreign policy present in the breast of the internal bourgeoisie.

## 2   Foreign Policy during the Lula Governments

Foreign policy was clearly a highly important instrument for the neo-developmentalist program. However, it should be understood in the framework of the political changes that took place in Brazil in the years 2000. The first thing to consider is the new configuration of the power bloc, that is the ascension of the internal bourgeoisie. The second is the new presence, for different reasons and to a lesser extent, of the ordinary people in national politics. In other words, changes in Brazilian internal politics associated to alterations in the international scenario are the explanation for the new foreign policy of the Lula governments.

According to Schutte (2012, p.8):

> The same discourse that reinstalled the State in the role of leader of the development process, mobilizing and rearticulating the State corporations and the public banks, guided the quest for a new insertion in the international scenario, which had to be as a function of the national development project, while at the same time, the national development guaranteed more resources and credibility to amplify international presence.

The international policy of the Brazilian State developed, above all, as a function of the fortification of the internal bourgeoisie, was marked by great differences from that of the FHC administrations. The creation of the South-South coalitions (IBSA, G-20, G-4 e BRICS) and Brazil's participation in them represented the resumption, in a new guise, of the 'third world' initiatives of the 1970s and 1980s[2] (Lima & Hirst, 2006).

"Unlike the FHC's government, when foreign policy was accessory to macroeconomic stability and had the function of guaranteeing international credibility, now, foreign policy, pro-active and pragmatic, is one of the feet of a government strategy standing on three additional pillars: maintenance of economic stability; resumption of the State's role in coordinating the neo-developmentalist agenda; and social inclusion and the formation of an expressive market of the masses."

The definition of the axes of the Brazilian State's international actions was guided by relations with the dependent states (the so-called South-South relations) intermediated by the creation of coalitions, the densification of South American integration, and a posture critical of the power asymmetry and

---

2  We agree with the proviso that Schutte (2012, p.21) made when he stated that "There is a tendency to confuse the emphasis on south-south articulations with an anachronistic 'third world-ism' normally associated with a critical vision of that policy. No doubt there are elements that hark back to the spirit of Bandung but the theme of non-alignment is no longer on the agenda. What remains is the identification of asymmetry that reinforces the concentration of wealth and political power. The 1955 conference in Bandung, Indonesia, placed on the agenda the acknowledgement of the right to development on the part of countries that had only recently freed themselves from colonization and of the Latin American countries, who sought their own national-developmentalist project. What is on the agenda now is real change in growth prospects, especially on the part of the so-called emergent economies".

inequitable rules in and of the international organizations. Furthermore, they sought to defend social policies designed to combat hunger and poverty.[3]

All those actions, as a set, contributed towards the Brazilian State's obtaining greater international projection and increasing its room for maneuver in relation to the imperialist states. Standing out against unilateral trade opening, the foreign policy reincorporated the quest for development as the central goal of the Brazilian State's international insertion. That is why, instead of attempting to draw closer to the imperialist States and adhere to international disarmament, intellectual property and other agreements, it sought coalitions with the dependent States and the strengthening of regional integrations as instruments for enhancing bargaining power in the international economic negotiations. It also sought to gain access to markets for exportation of its products and to territories in which to install its companies.

There were also sporadic conflicts between the Brazilian State and the United States on the international scene, such as Brazil's criticism of the invasion of Iraq, the shelving of the FTAA, the position against the installation of military bases in Colombia, the support for the Nuclear Agreement with Iran and others. As we will see later, those conflicts and the more critical posture in international organizations and negotiations show that the nature of the Brazilian State's insertion passed from a position of passive subordination to one of what could be called conflictive subordination.

That priority for South America had been declared even before Lula came to office. In December 2002, when Venezuela was facing a serious political crisis in the form of an attempted *Coup d'état* articulated by the opposition to President Hugo Chávez, Lula travelled to Caracas in a gesture designed to show concern with the direction the political crisis in that neighboring country was taking. Once there, he showed his disposition to contribute towards finding a peaceful solution and together with then President of Brazil, Fernando Henrique Cardoso, coordinated the Friends of Venezuela Group[4] (Cruz, 2003).

Following that, the nomination of Celso Amorim as Minister of Foreign Affairs and Samuel Pinheiro Guimarães to be Secretary-General revealed the reorientation that would be carried out. According to Saraiva (2011), the choice of those men reflected the strengthening of the group within Itamaraty that identified with the developmentalist/autonomist line of thinking. Other outstanding appointments were those of Marco Aurélio Garcia, an important

---

3  On this point, Lula's participation in the Economic Forum in Davos was outstanding. In front of the heads of the imperialist states he defended the need for global policies to combat hunger and extreme poverty.
4  This group was formed by Chile, Mexico, Portugal, Spain and the United States.

director of the Workers Party (PT) to the post of general advisor to the presidency for international affairs and, finally, Mauricio Bustani, former president of the OPCW, as Brazilian ambassador to the United Kingdom.

Later there would be changes in the organization of the Ministry itself with the creation of new departments and internal divisions with a view to strengthening the initiatives with the dependent States (South-South), as well as alterations to the reading list for candidates preparing for the examinations for the selective entry process for a diplomatic career (Mesquita, 2013).

Before passing to an analysis of the relation between foreign policy and the interests of internal bourgeoisie, it is important to describe how each of the aforementioned priority axes of the Lula Governments foreign policy was developed.

### 2.1   South-South Coalitions

The creation of the India, Brazil and South Africa Forum (IBSA) in 2003 inaugurated the South-South cooperation political strategy with three main themes: cooperation for development, combatting poverty and the defense of multilateralism. Alongside the G4 (group formed by Brazil, Germany, Japan and India) the IBSA Forum boosted the strategy of the efforts to democratize the UN Security Council. Pecequillo (2008, p.145–146) observed that:

> Unlike the FHC era when its UN tactic was a solitary effort, Brazil sought to articulate a framework of alliances. In addition to conquering Russia ... Great Britain and China's support, Brazil was alongside Japan, Germany and India in the G-4.

The most important coalition was the G-20. The group was created in 2003 during the Doha Round of the WTO's Development Agenda in Cancun and under the Brazilian State's leadership it brought together the main dependent States. Among them were India, Argentina, South Africa and Uruguay. The group had another important ally, the Chinese State. The coalition's mission was to strengthen the dependent States' struggles against the imperialist States in regard to the latter's illegal and unfair international trade practices, especially the agricultural protectionism of the United States and the European Union.

The idea of creating the G-20 came up prior to the Round when the United States and the European Union presented a joint proposal in which they maintained their support for subsidies for their farmers. When creating the G-20, the Brazilian State intended to present an alternative proposal that would counter the imperialist States' practices. That led to a crisis inside the Round showing that the negotiations would not be heading to unilateral concessions on the part of the dependent States anymore. The United States reacted immediately. Roberto Zoellick, US Trade Representative, blamed the Brazilian and Indian states for the crisis installed inside the WTO and some months later sent a letter to the G-20 members proposing a new round of negotiation on other bases (Carvalho, 2010).

It must be realized that the G-20 brought together dependent states with different interests. On the one hand were the Argentinean, Brazilian and Uruguayan states with postures essentially more offensive, defending the reduction of domestic subsidies and the opening of trade; on the other the Indian and Chinese states and those of the African countries had a more defensive posture, seeking merely for special safeguards for dependent states and differentiated treatment for certain products. It can be supposed that the more defensive posture of the Indian and Chinese states was linked to the existence of a national State and private bourgeoisie that ran the policy of those States. So, while in the other States, especially the Argentinean and Brazilian States, the presence of an internal bourgeoisie was the element determining a more offensive posture.[5] In that sense, the joint actions of the Brazilian and Indian states were a highly important aspect insofar as they brought together two States that represented quite different political interests.

Up until 2005 that coalition had obtained victory on three defensive issues: (I) the approval of the Framework Agreement in 2004 which foresaw the removal of the questions of government investments and purchases; (II) the incorporation of the bands formula, a proposal for special differentiated treatment for dependent States; (III) the Special Safeguard Mechanism making it possible to set up barriers (taxes and tariffs) whenever agricultural imports increased suddenly, jeopardizing local producers.

However, in 2008, when WTO president Pascal Lamy presented a package that foresaw, on the one hand, a gradual increase in the liberalization of agricultural products in the United States and the European Union, and on the other, the adoption of tariff cuts for industrial goods, the Brazilian State agreed to negotiate and ended by drawing away from the G-20 and losing the confidence and support of the Indian State (Pimenta, 2012).

Following that, in 2008, the Brazilian State became a part of the Financial G-20, an informal group created to discuss financial issues and led by the United States. The group endeavored to bring together the main economies of the imperialist and dependent States to debate the question of the under-valuation

---

5  Regarding the idea that there were internal bourgeoisies in Argentina and Brazil in the years 2000, see Boito and Rojas, 2007.

of the Chinese currency and to think of solutions for the financial crisis that was afflicting the United States economy (Mello, 2011).

Perhaps the most innovative and most difficult to analyze group that formed in the ambit of the South-South coalitions was the one that brought together, Brazil, Russia, India, China and South Africa known as BRICS. First identified by the Goldman Sachs agency in 2001, the acronym united the principal economies with great growth potential. Had it not been for the changes in the dynamics of the world economy after 2008, and the critical position those states found themselves in, then the BRICS would probably have persisted merely as a favored destination for investors. There are not really many elements of unity among them especially in terms of geographic proximity and cultural identities. Furthermore, the Brazilian State is an exception to the rule among them insofar as it does not have any atomic weapons.

Despite all that, "the Brics point to the third world agendas and concerns that suddenly disappeared in the context of the neoliberal reforms in the 1980s decade and reappeared in new attire in the first decade of the 21st century" (Kocher, 2011, p.168). The criticism levelled at the international financial system after the 2008 crisis made it possible for the BRICS to question the economic order imposed by the United States since the end of World War II and especially the dollar standard and the conditions the IMF imposed for conceding loans. In some way, the BRICS policy made a strong contribution to enhancing the Chinese State's political projection in the international scenario.

### 2.2   Haiti

The Brazilian State's contribution to the United Nations Mission to Stabilize Haiti (Minustah) should also be remembered. Having been at the head of the UN forces, the Brazilian State sought to involve the Latin American States in the process and then the Uruguayan and Chilean States sent troops to participate.

> Contrary to United Nations guidance, the Brazilian government chose not to create a specific contingent dedicated to that operation but instead to work a rotary system that enabled thousands of military personnel to take advantage of the opportunity to acquire practical experience.
> SCHUTTE, 2012, p.19

Due to the high degree of poverty and the Haitian State's extensive history of outside interventions and *Coup d'états*, the mission's difficulties were enormous. Furthermore, in 2010, the country was hit by an earthquake that devastated the capital, Port au Prince. Once again the Brazilian State showed enormous solidarity, contributing in the removal of the bodies and the rubble and authorizing 500 million reals in aid to assist the reconstruction in that country (Bracey, 2011).

## 2.3 Regional Integration

There can be no doubt that the main aim of the Lula Governments' foreign policy was regional integration and greater proximity with the newly elected governments, especially those who situated themselves in the political field critical of orthodox neoliberalism — Chávez in Venezuela, Kirchner in Argentina, Tabaré Vazquez in Uruguay and later, Evo Morales in Bolivia and Fernando Lugo in Paraguay, among others.

Two motives can explain that priority: (I) understanding regional integration to be the best instrument for boosting the region's political and economic position in the international sphere and especially the position of the Brazilian State; and (II) the advantages the Brazilian internal bourgeoisie could obtain with the increase in exportation of products and capitals to the region.

In that context there was notable drawing closer with the Argentinean State and indeed it was Lula's first international destination after taking office. In their election campaigns, both Lula and Kirchner had declared that regional integration would be their government's number one priority. On that occasion the two men revealed their strong disposition to 'relaunch' the MERCOSUR and take new steps along the path to regional integration (Vadell et al., 2009).

The commitments made at the Ouro Preto Summit in 2004 were designed to enhance the bloc's institutionalization and reduce asymmetries among the Member-States. They created the MERCOSUR Structural Convergence Fund (*Fundo de Convergência Estrutural do Mercosul*-FOCEM).[6] It is worth noting that Brazil promised to provide 70% of the financial resources for Focem which at the time were estimated at 70 million dollars. Those resources were mainly dedicated to social and infrastructure projects in the neighboring countries; Uruguay and Paraguay received 80% of the resources and Brazil and Argentina, 20%.

Another notable feature was the opening of a line of credit to finance the sales of machinery, components and parts manufactured in the MERCOSUR to Brazil. There was also the approval of credit for infrastructure projects in the neighboring countries, among them, the construction of a power transmission line connecting the Itaipu Hydroelectric plant to Asunción in Paraguay and the assembly and installation of a natural gas transmission duct in Argentina, among other projects. The BNDES also opened a branch in Montevideo to facilitate its business operations in South America.

---

6  The MERCOSUR Parliament (PARLASUR), the MERCOSUR Social Summits (*Cúpulas Sociais do MERCOSUR*) and the Permanent Review Court (*Tribunal Permanente de Revisão*) came into force.

In addition to strengthening the MERCOSUR, the Brazilian State sought to move forward with the project for close links between the MERCOSUR and the Andean Community of Nations (*Comunidade Andina das Nações*-CAN). In that way Ecuador and Colombia became associate members of the bloc and economic complementation agreements (*Acordos de complementação econômica*-ACE) were signed with Peru (2005), Ecuador, Colombia and Venezuela (2004) and Cuba (2006). Also, Venezuela's entry as a Member-State was approved (2005).[7]

The bloc signed agreements outside of the region with the Southern African Customs Union (SACU) in 2008 and with Israel (2007) and Egypt (2010). The Launching of the South American Community of Nations (*Comunidade Sulamericana das Nações*-CASA) during the 3rd Meeting of South American presidents in 2005 in Cusco, Peru, was the main regional integration political initiative as it gave rise to the creation of the UNASUR in 2008.

The strengthening of the MERCOSUR and the creation of the Casa contributed to ensuring a coordinated positioning of the South American States in the FTAA negotiations. Uruguay was the State that showed the greatest propensity to adhere to the agreement. However, after Tabaré Vazquez's election victory in 2004 that posture changed. In a conversation with minister Celso Amorim in 2005, the then president of Uruguay, referring to the possibility of closing a trade agreement outside of the MERCOSUR said the Uruguayan State would seek for an agreement that did not "wound the heart of the MERCOSUR"; in other words, one that did not decree the end of the Common External Tariff (Amorim, 2011, p.98). Shortly after that episode the FTAA proposal was shelved.

Honório (2013) considers that the Cusco meeting was a point of inflection in South American regionalism as it introduced new axes. At it: "themes such as the fight against poverty, the elimination of hunger, the creation of employment, access to health and education set the tone of that moment of regionalism in the region" (Honório, 2013, p.48–49).

Three years later, in 2008, under pressure from Hugo Chaves, the Casa gave rise to the Union of South American Nations (UNASUR) (Ruiz, 2010). That initiative enabled the Brazilian State to deepen political coordination among the South American States and to introduce new themes and priorities to the South American integration process in the form of infrastructure, development and security projects. UNASUR incorporated the IIRSA to the South American Infrastructure and Planning Council (*Conselho Sul-americano de Infraestrutura*

---

7  Venezuela only effectively entered the bloc in 2012 after the *Coup d'état* in Paraguay as the Paraguayan Congress refused to ratify that States entry to the bloc. After the Coup Paraguay was expelled from the MERCOSUR and Venezuela was able to ingress.

*e Planejamento*-COSIPLAN) and created various other councils in the areas of health, education, culture, science and technology, economics and finance, drugs and defense. The last mentioned was the most important, namely the South American Defense Council (*Conselho de Defesa Sul-americano*).

As the next chapter will show, those infrastructure projects have been the object great controversy in the analyses of the Brazilian State's role in Latin America. For now, it is sufficient to say that:

> The absorption of the IIRSA initiative by the formation of COSIPLAN and the formation of the South American Defense Council and support for the formation of the Bank of the South represent important innovations in the way Brazil acts on issues requiring coordination.
> VIGEVANI & RAMANZINI, 2013, p.26

Also outstanding were UNASUR's action against the military agreement between the United States and Colombia and against the attempted Coups D'état in Bolivia and Ecuador in 2008.

Another important issue was the initiative to achieve integration in the area of power supply. In the years 2000 there were various meetings in the ambits of MERCOSUR and UNASUR at which attention was called to the need for common projects in that area (Fuser, 2010). During Lula's first mandate alone, 15 agreements were signed between Petrobras and the Venezuelan State Corporation. Among the respective projects were the construction of the Abreu Lima refinery in Brazil and the exploration, by Petrobras, of gas and heavy oil in the Orinoco region (Bandeira, 2006).

Energy's strategic importance for regional development presented the Brazilian State with highly complex situations. That was the case with the renegotiations of the Petrobras contract with Bolivia and that of the Itaipu hydroelectric plant with Paraguay. In both cases, reviewing the contract meant fulfilling the electoral commitments of presidents Evo Morales and Fernando Lugo. The first in the light of the indigenous movement which had been fighting since the year 2003 for the nationalization of hydrocarbons, Bolivia's main source of revenue. The second counted on a review of the respective Treaty to increase the Paraguayan State's returns and enable investments in social and developmentalist policies. Despite the fierce criticism of the big media and the opposition, Lula reviewed both those contracts. According to Saraiva (2011) those acts of his indicate that the Brazilian State was more inclined to bear the costs of regional integration.

Lastly, in 2010, there was the creation of the Community of Latin American and Caribbean States. Insofar as it incorporated the institutional mechanisms of the Rio Group created in 1986, that new organization committed to seeking to establish political dialogues among its 33 member states and foster cooperation in joint regional development projects.

### 2.4 *Africa*

Special attention was also paid to relations between the Brazilian State and the African States. Similarly, in the relations with Latin America, there were two notable aspects: on the one hand South-South cooperation (closer alignment and policies of solidarity and combatting extreme poverty) and on the other, the expansion of exportation and an increase in the installation of Brazilian transnational companies.

As regards cooperation policy, the outstanding initiatives were: the efforts to underscore historical cultural and economic ties between Brazil and Africa via the strengthening of the Community of Portuguese-speaking Nations and the South Atlantic Peace and Cooperation Zone; Brazil's pardoning of African countries' foreign debts and support for local development; and the creation of the University for International Integration of the Afro-Brazilian Lusophony (*Universidade de Integração Internacional de Lusofonia Afrobrasileira* —UNILAB).

It must be remembered that the Brazilian State and the South African State, acted together in combatting agricultural protectionism in the WTO through the G-20. The Brazilian Panel on cotton, against the USA also ensured gains for African cotton producers. Lastly the South African State is a member of two important coalitions that Brazil also belongs to: the IBSA coalition and the BRICS.

Lula visited the African continent eight times and opened 68 diplomatic representations (embassies and consulates) in the region. On his first trip, in 2003, he visited Angola, Mozambique, South Africa, Namibia and São Tomé and Príncipe. On the second, in 2004, he revisited São Tomé and Príncipe and then went on to Cape Verde and to Gabon. In all those countries the president was accompanied by Ministers, businessmen and intellectuals. Schutte underscores how "in 2010, by means of the Alexandre Gusmão Foundation (*Fundação Alexandre Gusmão*-FUNAG), Itamaraty began its efforts to organize annual courses in Brazil for African diplomats sponsored by the Brazilian government" (Schutte, 2012, p.17).

According to Saraiva (2010, p.180), at the beginning of the 21st century, Brazilian foreign policy for Africa was of a technical cooperation nature and not merely assistance-orientated as it had been in the past. That author highlights the partnerships for the construction of production and logistics infrastructure in Africa, the cooperation initiatives to help in the fight against AIDS and the participation of institutions like Embrapa and Sebrae that helped the local development programs of various African States so much. The African continent was living a moment of growth and the partnership with Brazil seems to have been very beneficial.

In regard to trading policy, the outstanding feature was the huge increase in exports to African countries and the expansion of Brazilian companies operating in the region especially big companies like Vale, Petrobras, Odebrecht and so on. Vale has investments in Angola, Mozambique, Guinea, South Africa and in the Democratic Republic of Congo. In addition to its older investments in Angola and Nigeria, Petrobras expanded into Tanzania, Libya, Mozambique and Senegal. Odebrecht was involved in the construction of a big hydroelectric plant in Angola (Capanda) (Visentini, 2010). It is also important to add that in 2009 a Preferential Trade Agreement was signed between MERCOSUR and the Southern Africa Customs Union (SACU – Lesotho, Botswana, Namibia, South Africa and Swaziland).[8]

## 2.5 The Middle East

In the same way that it took place with the African continent there was policy of drawing closer to the Middle East. It began with President Lula's visit to five Arab countries, the United Arab Emirates, Syria, Lebanon, Egypt and Libya. It is noteworthy that despite the large community of Lebanese and their descendants in Brazil, the last Brazilian head of State to visit Lebanon had been the Emperor Dom Pedro II. The other five countries visited were of great importance either for regional integration or for bilateral trade. The concrete political result of those visits was the creation of the first South America-Arab Countries Summit which took place in Brasília in 2005 (Messari, 2006).

---

8  The relations between Brazil and Africa have also been a polemic point in the great debate among Brazilian foreign policy analysts. Unfortunately, it has not been possible to conduct such meticulous research into them as the research that is presented in the next chapter on the Brazilian State's role in South America. Nevertheless, it can be said right away that despite the fact that the relation between the Brazilian State and the African States is an unequal one, given that Brazil State's political and economic capacities are greater than those of the African States, the relation cannot be characterized as imperialist because there are no instances of the use of force, intervention in domestic policies, support for Coups D'état or other initiatives that could support such an allegation. The Brazilian corporations' performances, albeit directed at the extraction of natural resources does not characterize Brazilian presence in the region as an imperialist policy. Furthermore, Africa became an important recipient of direct foreign investments in the years 2000 and the European Union continues to be the main source of them. China has shown a more well-defined strategy and capacity to compete with and dislodge Brazilian presence on the continent (Iglesias & Costa, 2011).

It must also be borne in mind that Brazil condemned the United States' invasion of Iraq. However, its posture in relation to the Israel-Palestine conflict was somewhat dubious. While during the Brazil-Arab Countries Summit in Brasilia it had signed the Declaration of Brasilia which condemned the Israeli construction of a wall in Cis-Jordan and the Israeli State's terrorist policy, in the same year, Minister Celso Amorim visited Israel. Furthermore, there was the signing of a MERCOSUR-Israel trade agreement.

The Brazilian State's most daring position was the role it played as a rotary member of the UN Security Council in mediating the nuclear agreement between Turkey and Iran. That position, in addition to avoiding a possible outbreak of war between the United States and Iran marked Brazil's resumption of a critical attitude towards the nuclear non-proliferation treaty signed by FHC in 1998, resuscitating the inequality in access to technology as an element in the hiatus between the imperialist States and the dependent ones.

### 2.6 China

The Brazilian State's policy for achieving greater proximity with the People's Republic of China unfolded not only in the multilateral UN forums but also in the South-South, G-20 trade, G-20 financial and BRICS coalitions. The drawing closer of the two States was seen as part of a strategy for Brazil to obtain a seat on the UN Security Council and it also involved cooperation in the areas of science and technology.

Given that during the first decade of the 21st century, China had become an important economic pole, that partnership became very strategic. In 2004, Lula accompanied by nine ministers, six governors of Brazilian states, and four hundred businessmen visited that Asian country. On that occasion 14 treaties were signed between Brazilian and Chinese businessmen. In the very same year, the Chinese president came to Brazil and the Brazilian State decided to acknowledge China as a Market Economy. "In exchange for that recognition, Brazil hoped to gain China's support for its candidature for a seat as permanent member of the UN Security Council" (Becard, 2011, p.38).

The years that followed saw the creation of the China-Brazil High Level of Agreement and Cooperation Commission (*Comissão Sino-brasileira de Alto Nível de Concertação e Cooperação*-Cosban), the Brazil-China Strategic Dialogue and the Brazil-China Financial Dialogue and lastly, the Joint Action plan (Becard, 2011).[9] Among those initiatives were partnership arrangements with

---

9  Other fruits of those agreements in the late 1980s included the launching of three bi-national satellites (Becard, 2011).

Embrapa, cooperation in the area of biotechnology and of IT, the development of new materials, the policy for combating Aids, generic pharmaceutical products and others:

> The Joint Action Plan that Presidents Luiz Inácio Lula da Silva and Hu Jintao signed in April 2010 sought to impart an institutional quality to the Brazil China relations with the establishment of goals and the creation of mechanisms for permanent consultation and coordination between the two countries.
> OLIVEIRA, 2010, p.94

With the aim of incrementing bilateral relations, the Brazilian State launched its 'China Agenda', an instrument intended to foster business between the two countries and one that sought, above all, to increase the technological content of Brazilian exports.

From the economic standpoint, it must be underscored that in 2009, China became Brazil's leading trading partner, displacing the United States which had occupied that position for 80 years. However, increasing evidence of the dependence of the Brazilian economy on the Chinese economy and the asymmetrical nature of that relationship, given that Brazil exported mainly commodities (soy, iron ore and oil) and imported electronic products, clothing, toys and chemical products. That process intensified the 're-raw materialization' of the Brazilian export portfolio (Oliveira, 2010; IPEA, 2011a). Furthermore, there was an increase in Chinese direct foreign investment destined for the services, industry and agriculture sectors (IPEA, 2011a).

The two States' trading conflicts became more intense. The Brazilian State began to criticize the Chinese policy of exchange devaluation, accusing it of disloyal trading practices and even came to the point of opening a seminar in the ambit of the WTO to debate the issue. In addition, in 2008 the tires, footwear and textiles sectors adopted antidumping measures against China (CEBC, 2010).

### 2.7 *European Union*

In regard to the European Union, although there was no actual breaking off of relations, the differences prevailed, not only in the sphere of the WTO but also in regard to the negotiations for the MERCOSUR – European Union Agreement.

In the WTO, apart from the disputes in the ambit of the Doha Round, there was the contention concerning sugar. The panel on that issue began in 2002 in response to requests from the Brazilian and Australian States. They questioned the European Union's subsidies for its sugar exports, especially beet (Type C) sugar. Brazil argued that the same type of sugar produced in African, Caribbean and Pacific countries should be computed in the total of exports subsidized by the European Union. The body charged with finding a solution accepted the argument of the co-demanding States and in July 2006 the European Union was obliged to reformulate the global sugar regime (Pereira et al., 2012).

Another WTO Panel on boneless salted chicken cuts was set up in 2003 after the European Union had modified its tariff classification for the importation of chicken and raised the amount to be paid for the product to enter the European countries. Furthermore, it began to require a special safeguard that called for an increased level of salt in the product to ensure its long-term conservation. The Brazilian State questioned that measure alleging that it constituted unfair treatment that violated Article 28 of the GATT. The appeal board of the WTO recommended that the European Union should alter the measurements it had imposed and negotiate quotas with the Brazilian State for the importation of such chicken products (Pereira et al., 2012).

There were two important rounds of the negotiations of the MERCOSUR-European Union Agreement, one in 2004 and the other in 2010. In the first, the UE attempted to present a proposal for gradual, restricted liberalization of agricultural trade which the MERCOSUR did not accept. Six years later, the MERCOSUR included the automotive sector in the liberalization proposal and amplified its industrial offer, but the European offer fell far short of expectations and so the agreement was not concluded.

### 2.8 The IMF

In regard to the IMF, although Lula respected and maintained the agreement that FHC had signed in 2002, "already in 2003, President Lula's wish to reduce close relations with the Fund was readily apparent" (Tude & Milani, 2013, p.88). Two years later, in 2005, Lula announced that he would not renew the agreements and anticipated payment of the US$ 10.8 billion of the Special Drawing Right and around US$15 billion referring to loans that Brazil had taken out with the fund. From 2007, Lula began to underscore the Brazilian State's financial independence from the IMF and adopted a critical discourse in regard to the Fund's policies of austerity and other conditionalities.

In 2009, having gone from being an IMF debtor to being a creditor President Lula exalted his criticism even further, underscoring the institution's inefficiency in containing the United States' financial crisis (Tude & Milani, 2013). From then on, the struggle for a profound institutional transformation was the guideline for the Brazilian State's relations with the IMF. In that aspect President Lula's participations in the financial meeting of the G-20 and the

BRICS meeting were outstanding. In both the stance of criticism in regard to the policies of austerity that the fund dictated to its borrowers were notable.

## 2.9 The United States

The nomination of Celso Amorim and Samuel Pinheiro right after Lula took office showed that Brazil's posture in the face of the FTAA was going to be more emphatic. That fact, together with the support for Venezuela and the criticism of the invasion of Iraq produced a certain cooling effect on Brazil and the United States' bilateral relations. Despite those tendencies to distancing Lula endeavored not to draw away from the United States entirely and in June 2003, visited that country again and received a warm, friendly welcome. On that occasion Lula stressed the need for closer proximity with the United States particularly in the aspects of joint action against terrorism and aid to Africa.

On the other hand, in that very year 2003, Lula took back the proposed agreement between the United States and the Brazilian State for the construction of the American base in Alcântara from the ambit of the Congress and shelved it (Bandeira, 2004). As time went by the stalemates in the FTAA negotiations became ever more apparent. "The issues that Brazil was interested in negotiating were precisely those on which the United States was not disposed to concede anything and vice versa" (Vigevani & Mariano, 2006, p. 346). Both understood that the most sensitive issues namely, agricultural protectionisms, services, property, government purchasing, and intellectual property should be negotiated in the sphere of the WTO.

Again in 2003, the Doha Round in Cancun was a fiasco for the United States. Under the leadership of the Brazilian State, the dependent states declared that they were not disposed to accept the unilateral opening of their economies unless the United States and Europe were prepared to give way on their agricultural protectionism.

The Brazilian State did not want to bear the political cost of the failed negotiations and that was why the Lula government did not abandon them. Above all, it feared isolation if the bilateral agreements between the United States and the other Latin American States were to materialize. Accordingly, during the meeting in October 2003, it proposed making the FTAA negotiating rules more flexible. That proposal for a 'Light FTAA', as it came to be known, foresaw the possibility of different levels of commitment between the Latin American countries and the United States and the signing of bilateral or multilateral agreements.

The Brazilian State also invested in other strategic actions to boost its bargaining power: 1) relaunching the MERCOSUR; 2) creating international coalitions (IBAS and G-20); 3) strengthening the new regional integration projects;

and 4) drawing closer to progressive countries that were against the FTAA (Venezuela). As is well known, during the Mar del Plat Summit in Argentina, the FTAA project was finally shelved.

There were still disputes between the two countries, pending settlement within the WTO especially one associated to the Cotton Panel opened by the Brazilian State during the FHC administration (2002). Through the Panel, the Brazilian State hoped to shed light on the harmful effects of the United States' policy of subsidizing its domestic agriculture and in that way boost Brazil's efforts, in the Doha Round, to obtain an agricultural subsidies reduction. It was an innovative initiative and therefore challenging because although the arguments and the adopted strategy were juridically well-founded, there was no extant jurisprudence that the Brazilian State could cite to its advantage (Azevêdo, 2010).

In 2005, the WTO body charged with settling disputes adopted its final declaration regarding the merit of the case and fully met the expectations of the representatives of the Brazilian State. The main aspect of the decision was the acknowledgement that the subsidies the United States paid to its cotton farmers artificially reduced the international price of cotton, harming Brazilian (and African) cotton producers. Nevertheless, in the years that followed the United States made very few corrections to its programs and that led the Brazilian State to request the setting up of an 'Implementation Panel'. That panel showed that the United States policies continued to cause harm to Brazilian producers and so the Brazilian State took the dispute to its ultimate stage, which was retaliation (Azevêdo, 2010).

The Brazilian State also won the retaliation case in 2009 and it was duly licensed to apply cross-retaliation which meant the possibility of applying countermeasures in the fields of intellectual property and services. Fearful of the countermeasures that might be taken, after a period of bilateral negotiations concluded in June 2010, the United States agreed to make monthly payments into a fund designed to support Brazilian cotton farming. Those financial resources could be used for improving cotton crop logistics or in programs of cooperation with other dependent states producing cotton such as the African States forming the Cotton 4 group (Benin, Burkina Faso, Chad and Mali) (Azevêdo, 2010).

The Brazilian State also opened a Panel at the WTO in 2009 on the anti-dumping measures the United States was taking in regard to the orange juice it imported from Brazil. The Panel decided in Brazil's favor and introduced formal jurisprudence in the WTO that ended by marking the United States posture in regard to its behavior in regard to that kind of trade issue (Pereira et al., 2012). There were other actions in which Brazil and the United States had divergent, conflicting international policy stances such as their positions regarding the negotiations on Iran's production of enriched uranium in 2010, and the refuge afforded to President Manuel Zelaya in the Brazilian embassy in Honduras in 2009, the Brazilian State's opposition to the installation of United States military bases in Colombia, and others.

According to Amorim Neto (2011), between 2003 and 2008 the Brazilian State registered its lowest level of general convergence with the United States in the voting at the UN General Assembly sessions since 1946. On the other hand, in March 2007, President George W. Bush visited Brazil and, on that occasion, the United States revealed its interest in gaining access to a new energy matrix, namely ethanol. The Brazilian State welcomed the idea of a bilateral agreement on biofuels but nothing concrete came about because maize farmers in the United States questioned the deal and lobbied the US Congress not to accept the agreement (Pecequillo, 2008). Another delicate question was the fact that as soon as the discovery of the pre-salt oil deposits was announced, the United States reactivated its 4th International Fleet indicating the possibility of an imminent geopolitical dispute.

## 2.10  *Defense Policy*

The Brazilian State, in turn, made a point of fortifying its national defense policy and contributed towards the creation of the South American Defense Council. The former initiative was notable for the announcement, in 2005, of a new National Defense Policy and following that, the elaboration of a National Defense Strategy (*Estratégia Nacional de Defesa*-END), presented in 2008 (Soares, 2011). "The departure point for the strategic formulation for Defense is the realization that the country is increasingly occupying an outstanding position in the international context. That new patamar of international insertion requires 'a new posture in the field of defense'" (Soares, 2011, p.76–77).

The END was organized around three axes. The first concerned three decisive sectors for national defense, namely the nuclear, cybernetics and space sectors. The second was centered on a resumption of the activities of the national defense industry and counted on the mastery and development of national technology to increase the State's defense capacity. The third axis concerned the composition of the armed forces which should be guided by the principle of a universalist recruitment (Ministério da Defesa, 2008).

Furthermore, the Brazilian State refused to sign the additional protocol to the Nuclear Non-proliferation Treaty (NPT) which allowed for the inspection of any nuclear products, equipment or installations, even those not declared by the State (Goldemberg, 2010). Other defense-related events were the 2008 signing of the Brazil-France Military Agreement and complementary Law n.136

dated August 25, 2010. The agreement can be seen as a complement to the END and specifically concerned the construction of five submarines, a naval base and a shipyard. In turn, the complementary Law amplified the policing power of the Navy and the Airforce in regard to trans-frontier infractions. Both sought to increase the Brazilian State's defense capacity in the regions of the pre-salt deposits and the Amazon.

On the other hand, in 2010, the government reestablished the Military Agreement with the United States,[10] which provided for technical cooperation between the two states in the areas of research and development, logistics support and the acquisition of equipment and services. That shows the hybrid nature of the Brazilian State's posture; at the same time as it distanced itself from the USA it did not relinquish cooperation with the leading imperialist state in the hemisphere.

### 2.11 The Lula Governments' Foreign Policy and the Neo-developmentalist Front

Now that the main axes of the Brazilian State's performance in the international scenario during the Lula governments have been described it is time to pass on to the actual analysis of the relation between foreign policy and the neo-developmentalist front bearing in mind that the interest here is centered on the internal bourgeoisie.

In the following pages an attempt will be made to answer the following questions: (I) what were the relations between foreign policy and the neo-developmentalist front? (II) in what ways did the foreign policy succeed in guaranteeing the strengthening of the internal bourgeoisie?

To that end the text is divided into five parts: 1) the Brazilian State's position in regard to imperialism; 2) the political performance of the neo-developmentalist front; 3) the internal bourgeoisie and the south-south foreign policy; 4) the unstable equilibrium of commitment and the foreign policy; and 5) the party-political dispute and foreign policy.

### 2.12 The Brazilian State's Position in Regard to Imperialism

In order to discuss the State's position in regard to imperialism, it is important to remember that what is being defended in this work is not the existence of a mechanical relation between the actions of the State and the benefits accruing to the internal bourgeoisie but instead the affirmation that the Brazilian State used its greater autonomy of action to adopt positions whose direct result was

---

10  A similar agreement had been signed by Getúlio Vargas in 1952 and revoked by Geisel in 1977.

to attend to the economic interests of the big internal bourgeoisie. In other words, the State set out to construct an image that reflected and at the same time expanded the economic capacity of the internal bourgeoisie.

Obviously, not all of the actions were intimately linked to the economic interests of the internal bourgeoisie. However, the strategic objective of the quest for greater autonomy in the international scenario was coherent with those interests and after all, that quest was of no interest to big international capital. Actually, for the State to able to achieve the strengthening of that fraction of the bourgeoisie, it needed to obtain a greater margin for maneuver in the international scenario. That is why actions such as Brazil's leadership of the troops in Haiti, its sheltering of Manuel Zelaya in the Brazilian embassy in Honduras and the nuclear agreement with Iran, even if they do not seem to represent the interests of the big internal bourgeoisie, they certainly had an important aspect in regard to the relations between the Brazilian State and imperialism. The withdrawal, albeit merely sporadic, made it possible for the State to demonstrate greater autonomy so that the internal bourgeoisie could gain more space not only in the internal market but also in the world markets and especially in the markets of the dependent States.

Nevertheless, that new role of the Brazilian State in the international scenario was taken on without abandoning or rupturing relations with the imperialist States and for that very reason, the Brazilian State adopted a more conflictive posture; there was no substantial change in the Brazilian State's position in the international power structure. According to Myamoto (2011, p.130), "Brazil seemed to repeat, in part, the old strategy that the military governments had adopted, of wishing to obtain benefits from the First and Third worlds, simultaneously". To Peccquillo (2008), that contradictory relationship configured a combination of the main axes of the foreign policy: the vertical (bilateral) one and the horizontal (multilateral) one.

Unlike those authors, we would argue that the maintenance of relations and the existence, at the same, of sporadic conflicts between the Brazilian State and the imperialist States confirm the hypothesis of the fortification of the internal bourgeoisie inside the power bloc. As was shown in the theoretical chapter, that fraction had no intention of breaking the bonds of dependence on foreign capital and was not even willing to accept greater confrontation of imperialism. The internal bourgeoisie was characterized by an ideological-political dissolution that did not permit an anti-imperialist posture. In that sense we would classify the Brazilian State's political position at the time as one of conflictive subordination.

Such a characterization does not imply assuming that the overall set of the State's international actions was subordinated to imperialism It is rather, the position that the State occupied in the international scenario at a certain political conjuncture, or, in other words, the relations of the power bloc in Brazil with imperialism. That is because, according to the theoretical reference explained earlier in this book, to identify the role the State plays in the international power structure, relations among classes and class fractions inside the respective national social formation and their relations with imperialism must be taken into account. In that vein, it seems evident that the policy cannot be considered anti-imperialist or independent, given that to assume an anti-imperialist position, a composition of the anti-imperialist forces within the national social formation would be necessary, that is, a national bourgeoisie allied with the people's classes acting in and directing a revolutionary process. As has been clearly demonstrated, neo-developmentalism is much weaker than that, both internally and externally.

Nevertheless, that conflictive aspect indicates a considerable change in comparison with the 1990s. It can be seen that the Brazilian State in the person of President Lula, took on a more outstanding international role than in the period of his predecessor and, however small the concrete results of those initiatives may seem from the standpoint of the international power structure, there was a great difference in comparison with the foreign policy of the FHC governments. That said, it is now appropriate to describe the way the neo-developmentalist front organized itself politically in the light of foreign policy in the Lula governments.

### 2.13    *The Political Organization of the Neo-developmentalist Front*

From 2003 on, the Brazilian Business Coalition (*Coalizão Empresarial Brasileira*-CEB) and the National Campaign against the FTAA (*Campanha Nacional Contra a Alca*), protagonists, as the preceding chapter showed, of the mobilizations of the internal bourgeoisie and the ordinary people's sectors against the FTAA negotiations, played a lesser role. That was because of the FTAA was no longer a threat.

The non-Bourgeois sectors that were part of the National Campaign against the FTAA divided and after the Light FTAA proposal and the decision for the Brazilian State to head the Minustah mission in Haiti. Those two issues caused a lot of discomfort for the Brazilian left as a whole and together with other domestic policies contributed to the formation of three political camps: those opposing the government, (PSTU and PSOL), those that formed the government's support base (PT and CUT) and those sectors that gave critical support to the government (MST and Consulta Popular).

The last two camps could count on the actions of the Brazilian Network of Integration for the Peoples (*Rede Brasileira de Integração para os Povos*-REBRIP) an organization that brought together social movements and trade unionism most of which had been part of the National Campaign against the FTAA. During the Lula governments, it had accompanied the FTAA negotiations in the WTO as well as the MERCOSUR-European Union agreement and the regional integration projects. The MST added considerable weight to its international articulation, the *Via Camponesa*.

In turn, the various sectors that integrated the internal bourgeoisie began to accompany the international negotiations via their foreign trade departments and the bureaus of the national associations and state federations (Lohnbauer, 2010). The Brazilian Business Coalition, continued accompanying the MERCOSUR-European Union negotiations in 2004 and advising certain research projects for the CNI but over the years its functions began to fade away and CNI began to involve itself directly in the studies and the accompaniment of the more important international negotiations (Cruz & Silva, 2011).

Entities representing agribusiness created the ICONE and that institute began to accompany the main economic negotiations involving their sector's interests. That entity, alongside the CNA, played a highly important role in defining the Brazilian State's posture at the 2008 meeting of the WTO's Doha Round which resulted in the dismantling of the G-20-commercial (Carvalho, 2010; Iglesias, 2007). After the recognition of China as a market economy in 2004, the mining, energy, paper, cellulose, food and construction sectors, interested in increasing their exports to China or in endeavoring to increase the direct performance of the branches of their companies in Chinese territory, formed the Brazil-China Business Council (*Conselho Empresarial Brasil-China*-CEBC).

The big economic groups in the areas of construction, mining, oil, food, automobiles etc. have historically always acted more autonomously in relation to the federations or other class representative entities as they have more direct relations with the State. In those international negotiations that were directly addressing their interests they preferred to send their own representatives (president, officers etc.).[11] In general, despite the organizational pulverization within the internal bourgeoisie, it continued acting conjointly. One could say that the strategy that the State used succeeded in ensuring benefits for different sectors, especially in regard to the question of access to international

---

11   For example, Boito Jr. (2012, p.71) reports that "The big companies that have invested heavily in Venezuela support the Chavez government. Marcelo Odebrecht, General president of the Construction Corporation that bears his name and surname and which takes on big construction projects in that country has defended the Chaves government and criticized the major Brazilian press for diffusing, according to him, a negative, deformed image of the Venezuelan president".

markets and the defense of an equilibrium between the dependent States and the Imperialist States in the international economic negotiations.

Furthermore, despite the contradictions that existed between the interests of the industrial bourgeoisie and agribusiness, it would seem that at the current stage of the development of capitalism the division between those two sectors is not so accentuated. That is because many of the agricultural products are processed and packaged and accordingly agribusiness also organizes itself in the state federations and the CNI itself. As an example, within the FIESP structure, there is a Department of Agriculture, and it has a Higher Council of Agribusiness (*Conselho Superior do Agronegócio*). There are many cases of seeking an equilibrium between the interests of those two sectors. Ever since the time of the FTAA negotiations, the two sectors have acted jointly and sought to present common claims and demands to the Brazilian State in regard to the international negotiations.

During the WTO and the MERCOSUR-European Union negotiations, the two sectors endeavored to find a formula for equilibrium between the access of agribusiness to the markets of the imperialist States and the opening up of the internal markets to industrialized products produced in those States. Another example of such efforts was the Cotton Panel in the WTO against the United States. Even though the Brazilian State did eventually get the right to retaliate against the United States, Azevêdo (2010) states that it was only not applied in 2008 because the industrial bourgeoisie was fearful of a counterretaliation and the deleterious effects on the extant partnerships between United States corporations and Brazilian companies. In that light the Brazilian State agreed to new bilateral negotiations which eventually led to the 2010 agreement.

As explained in Chapter 1, the existence of a fraction is circumstantial and temporal. The agglutination of the segments that integrate a fraction is determined by the pertinent effects produced by the State policy and by the international political and economic contexts. In general, there are conflicts in the interior of any fraction but the points of unity are superior to them, otherwise the fraction will take on a new outline. Later, the burgeoning crisis that developed in the heart of the internal bourgeoisie will be described but at this point it is more appropriate to discuss the relations between the interests of the internal bourgeoisie and the south-south foreign policy.

## 2.14   *The Internal Bourgeoisie and the South-South Foreign Policy*
Considering that what determined the south-south foreign policy was the internal bourgeoisie's trajectory of political ascension and the support received from the people's organizations and trade union organizations that integrated the neo-developmentalist front, the Brazilian State required greater autonomy

in the international scenario in order to ensure protection for the internal market, increased exportation and the boosting of the internationalization of Brazilian companies. The shelving of the FTAA proposal, the postponement of the MERCOSUR's negotiations with the European Union and participation in the WTO were all part of the Lula government's policy of not accepting unilateral trade opening, thereby protecting the internal market, and of confronting the imperialist States on issues related to agricultural subsidies. In general, as will be shown below, Brazil's internal bourgeoisie supported those initiatives.

Having described, in Chapter 2, the role the FTAA negotiations played in agglutinating the internal bourgeoisie and in mobilizing the people's sectors that integrated the neo-developmentalist front, the points to be examined now are the WTO negotiations, and the MERCOSUR – European Union negotiations:

The Ministry of Agriculture and Livestock Production (*Ministério da Agricultura e Pecuária*-MAPA) was given the task of accompanying the WTO negotiations alongside the Brazilian Ministry of Foreign Affairs. To that end it created a Technical Group (TG) to debate with businessmen and Trade Unions, the proposals the Brazilian State would defend at the meeting of the G-20. The TG was made up of civil servants from the Ministry of Agriculture (*Ministério da Agricultura*), the Ministry of Agrarian Development (*Ministério do Desenvolvimento Agrário*), the Ministry of Foreign Affairs (*Ministério das Relações Exteriores*), the Ministry of Development, Industry and Foreign Trade (*Ministério do Desenvolvimento Indústria e Comércio Exterior*), and representatives of the National Confederation of Agriculture (*Confederação Nacional da Agricultura*-CNA), the ICONE and the National Confederation of Workers in Agriculture (*Confederação dos Trabalhadores na Agricultura*-CONTAG).

The Brazilian State's performance in the G-20 was only possible because, influenced by the interests of the neo-developmentalist front it adopted both offensive and defensive positions. The offensive ones were the liberalization of agricultural, which had to do with the interests of the agribusiness sector and the defensive ones were protection of the internal market and the small farmer, which addressed the interests of the small-scale agriculturists whether wage earning and/or settled.

Agribusiness did not readily accept that composition, however. It saw that its interests would be put aside in the light of the Indian State's position which sought special safeguards for the dependent States. The situation was exacerbated after the WTO Ministerial Conference in 2005 when the G-20 obtained gains in that very direction. ICONE director Marcos Jank declared that the gains obtained only fulfilled the expectations of the small-scale farmers and accordingly failed to correspond to those of the Brazilian exporting sector. Agribusiness then began to pressure the Brazilian State to get the imperialist states to open their agricultural markets (Carvalho, 2010).

The disputes between agribusiness and the wage-earning workers divided the technical group organized by the Ministry of Agriculture and Livestock Production and not only the entities that represented those two segments, Contag, CNA and ICONE, but also the Ministry of Agriculture and the Ministry of Agrarian Development (Ramanzini, 2012). That all goes to show that the disputes in the heart of the neo-developmentalist front were internalized and produced disputes among various other entities of the State apparat.

Those disputes went on until 2008 when the Brazilian State yielded to the pressure from Agribusiness and decided to accept the package that Pascal Lamy had proposed. According to Carvalho (2010, p.420):

> The increased divergence between the offensive and defensive interests inside the G-20 and the agribusiness pressure eroded Brazil's capacity to continue negotiating based on that group and contributed to the country's distancing itself from the G-20 in July 2008 and its acceptance of the WTO proposal.

In other words, an important segment of the internal bourgeoisie, agribusiness, ended by exerting a greater influence on the actions of the Brazilian State than the others.[12] The MST and Contag in turn threatened to block roads and occupy farms and public buildings if the president did not sign a WTO agreement (CUT, 2008).

The Brazilian industrial bourgeoisie took a positive view of the Doha Round as the center of the Brazilian foreign policy strategy during the Lula governments (Tachinardi, 2006; Neto, 2008). The CNI considered that the following elements should form the base for the multilateral negotiations: opening up the agricultural sector of the imperialist States, improving mechanisms for settling controversies, striking a balance between the gains for the agriculture sector and possible negative consequences for the industrial and services sectors (CNI, 2006c). The CNI showed that it was willing to make concessions in the industrial area if gains for agribusiness were effectually obtained but it stated that it would not accept unilateral, unequal trade opening concessions.

---

12   It is worth noting that Agribusiness was also represented in the Sugar, Cotton and Orange Juice Panels opened by the Brazilian State in the WTO (Iglesias, 2007).

In 2008 the FIESP held a meeting at its headquarters with ambassador Roberto Carvalho to present what it considered to be the acceptable limits for negotiations with the WTO.

There was a perceptible degree of disbelief in the possibility of an agreement, on the part of the industrial bourgeoisie. the sector could not see any great advantage in the agreement's possible approval because it was well aware that its competitors, China among them, would also be benefited which could mean that the gains in terms of the industrial sector's access to markets might be very small (CNI, 2010). Thus, as soon as the failure of the 2008 WTO meeting was apparent, CNI president Monteiro Neto wrote an article expressing how he regretted the collapse of the negotiations and stating that the time had come to think in terms of a new 'Post-Doha' agenda. He argued that it would be important to seek for new regional agreements and make progress on other issues such as investments protection, rules for services and government purchases, and others (Neto, 2008).

According to the CNI document, the new preferential trade agreements that Monteiro mentioned should take into account the following elements: 1) the size of the importing market; 2) the opportunities for Brazilian exports; and 3) the elimination of barriers against Brazilian products. In 2006 the CNI had identified the following States and regional blocs as candidates for such agreements: the United States, the European Union, Mexico, India, South Africa, and the Gulf Cooperation Council (CNI, 2006a). In 2010, the list was repeated (CNI, 2010).

In regard to the MERCOSUR-European Union negotiations, there was also perceptible divergence of interests between the industrial bourgeoisie and the agribusiness sector. According to Cruz and Silva (2011, p.61):

> In general, the positioning of the CEB presented convergence with the Brazilian government's position in the negotiations. Up until 2004, while the negotiations were still ongoing, the CNI conducted a series of consultations with the private sector and defined the positioning on questions on the negotiating agenda. CNI representatives' declarations indicated the defensive posture of industrial sectors like the automotive, textiles and footwear [sectors]. in relation to the entrance of European industrial goods. While the agricultural sector sought for European opening for their products. The CEB in its aspect as the vocalization of the business sector, albeit an institution created in the ambit of the Confederation of Industry, also articulated with the agricultural and agribusiness sectors for the dialogue with the government.

In the wake of the breakdown of the negotiations the agribusiness representative went so far as to accuse the Brazilian diplomats of 'ill will' in the negotiations (Cruz & Silva, 2011).

In 2010 when the negotiations were resumed, there was closer proximity of a segment of the industrial bourgeoisie, the textiles segment, with agribusiness. The textiles sector began to show greater interest in access to the European market (Cruz & Silva, 2011). However, in a letter delivered to the Ministry of Foreign Affairs the CNI continued to state that the agreement would bring with it negative impacts for the industrial sector. According to the president of the Brazilian Business Coalition (*Coalizão Empresarial Brasileira*-CEB) an agreement between the two blocs should take into consideration the internal conditions of each economy (Leo, 2010).

Once again, the negotiations made little progress; it was merely decided to continue the meetings between the two blocs. One reason for the scant progress was that the European Union's offer to the agricultural sector fell far short of expectations. Furthermore, the Argentinean State, an important member of the MERCOSUR, began to show less interest in the agreement in view of the possible deleterious effects that it might have on its industrial park. Based on that, the Brazilian agribusiness sector, which was the one most interested in the agreement, began to vociferate the need for MERCOSUR to become more flexible so that an agreement with the European Union could be finalized without the endorsement of the Argentinean government.

On the other hand, the central organization of Trade Unions and their Confederations (Unified Workers Central) (*Central Única dos Trabalhadores*-CUT) and the *Via Campesina*, an organization that brought together entities such as the Landless Rural Workers Movement (*Movimento dos Trabalhores Rurais Sem Terra*-MST), the Small Farmers Movement (*Movimento dos Pequenos Agricultores*-MPA) and the Movement of those Affected by Dams (*Movimento dos Atingidos por Barragens*-MAB), reacted critically to the MERCOSUR proposal to liberalize the agricultural and agribusiness sectors in up to 90%. In a letter to minister Celso Amorim, the secretary for Foreign Affairs of the CUT, João Vaccari Neto, argued that the European Union's offers were very small in comparison with the offers of the MERCOSUR States. The representative of the MPA, in turn, stated that the opening of important sectors of the Brazilian market to the Europeans could do great harm to small farmers (Agencia Carta Maior, 2004). The MST organized a protest demonstration of over 100 militant members in front of the Itamaraty building. According to Rogério Mauro, member of that movement's national coordinating body, if the agreement were signed it would jeopardize large sectors of Brazilian society and only benefit agribusiness exportation (Radiobrás, 2004).

In 2007, alongside the Union Centrals and Confederations of Argentina, Venezuela, South Africa, Namibia, Egypt, Tunisia, India, Indonesia and the Philippines, CUT delivered a letter to the ambassadors participating in the WTO Non-Agricultural Market Access (NAMA) negotiations. In it those entities stated that the formulae and enhanced flexibility proposals would be unacceptable as they favored the economies of the imperialist States and would produce negative effects on employment and local industries in the developing countries (CUT, 2007).

In short, just as it had been in the FTAA negotiations, so the position of the imperialist States in the Doha Round of the WTO and in the MERCOSUR-European Union negotiations contributed towards the internal bourgeoisie's maintaining itself as the same fraction and, at the same time, to ensuring the support of the union centrals and confederations and the people's social movements so that the Brazilian industry should not be exposed to entirely unequal competition that would lead to further unemployment.

The differences between the industrial bourgeoisie and the agribusiness sector were no longer so sharp as neither accepted a unilateral opening of the industrial and services sector markets without there being a counterpart concession for agricultural products. As neither the United States nor the European Union were disposed to relinquish their agricultural protectionism, the negotiations made no progress.

In addition to having rejected the agreements which were unfavorable for the internal bourgeoisie and workers in industry, the Brazilian State began to invest in policies to guarantee the expansion of the sales of manufactured products and the intensification the Brazilian transnational companies' performance in other territories. Thanks to the currency exchange rate devaluation, the reduction in interest rates, the policy of stimulating the formation of the great 'national champions', the boosting of South American integration and the strengthening of relations among the dependent States, the Brazilian State obtained considerable benefits for the internal bourgeoisie and there was notable support of that fraction for the State's main initiatives. Among those initiatives were:

The MERCOSUR became a favored sphere for the industrial bourgeoisie. The CNI accompanied the bloc's meetings and continued to participate in the Social and Economic Consultative Forum (*Foro Consultivo Econômico e Social*-FCES). The Confederation supported the measures to strengthen integration with the creation of the Focem (CNI, 2005, p.3–4) and paid close attention to the bloc's external negotiations with the European Union, Israel, Egypt and the SACU.

The Brazilian internal bourgeoisie was not only interested in 'relaunching' the MERCOSUR, but it also recommended "progress with the creation of a free trade area in South America" (CNI, 2006b, p.156). In addition, its documents underscored the entity's interest in investments in transportation and logistics infrastructure (CNI, 2007b). It also began to call for protection for Brazil's direct foreign investments and increased financing for the internationalization of Brazilian companies (CNI, 2010). According to material in the Industry Review (*Revista da Indústria*) (Cunha, 2005, p.30):

> The boom in Brazilian exports has made it possible for a scenario to materialize which a little over a decade ago seemed impossible. With the elevation of overseas sales, national brands are beginning to consolidate their space in various markets, while the image of the country is associated to their competitiveness. "In this new millennium, the Brazilian companies have risked even higher flights and begun to install branches in the exterior. Internationalization is a tendency which, albeit still at an incipient stage, is increasingly taking over Brazilian industries' strategy" ponders Roberto Gianetti da Fonseca, director of the International Relations and Foreign Trade Department of the FIESP.

The IBAS forum also aroused the interest of the Brazilian internal bourgeoisie. Its representatives perceived the trading and investment opportunities, especially in the mining, energy, infrastructure, and logistics sectors. Since 2005, the CNI has been part of the IBAS Business Council and, together with the other business entities of India and South Africa, had expressed interest in obtaining a Free Trade agreement among the States as witness the excerpt below (Conselho Empresarial IBAS, 2007):

> Considering that MERCOSUR and SACU have signed a Preferential Trade Agreement, as have India and MERCOSUR, and the fact that the discussions of a Preferential Trade Agreement between India and Sacu are making progress, it may be appropriate to consider a MERCOSUR-SACU-India Preferential Trade Agreement.

In 2008, the CNI received the visit of an Indian businessmen's mission and from then on defended an increase in State investments in marine infrastructure and transportation to guarantee the flow of trade among the countries. The internal bourgeoisie's interest in Africa was apparent not only in the official visits of the Brazilian State but also in the innumerable business missions to that continent. As has already been mentioned, many of the trips made by the President and by his Minister of Foreign Affairs were accompanied by businessmen interested in investing in, and trading with the African countries.

It is worth noting that between 2000 and 2005, the National Industrial Training Service (*Serviço Nacional de Aprendizagem Industrial*-SENAI) an entity connected to the FIESP, acted together with the Brazilian Cooperation Agency in the creation and maintenance of the Brazil-Angola Professional Qualification Center (*Centro de Formação Profissional Brasil-Angola*) (site: Agência Brasileira de Cooperação). The internal bourgeoisie also supported the re-equipping of the Brazilian air force and navy and the preference given to the national defense industry in the respective government purchasing (Camargo, 2007/2008).

Lastly, the following excerpt from the *Review of Industry* shows the industrial bourgeoisie's acknowledgment of the benefits it accrued from the south-south relations:

> Brazil is increasingly recognized as an important global player. While the Federal Government seeks to enhance the country's image, FIESP's intense international agenda last month indicates that São Paulo industry is confirming itself as the strong link among markets beyond our borders. 'Establishing partnerships with emerging markets is an opportunity to amplify Brazilian trade. Those economies are complementary to the main sectors of our economy' declares ambassador Rubens Barbosa.
> CUNHA, 2004, p.10

One of the economic results that proves our hypothesis was the increase in Brazilian direct foreign investment. An analysis of the geographic distribution of the branches of companies that became transnational shows that in 2010, more than 48% of Brazilian transnational companies were operating in South America, Central America or Africa. As those are smaller markets, in relative terms that 48% is even more significant (Fundação Dom Cabral, 2011).

The data on the evolution of Brazilian exports to dependent and imperialist countries (Figure 4) reveal that there was an exponential increase in the exportation of basic products and (manufactured and semi-manufactured) industrialized products to the dependent countries. Once again if we bear in mind the relatively small weight of those States economies, the proportional increase was far greater. Taking as the reference the differences between the first and last years of the government (2003 and 2010), the exportation of basic and industrialized products to dependent countries leapt up from 7.9 billion to 52.2 billion dollars and from 21.8 billion to 63.3 billion dollars respectively.

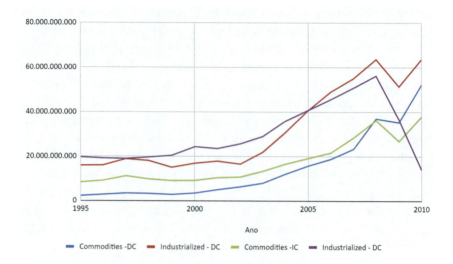

FIGURE 4    Brazilian exports to imperialist countries (IC) and dependent countries (DC) by destinations and by values – in billions of dollars
DATA: MINISTRY OF DEVELOPMENT, INDUSTRY AND FOREIGN TRADE; ELABORATED BY THE AUTHOR

Altogether that was an increase of 288.8%, whereas exports to the developed countries increased by a mere 22%.

The data and the evidence presented above confirm the relation between the south-south foreign policy and the economic benefits that accrued to the internal bourgeoisie. Having proved that, it is time to identify an aspect of the growing contradiction between the industrial bourgeoisie and agribusiness in regard to that south-south foreign policy.

## 2.15    *Contradictions among Sectors Composing the Internal Bourgeoisie*

The growing conflict among the different segments making up the internal bourgeoisie centered on the Brazilian State's increasing proximity with the Chinese State. Since 2004 when the Brazilian State recognized China as a market economy the industrial bourgeoisie had been highly critical (Vigevani & Cepaluni, 2011). as can be seen from the following excerpt:

> FIESP president Paulo Skaf declared emphatically "The People's Republic of China is absolutely not a market economy" and that FIESP was constantly receiving information from Brazilian companies registering internal losses due to the importation of Chinese products and the practice of dumping prices.
> MARQUES & RIOS, 2004, p.21

China worried the manufacturing industry not only because of the threat to the internal market, but also the fact that increased importation of Chines goods by the other South American States jeopardized the exportation of Brazilian products to them. According to Onuki and Oliveira (2007, p.13) the FIESP not only participated in public hearings and endeavored to raise awareness via the media but instigated a Parliamentarian of the Federal Legislative to present a Legislative Decree that would make any recognition of China as a market economy impossible.

Given the substantial change in the Brazilian balance of payments after 2008 that contradiction in the heart of the internal bourgeoisie became even greater. On the one hand there was the euphoria of the agricultural and mining sectors who increased the volumes of their exports to China and began to call for greater commitment between the two States, supporting the Brazil-China bilateral agreement signed in 2009 (CEBC, 2010). On the other hand, the increase in the volume of imports of manufactured products from that Asian country to Brazil made the industrial bourgeoisie raise the tone of its criticism. Everything went to show that if the losses of the manufactured good sector persisted then the contradiction could become exacerbated and, in that case, the industrial bourgeoisie would be able to count on the support of the union confederations and centrals in defense of Brazilian industry.

In addition to those points of conflict in the heart of the internal bourgeoisie, it is important to analyze other international actions of the Brazilian state which, in the political arena, apparently did not represent the internal bourgeoisie's interests.

## 2.16   *The Unstable Equilibrium of Compromises and Foreign Policy*
What can be said about those foreign policy initiatives which apparently did not enjoy the support of the internal bourgeoisie? It can be affirmed that those actions fit in very well with the idea of an unstable equilibrium of compromises between the classes and class fractions and the Brazilian State. The explanation follows in the coming paragraphs.

The trade disputes between Brazil and Argentina in the ambit of the MERCOSUR, Venezuela's ingress to the bloc and the reviews of the Petrobras contract with the Bolivian State and the Itaipu hydroelectric plant contract with the Paraguayan State were the main points of the supposed friction between the interests of the internal bourgeoisie and the foreign policy. Those points make it possible to get a more detailed perception of the internal bourgeoisie's political-ideological stance and show how the State sought to safeguard the bourgeoisie's more strategic interests even though the bourgeoisie failed to realize that at first. That is good reason to believe that the idea of an unstable equilibrium of compromises is appropriate for explaining the cases and they will be examined separately, one by one.

In regard to MERCOSUR, it is apparent that over the years the internal bourgeoisie spoke out more and more against the increasing protectionism of the Argentinean State. After 2004 when that neighboring State adopted protectionist measures for footwear and household appliances, both the CNI (2005) and the FIESP called on the Brazilian State to intervene to avoid setbacks in the bloc's trading integration. The text below, taken from a message of FIESP president Paulo Skaf (Skaf, 2005, p.78) is an example:

> If it is true that the solution for the MERCOSUR's problems is precisely its consolidation, as the government has repeatedly said, then let the necessary measures and concrete understandings in that direction be effectuated. It is obvious that in the ambit of that goal the adoption of restrictive measures and protectionism for the national industries of the member countries are not appropriate.

From then on, the internal bourgeoisie began to adopt a more critical posture in regard to the neighboring State. In 2006 when the Competitive Adaptation Mechanism (*Mecanismo de Adaptação Competitiva*-MAC)[13] was signed, CNI president, Armando Monteiro Neto, declared that "the mechanism would go against the spirit of integration of the MERCOSUR and generate a climate of retrogression in the bloc's development" (Folha de São Paulo, 2006).

The issue came to a head when in 2009 the Argentinean State, in a bid to protect its own industries, demanded certificates of importation known as non-automatic licenses for importation of a series of Brazilian products. As those measures jeopardized Brazilian exports, even though it acknowledged the superiority of Brazilian industry vis-à-vis Argentinean industry, the CNI was emphatically critical of them and even went so far as to call for the establishment of a WTO panel against Argentina (CNI, 2009c) and the adoption of retaliatory measures. To that end it edited technical notes and sent letters to the Minister of Foreign Affairs, Celso Amorim and to the Minister of Development. Industry and Foreign Trade, Miguel Jorge (CNI, 2009a).[14]

---

13   The MAC is a protocol that provides for the application of protectionist measures on the part of MERCOSUR member States whenever the importation of a product registers a substantial increase for a relevant period of time, thereby harming or threatening the domestic industry.

14   It is important to observe that CNI vociferated the most critical position in regard to the bloc more than the FIESP did. The latter seems to have adopted a more strategic vision in relation to the MERCOSUR. In an interview conceded to the program 'Roda Viva' of the TV

Against that background and the difficulties encountered in other trade negotiations like the Doha Round of the WTO and the MERCOSUR-European Union Agreement, the Brazilian internal bourgeoisie raised the tone of its complaints and began to defend the idea of making the bloc more 'flexible' so that the Brazilian State could start to seek for bilateral agreements. Actually, one could say that that the internal bourgeoisie switched to defending the improvement of the Customs Union to the detriment of effectuation of the free trade area (CNI, 2010; Cruz & Silva, 2011).

Despite all those issues, the internal bourgeoisie never stopped stating that the MERCOSUR was an important space for Brazilian industry, not just for exporting its manufactured goods but also for making direct foreign investments and it reaffirmed that the Brazilian State should take on the leadership of the bloc, abiding by the regulations and contributing to the coordination of the respective national development policies (CNI, 2010). That was why it fell to the Brazilian State to think strategically about the way to deal with the trading conflicts that arose inside the bloc. The CNI considered it important to find measures that could ensure MERCOSUR's continued existence in the long term and that, in turn, involved strengthening the Member States' economies given that MERCOSUR was of strategic interest to Brazil's internal bourgeoisie. In the name of the stable equilibrium of compromises it was possible that there would be losses at first for the Brazilian internal bourgeoisie as there would be drops in sales of some products to Argentina, but in the long run it would safeguard the bloc's existence and ensure its strengthening.

Venezuela's admission to the MERCOSUR was another point that demonstrated the contradiction between the State decision and the interests of the internal bourgeoisie. By adopting a technical tone, the internal bourgeoisie endeavored to manifest its reservations in regard to that admission. The long note that the CNI published on that issue warned about the formal procedures that were necessary before that new State could be incorporated to the bloc. The CNI stated that the adherence to a free trade area would be the most difficult issue given the commitments already made and implemented under the terms of the Economic Complementation Agreement 59 (*Acordo de Complementação Econômica* 59). Actually, the real motive was fear of contamination of the bloc's external actions due to President Hugo Chaves'

---

Cultura channel, on May 28, 2012, Paulo Skaf went so far as to defend the need for Brazil to revert to an economic surplus in its bilateral trading given that a crisis in Argentina could affect the Brazilian economy. Furthermore, he recommended that the government should extend its government purchasing policy to [include] Argentinean products.

antiimperialist posture. The following texts are taken from the said long CNI (2006a, p.10) note:

> The Bloc's low level of participation in more important agreements from the economic point of view means reduced immediate difficulties in this area. However, the agreements in negotiation and future initiatives will be subject to coordination with the new member, which must increase the difficulty to define common positions of the bloc in the trade negotiations.

"The eventual re-launching of the MERCOSUR-EU negotiations could be an important test. The intra-MERCOSUR difficulties in the industrial products offer (e.g., the automotive sector) and the negotiations in the agricultural area will acquire additional complexity with the entrance of Venezuela, especially in MERCOSUR's understandings with the USA."

Ever since the year 2000, Brazil had maintained surpluses in its trading with Venezuela. In another note, the CNI (2006a) recognized that there would be many opportunities for Brazilian construction and energy companies. Everything goes to show that the Brazilian bourgeoisie seemed to believe that in spite of the economic gains to be had, it was not worth incurring any political costs that would affect the bloc's image in the eyes of the imperialist States. That being said, the question that arises is: would that not be evidence of the internal bourgeoisie's dependent nature and political-ideological weakness?

During the Chaves governments the Venezuelan State policy was the policy of the national (State) bourgeoisie in antiimperialist alliance with the classes of ordinary people, whereas the Brazilian State's policy was the policy of the internal bourgeoisie in a neo-developmentalist front. It could be said, therefore, that the internal bourgeoisie rejected the antiimperialist posture of the Venezuelan national (State) bourgeoisie because it did not want to break off relations with the United States.

So, what was in play in regard to the review of the Petrobras contract with Bolivia and the Itaipu contract with Paraguay? In both cases the Brazilian government was facing partner governments with fragile economies that had elected presidents that were critical of neoliberalism. It was up to the Brazilian State to contribute to ensuring that those government's political programs went into effect and that the respective countries experienced economic development. It was in the Brazilian State's interest to maintain political proximity with neighboring States and see that the economies of those countries became more robust because the Brazilian internal bourgeoisie would benefit from increased exportation to them of manufactured goods and from the installation of branches of Brazilian companies in those countries. Strategically, those initiatives strengthened the regional integration processes and required that the Brazilian State should bear the costs of the said processes.

Another aspect of the review of those contracts was that they ensured the medium and long-term maintenance of access to those sources of energy of fundamental importance to the Brazilian industrial bourgeoisie. Thus, these cases demonstrate that generally, when the bourgeoisie criticized those actions, it only thought about its own immediate interests and had no interest in more strategic aspects which were left for the State to deal with. In the case of Paraguay for example, some years after the contract review the FIESP began to encourage businessmen to install companies in that country in view of the low payroll and energy costs.

It should be remembered that in the case of Petrobras in Bolivia, it was the national and international capital that most endeavored to revert the prospect of nationalization and the contract review because those actions lowered the profits of the company's shareholders. Strangely enough most of the points discussed above were supported by the social and union movements that were part of the neo-developmentalist front.[15] In other words, the actions of the Brazilian State sought primarily to address the interests of the internal bourgeoisie but at the same time some of its actions only enjoyed the support of the trade unions and people's movements. Those issues provided space in which the conservative sectors and the party-political opposition could act in their endeavors to publicly wear down the government. The next item addresses that aspect.

### 2.17   The Party-Political Dispute and Foreign Policy

One fact that draws attention is that part of the actions that were a source of conflict between the Brazilian State and the United States such as Venezuela's

---

15   During the Conference to mark 10 years of the Foreign Policy held in July 2013 at the Federal University of the ABC, on the part of the social movements and union movements that formed the government's support base, namely the Unified Workers Central (Central Única dos Trabalhadores-CUT), the National Union of Students of Brazil (União Nacional dos Estudantes do Brasil-UNE), the Central of Men and Women Workers of Brazil (Central dos Trabalhadores e Trabalhadoras do Brasil-CTB) and the Landless Rural Workers Movement (Movimento dos Trabalhadores Rurais Sem Terra-MST), there were positive statements about the government's proximity with the leftist governments of South America, its support for the review of the Petrobras contract with Bolivia and the Itaipu Treaty with Paraguay, its support for Manuel Zelaya in Honduras, its support for the Iran nuclear agreement etc. The texts of Fátima Mello (2010) and João Antonio Felício (2010), representatives of the REBRIP and the CUT respectively, also confirm that position.

ingression in the MERCOSUR, the review of the Petrobras contract in Bolivia and others were criticized by the big press and the party-political opposition to the government. That shows that the dispute between the orthodox neoliberal field and the neo-developmentalist was also reflected in foreign policy matters. The truth is that the parliamentary opposition and the big press used these and other issues to harass the government. According to Cruz (2013, p.13):

> For the opposition, the foreign policy emerges as a favorable area because in it the attack on the government can be conducted at a minimum cost given the great majority of the population's indifference to international issues whose implications for their daily lives are highly remote and obscure.

"In the small space of the public, moderately informed on such themes, the opposition confronts the government in conditions of a relative equilibrium of forces and can express the virulence of its criticism without restrictions. We had a sample of that fact in the uproar surrounding President Ahmadinejad's visit to Brazil; in the discussion of the military agreement between Colombia and the United States; in the debate on Venezuela's adherence to the MERCOSUR, and in the polemic associated to the performance of Brazilian diplomacy during the crisis in Honduras. These last two episodes are highly revealing."

It should be remembered that Venezuela's ingression in the MERCOSUR was approved by the bloc's member States in 2005, but the Brazilian Senate's approval only occurred almost four years later at an agitated Senate session on December 15, 2009 (Cruz, 2013). In regard to the class representatives of entities composing the internal bourgeoisie it is important to bear in mind that:

> [Many of the] public leaders of the preceding government went on to run some of the main exportation entities. Former Minister of Agriculture. Pratini de Moraes was in the ABIEC from 2005 to 2009, ex-Secretary of the Ministry of Agriculture Pedro Camargo Neto has been in the ABIEPECS since 2006, Marcos Junk, former special advisor to the Ministry of Development, Industry and Trade, ex-president of the ICONE has been engaged in the UNICA since 2007 and former Minister of Agriculture, Francisco Turra has remained in the UBABEEF since 2008
> LOHNBAUER, 2010, p.78

Considering the national and state entities, that relationship was maintained. Rubens Barbosa, President of FIESP's Foreign Trade High Council, was ambassador in London and Washington during the FHC governments. Armando

Monteiro Neto, President of the CNI from 2002 to 2010 was affiliated to the PSDB from 1990 until 1997. After that he joined the PMDB, and in 2003, the PTB. He was elected to the House of Representatives for three successive mandates from 1999 to 2011 on a PTB ticket.

The political entities do not necessarily express the class position but rather individual's positions or sector's positions. Accordingly, in spite of the existence of criticism it is not possible to state that the interests of that fraction were not favored by the State.[16]

There was, indeed, harsh criticism of the Brazilian State's international actions. Rubens Barbosa (2008) for example, stated that there had been an excessive 'ideologization' of foreign policy. In the FIESP and CNI documents there are recurrent demands for fortifying the Chamber of Foreign Trade (*Câmara de Comércio Exterior*-CAMEX), linked to the Ministry of Development, Industry and Foreign Trade. According to the two entities, to avoid what they call the 'ideologization' of the Brazilian State's stance in the international economic negotiations, they should be left to CAMEX which had a more pragmatic character than the Ministry of Foreign Affairs.

The question is: if the excerpt from the CNI document is taken as an example, can all that has been stated above be put aside and the affirmation be made that the internal bourgeoisie was not benefited by the Lula governments' foreign policy? Let us see:

> In recent years the country has taken on a protagonist role in the World Trade Organization's Multilateral trade negotiations, but it is still acting with great difficulty in the terrain of preferential agreements.
>
> The priority placed on south-south preferential trade agreements has not produced significant results, and that has translated as underly ambitious arrangements with other emergent economies (India and South Africa) in an agenda that is commercially irrelevant in the country's geographic region, Latin America.
>
> Despite the lack of results from the preferential [trade] negotiations, Brazilian exports have shown a good performance, benefiting from a highly favorable international panorama. The results would have been even better if the negotiations had been materialized.
>
> CNI, 2010, p 187

---

16  On this point we disagree with Bezerra (2008) and Cruz and Silva (2012) when they state that the Brazilian businessmen were against the south-south foreign policy.

So, the question that remains is: which negotiations could have been materialized? the FTAA ones? the MERCOSUR-European Union ones? That is not exactly what it is all about. That kind of posturing on the part of the bourgeoisie shows that it is always dissatisfied and wanting more, especially in times of international financial crisis; the quest for new markets always reappears.

The truth is that the internal bourgeoisie's agenda still included agreements with the United States, with the European Union, Mexico, India, South Africa and others. That is because they are highly important markets, not only for agricultural products but also for manufactured ones. Nevertheless, the rhythm and the possibility of that kind of agreement materializing did not depend of the posture of the Brazilian State alone but also on the other power blocs' interests and on the political stances of their respective States and especially of the imperialist States and those of the MERCOSUR. It is in that sense that the positions in defense of greater flexibility in the integration of the South American bloc appears, given that the MERCOSUR could have become an obstacle to the approval of agreements with other States or blocs. However, there could hardly have been any agreement that would have brought mutual benefits for all the different sectors that made up the internal bourgeoisie.

The fact is that the opposition seems to have taken advantage of that context to gather support for the internal bourgeoisie and corrode the government. The following is an excerpt from an interview that FHC granted to the *Valor Econômico* in 2012:[17]

> We never got down to a real discussion of the FTAA (Free Trade Area of the Americas) when the Americans were interested in it. Afterwards they lost interest, along with the Brazilian government, and they made bilateral agreements with various countries here in Latin America. We never got around to seriously thinking about a negotiation with the United States, we were always afraid. That 'we' means all of us. The political sector, because of ideology, the business sector from fear of competition, and the government, because of being unclear as to what Brazil's interests were. We just kept the FTAA lukewarm in a bain-marie. Despite all the hullabaloo, we never did anything, never took a single step to strengthen the FTAA. So I ask myself: could it be that now we are no longer in a condition to think more freely? Not to do it. We ended up very isolated in the MERCOSUR. We did not manage to establish relations between

---

17   It is worth noting that during the 2010 electoral campaign the PSDB candidate, José Serra followed the same line of argument as FHC. On that issue see Ennes (2010).

MERCOSUR and Europe; I tried but it didn't work. We did not make the FTAA and we did not get ahead very much with any other bloc, nor with any countries. Brazil has an automotive agreement with Mexico, A free trade agreement, or something similar, with Israel and I don't who else, if there are any others. So we are very much unarmed. As it all coincided with our having this boom in China, the commodities boom, the question lost its importance. The moment the favorable [trade] flows with China diminish, there will be a need for other markets. So, what then?

As is well known, despite the party-political dispute the PT candidate in the presidential elections, Dilma Rousseff was elected in 2020 and in regard to the relations between foreign policy and the internal bourgeoisie, there were no alterations.

CHAPTER 4

# Brazil and South America

The Lula Governments' foreign policy and the burgeoning wave of internationalization of Brazilian companies led some authors to state that the Brazilian State had taken on an imperialist or sub-imperialist role in South America. This chapter[1] makes a critical presentation of the analyses of Virgínia Fontes (2010), Raul Zibechi (2012) and Mathias Luce (2007) and defends the view that the Brazilian State's position was actually highly important for the maintenance of progressist governments in the region. Then comes an examination of the role and interests of people's movements and trade unionism in relation to the regional integration processes.

## 1   Brazilian State and South America: Imperialism, Sub-imperialism and Neo-developmentalism

### 1.1   *Brazilian Imperialism*

Virgínia Fontes (2010) and Raul Zibechi (2012) argue that Brazil has played an imperialist role in the region. They hold that weakening of the United States' hegemony and the predominance of finance have configured a 'new imperialism'. Virgínia Fontes describes the current stage of capitalism's development as 'capital-imperialism' based on three elements: 1) the predominance of monetary-capital; 2) the performance of pension funds in the stock markets, which transforms workers into instruments of capital accumulation and valorization; and 3) capitalist expansion beyond national borders. She also considers that Brazil has reached the stage of capital-imperialism and accordingly has joined the group of imperialist countries, albeit in a subaltern condition (Fontes, 2010, p.306).

Raul Zibechi (2012) states that the international division of labor is organized among central States, semi-peripheral States and peripheral States. Each long historical cycle has seen the economic and military hegemony of a great State – England in the 19th century and the United States in the 20th century. The author proposes that ever since its defeat in Vietnam in 1968, the

---

[1] This chapter is a modified version of the article, "A tese do imperialismo brasileiro em questão" ("The Thesis of Brazilian Imperialism in Question") published in *Revista Crítica Marxista* n°36 (*Marxist Critiques Review* n°36, 2013).

hegemony of the United States has been waning, and that the destruction of the World Trade towers in 2001 and the acute economic crisis in 2008 accelerated that process. In that scenario, he argues, there would be space for the ascension of new powers. Thus, Brazil would be a regional power ascending to the position of a global power. According to Zibechi (2012, p.262):

> since the first decade of the 21st century, a tendency has solidified that had revealed itself forcefully during the military regime and was soon abandoned only to flower again in all its intensity with the Lula government. That tendency is the wish to convert Brazil into a global power.

A reading of those authors raises the following question: is it possible to think about imperialism without considering the military, economic, technological and political capacity of the Brazilian State and Brazilian social formation? Despite the changes in the productive sphere (trans-nationalization) and the form of accumulation (financialization), the political and military dimension of the Leninist theory of imperialism cannot simply be disregarded. Above all, the correlation of forces in the international sphere cannot be subjected to such an equivocated analysis.

Fontes and Zibechi's concepts of imperialism concentrate on the economic sphere, or rather, on the increase in Brazilian direct foreign investment, as an instrument for dominating the South American social formations. What they lack is a more rigorous analysis of the political relations among the States. Obviously, the internationalization of Brazilian companies to other territories is full of contradictions; it increases the concentration of Brazilian capital and the exploitation of natural resources and wage-earning labor in those social formations. Nevertheless, it does not override the imperialism of the United States and the fractions of the bourgeoisie associated to it. Those forces still perform the dominant role in global geopolitics, and they have strongly opposed progressist governments in South America.

A considerable portion of Brazilian investments in South America were linked to fortifying developmentalist policies that depend on external investment. The respective governments, mostly national-developmentalist, did not have the resources or structure to execute works in the period they wished to and accordingly contracted Brazilian companies backed by the financing of the National Social and Economic Development Bank (*Banco Nacional de Desenvolvimento Econômico e Social*-BNDES). Projects like the construction of the Metro in Caracas, the port of Mariel in Cuba, the Amazon Highway in Bolivia and the hydroelectric plant in Ecuador were not projects or initiatives of the Brazilian State.

Furthermore, the Brazilian State never used military force to guarantee the activities of the Brazilian companies, not even in some cases like the hydroelectric dam construction in Ecuador or the highway in Bolivia against which there were strong grassroots mobilizations that even led to the suspension of the work in progress. Actually, those mobilizations were signs of the contradictions generated by the development of capitalism. There are contradictions between the pre-capitalist modes of production of indigenous peoples and riverside dwellers that still survive in the midst of a social formation dominated by the capitalist mode of production and the conflicts between bourgeois classes and class fractions and the dominated classes, that is, capital-labor conflicts. There was a large-scale mobilization in Brazil too, against the construction of the Belo Monte Hydroelectric Plant. In other words, the region was experiencing a development cycle that brought with it both progressist and contradictory aspects.

Fontes and Zibechi took pains to distinguish their views from those of Marxist Ruy Mauro Marini (1974) and his theory of dependency which introduced the concept of sub-imperialism in his analysis of the Brazilian State in the 1970s. According to Fontes and Zibechi, Marini's theory failed to explain Brazilian capitalism's new stage of development because the main structural feature of dependency, scarcity of the internal market, was no longer a reality of the Brazilian social formation. Zibechi argues that Brazil has converted itself into a country of middle classes and achieved a degree of autonomy in capital accumulation through the dynamics of exportation and the changes made in the productive structure. That author states that Brazil is not dependent and neither does it perform as a sub-power as Marini purports. Zibechi believes that Brazil is on the way overcoming its peripheral condition and becoming a power as the Military of the *Escola Superior de Guerra* (War College) had envisioned in the 1970s.

While it is true that during the Lula governments there was a drop in unemployment and an increase in the credit offer for consumers, that does not mean that Brazil was a country of middle classes. Most of the jobs that were created only required a labor force with a low level of qualification and paid correspondingly low wages. Furthermore, there was no autonomous development of Brazilian capitalism. Dependency is an intrinsic characteristic of Latin American economies and politics, and it expresses the relationship between the external conditioners and the internal structures (Cardoso & Faletto, 1981). The Brazilian bourgeoisie does not have sufficient political and economic force to become autonomous. Just as the old developmentalism (1930–1980) never succeeded in overcoming dependency, so the neo-developmentalism also failed to do so because overcoming dependency requires structural reforms.

TABLE 2   Latin America and the Caribbean: Foreign direct investment inflows by receiving country or territory 2000–2011 (millions of dollars and relative difference in percentages)

| Country | 2000–2005[a] | 2006 | 2007 | 2008 | 2009 | 2010 | 2011 | Absolute difference 2011–2010 | Relative difference 2011–2010 |
|---|---|---|---|---|---|---|---|---|---|
| South America | 38004 | 43539 | 71977 | 92868 | 55492 | 89911 | 121500 | 31631 | 35 |
| Argentina | 4296 | 5537 | 6473 | 9756 | 4017 | 7055 | 7243 | 188 | 3 |
| Bolivia (Plurinational State of) | 350 | 278 | 362 | 508 | 426 | 672 | 859 | 187 | 28 |
| Brazil | 19197 | 18822 | 34585 | 45058 | 25949 | 48506 | 66660 | 18154 | 37 |
| Chile | 5047 | 7426 | 12572 | 15518 | 12887 | 15373 | 17299 | 1926 | 13 |
| Colombia | 3683 | 6656 | 9049 | 10620 | 7137 | 6899 | 13234 | 6335 | 92 |
| Ecuador[b] | 839 | 271 | 194 | 1006 | 321 | 158 | 568 | 410 | 259 |
| Paraguay[b] | 48 | 95 | 202 | 209 | 95 | 228 | 149 | -37[c] | -20[c] |
| Peru | 1604 | 3467 | 5491 | 6924 | 5576 | 7328 | 7659 | 331 | 5 |
| Uruguay | 393 | 1493 | 1329 | 2106 | 1620 | 2483 | 2528 | 45 | 2 |
| Venezuela (Bolivarian Republic of) | 2546 | -508 | 1620 | 1195 | -2536 | 1209 | 5302 | 4093 | 339 |

SOURCE: CEPAL BULLETIN, 2011, P.34

TABLE 3  Latin America and the Caribbean: Foreign direct investment outflows by country 2000–2011 (millions of dollars and relative difference in percentages)

| Country | 2000–2005[a] | 2006 | 2007 | 2008 | 2009 | 2010 | 2011 | Absolute difference 2011–2010[b] | Relative difference 2011–2010[b] |
|---|---|---|---|---|---|---|---|---|---|
| South America | 7040 | 35481 | 14536 | 35141 | 3197 | 31134 | 12579 | -18555 | -60 |
| Argentina | 532 | 2439 | 1504 | 1391 | 712 | 965 | 1488 | 523 | 54 |
| Bolivia (Plurinational State of) | 1 | 3 | 4 | 5 | -4 | -53 | -8 | 46 | 86 |
| Brazil | 2513 | 28202 | 7067 | 20457 | -10084 | 11588 | -9297 | -20885 | -180 |
| Chile | 1988 | 2212 | 4852 | 9151 | 7233 | 9231 | 11822 | 2591 | 28 |
| Colombia | 1156 | 1098 | 913 | 2254 | 3088 | 6562 | 8289 | 1727 | 26 |
| Paraguay[b] | 5 | 4 | 8 | 8 | ... | ... | ... | ... | ... |
| Peru | 22 | 0 | 66 | 736 | 398 | 215 | 111 | -104 | -48 |
| Uruguay | 15 | -1 | 89 | -11 | 16 | -44 | 1 | 45 | 102 |
| Venezuela (Bolivarian Republic of) | 809 | 1524 | 33 | 1150 | 1838 | 2671 | 173 | -2498 | -94 |

SOURCE: CEPAL BULLETIN, 2011, P.62

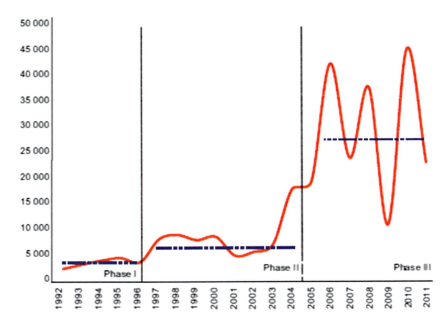

FIGURE 5    Latin America and the Caribbean: Outward foreign direct investment, 1992–2011 (in millions of dollars)
SOURCE: ECONOMIC COMMISSION FOR LATIN AMERICA AND THE CARIBBEAN (ECLAC), ON THE BASIS OF OFFICIAL FIGURES AS AT 16 APRIL 2012

Be that as it may, it is necessary to reflect on the current stage of dependency of the Latin American economies. It is well known that in the period from 2003 to 2007 South America was benefited by the increased demand for commodities and an increase in their prices and that after 2008 the region received a high flow of direct foreign investment from the imperialist countries and there was increased importation of industrialized products from China. As Table 2 shows, Brazil was the main receiver of foreign investment in the region.

The Brazilian transnational companies are mainly concentrated in the construction, food, steel and mining sectors and in the government's words they are the 'national champions'. They are sectors with low technological intensity, and they can count on the State to strengthen them to face up to foreign capital. Brazilian direct foreign investment in the region has not been greater than imperialist direct foreign investment mainly coming from the United States and Europe. Actually, in recent years the exportation of capitals has intensified throughout the region (see Figure 5).

Brazil is not the only country to make direct foreign investments (Table 3). Argentina, Mexico, Chile, Colombia, Venezuela and others also have big companies that are active in other territories. According to the Informative Bulletin issued by ECLAC, Chile was the country that made the most foreign investment in 2011. The main destination for the Chilean investments were Brazil, Colombia and Peru (CEPAL, 2011, p.63). The table below reveals how Brazilian Direct Foreign Investments (BDFI) were very high in 2006, 2008 and 2010 whereas in 2009 and 2011, the BDFI was negative. That was due to two facts: 1) the elevation of loans among company branches that had to send part of their profits to the Brazilian affiliate companies that were in financial difficulties; and 2) the acquisition of shares in companies operating in Brazil namely, the CPFL in the wind energy sector and the Portugal Telecom company (CEPAL, 2011, p.63).

In short, there is a new tendency that is not restricted to Brazil alone and even though the country is one of the main exporters of capitals in the region, that is not sufficient to characterize it as an imperialist State.

### 1.2    Brazilian Sub-imperialism

Mathias Luce (2007) sought to update Marini's concept of sub-imperialism. According to Marini, sub-imperialism was defined by: 1) a new division of labor that made it possible for dependent social formations to become exporters of manufactured products to their neighbors: 2) a dependent economy achieving the stage of monopoly and financial capital; 3) the State playing a role such as Brazil did during the period of military dictatorship opposing grassroots and people's struggles and supporting *Coup d'états* in Uruguay, Bolivia and Chile. In short, Marini's idea was that Brazil acted in the region as the United States' 'right hand man' and supporter (1974, p.124).

Luce (2007) considers that the Lula government's regional integration policy was determined by Brazil's sub-imperialist nature, albeit the aspect of military coercion was not strictly applicable. The author states that it was up to the Brazilian State to perform the role of the United Sates' agent in the region and that it constituted a sub-imperialism ruled by consensus. Furthermore, in the aspects of economic liberalization and political stabilization, Brazil's foreign policy at the time was orientated by its 'antagonistic cooperation'[2] with the United States.

---

2   According to Marini (1974, p.22) 'antagonistic cooperation' refers to the productive and economic integration of Latin America to the imperialist economy; it is dependent and subaltern and fails to eliminate the conflicts inside and between the national and international bourgeoisies. The Latin American bourgeoisies will endeavor to obtain greater advantages in the productive reorganization process and that could produce some clashes between the interests of the United States and those of the Brazilian State.

Luce explains how, at the same time that the Brazilian State rejected the United States' proposal for a Free Trade Area of the Americas (FTAA), it guaranteed a favorable environment for foreign corporations by means of the South American Free Trade Area (*Área de Livre Comércio Sul-americana*-ALCSA), and the Initiative for South American Regional Integration in Infrastructure (*Integração em Infraestrutura Regional Sul-americana*-IIRSA). The author adds that those initiatives were equally orientated towards open regionalism, that is, an integration proposal exclusively directed at free trade and productive integration.

Regarding stabilization, Luce argues that although the Brazilian State did manage to impede the advance of United States militarization in the region, it acted in a way that neutralized the antiimperialist struggles on the continent, especially those in Venezuela, Ecuador and Bolivia. In Luce's words "it can be seen that the Brazilian government, at least indirectly, furthered the intentions {of the USA} to neutralize Chavez" (Luce, 2007, p.50).

There do not seem to be sufficient reasons to state that the Brazilian State's role in South America is sub-imperialist. That is because the most important episodes in recent years suggest a very different role. Those episodes were the coups d'états and attempted coups in the region: in 2002 in Venezuela, 2003 and 2008 in Bolivia, 2008 in Ecuador and in Honduras, and in 2012 in Paraguay. Even before taking office as president, Lula had organized the 'Friends of Venezuela' group in support of Chavez. In 2008 the Brazilian State coordinated the intervention of the South American Union of Nations (*União das Nações Sul-americanas*-UNASUR) and sheltered the deposed president of Honduras, Manuel Zelaya, in the Brazilian embassy when the United States defended the usurpers. The Brazilian State, albeit without adopting an openly anti-imperialist discourse like Venezuela and Cuba, acted autonomously and in diametrical opposition to the interests of the United States.

Furthermore, it is worth remembering two other facts that demonstrate a posture of cooperation and support in sustaining the new governments in the region, namely, the revision of the Petrobras contract in Bolivia in 2006 and the revision of the Itaipu Hydroelectric Plant Treaty with Paraguay in 2009 (Hirst et al., 2010). Another such fact was the role the Brazilian State played in ensuring Venezuela's admission to MERCOSUR.

In the military sphere, it should be remembered that Brazil came out against the installation of United States bases in Colombia and in favor of closing the Manta military base in Ecuador. It also stimulated the creation of the South American Defense Council (*Conselho de Defesa Sul-americano*-CDS) in the ambit of UNASUR. From the symbolic point of view, the CDS is an important initiative that could endow the region with greater autonomy in the face of United States imperialism. It is the first military organization on the continent that the

United States are not part of. Furthermore, the Brazilian State is re-equipping its navy to enhance its military autonomy. According to José Luis Fiori (2011, p.18):

> In September 2009, Brazil signed a strategic military agreement with France which must alter Brazil's relations with the USA and in a few years transform it into the greatest naval power in South America with the capacity to construct conventional and atomic submarines and produce its own fighter-bombers. That decision does not mean there is an arms race between Brazil and its continental neighbors, much less with the USA, but it does signal an important change in Brazil's international position and its decision to enhance its political-military vetoing power. In the same period, Venezuela and Argentina signed financial and military agreements with Russia, while Chile and Colombia maintained their relatively high levels of [military] expenditure, the highest on the continent, 3.4% and 4% of the two countries' GDPs, respectively. However, despite the new purchases and new armaments, none of the South American countries has acquired, or has the capacity to project its military power beyond its borders. What they are signaling, in an increasingly explicit manner, is their decision to impede eventual foreign interventions in their territories. That is an unequivocal sign of the increase in competitive pressure on the continent and the increase in United States military pressure in South America.

It should be borne in mind that the signing of the Brazil-France agreement and the creation of the UNASUR CDS took place after the USA reactivated its Fourth Naval Fleet in 2008, right after the announcement of the discovery of the pre-salt oil deposits in Brazil.

The Brazilian State encountered great challenges in regard to regional integration, especially in connection with MERCOSUR. They were: 1) correcting the inequalities among the member States; and 2) curbing the advance of importation from China. Thus, the priority set on the main regional economic bloc was not sufficient to eliminate the contradictions among the Brazilian, Uruguayan, Argentinean and Paraguayan bourgeoisies. Despite the political disposition of the heads of State (Lula and Kirchner-Kirchner) to fortify the bloc with the creation of the PARLASUR, the Fund for the Correction of Asymmetries and the admission of new partners (Bolivia and Peru and later Venezuela), it was not possible to eliminate the trade conflicts. In turn, the Brazilian State endeavored to boost political integration with the creation of UNASUR; it played an important role during the region's political crises, and is considerably different from the other bodies previously created in the interests of integration.

TABLE 4　API project details

| # | HUB | API project name | Countries involved | Amount |
|---|-----|------------------|--------------------|--------|
| 1 | AMA | PAITA – TARAPOTO – YURIMAGUAS ROAD, PORTS, LOGISTICS CENTERS AND WATERWAYS | PE | USD 568.9 |
| 2 | AMA | CALLAO – LA OROYA – PUCALLPA ROAD, PORTS, LOGISTICS CENTERS AND WATERWAYS | PE | USD 2,529.4 |
| 3 | AMA | NORTHEASTERN ACCESS TO THE AMAZON RIVER | BR / CO / EC / PE | USD 105.5 |
| 4 | AND | CARACAS – BOGOTÁ – BUENAVENTURA / QUITO ROAD CORRIDOR | CO / EC / VE | USD 3,350.0 |
| 5 | AND | COLOMBIA – ECUADOR BORDER INTERCONNECTION | CO / EC | USD 223,6 |
| 6 | AND | COLOMBIA – VENEZUELA BORDER CROSSINGS CONNECTIVITY SYSTEM | CO / VE | USD 5,0 |
| 7 | AND | DESAGUADERO BINATIONAL BORDER SERVICE CENTER (CEBAF) | BO / PE | USD 4,0 |
| 8 | AND | AUTOPISTA DEL SOL EXPRESSWAY: IMPROVEMENT AND REHABILITATION OF THE SULLANA-AGUAS VERDES SECTION (INCLUDING TUMBES BYPASS) | PE | USD 90,3 |
| 9 | CAP | CONSTRUCTION OF THE SALVADOR MAZZA – YACUIBA BINATIONAL BRIDGE AND BORDER CENTER | AR / BO | USD 23,0 |
| 10 | CAP | ARGENTINA – BOLIVIA CONNECTION THROUGH LA QUIACA – VILLAZÓN | AR / BO | USD 227,0 |
| 11 | CAP | PARANAGUÁ – ANTOFAGASTA BIOCEANIC RAILWAY CORRIDOR | AR / BR / PA / CH | USD 944,6 |
| 12 | CAP | FOZ DO IGUAÇU – CIUDAD DEL ESTE – ASUNCIÓN – CLORINDA ROAD CONNECTION | AR / BR / PA | USD 316,0 |
| 13 | CAP | ITAIPU – ASUNCIÓN – YACYRETÁ 500-KV TRANSMISSION LINE | PA | USD 255,0 |

TABLE 4  API project details (*cont.*)

| # | HUB | API project name | Countries involved | Amount |
|---|-----|------------------|--------------------|--------|
| 14 | GUY | REHABILITATION OF THE CARACAS – MANAUS ROAD | BR / VE | USD 480,0 |
| 15 | GUY | BOA VISTA – BONFIM – LETHEM – LINDEN – GEORGETOWN ROAD | BR / GU | USD 250,0 |
| 16 | GUY | ROUTES INTERCONNECTING VENEZUELA (CIUDAD GUAYANA) – GUYANA (GEORGETOWN) – SURINAME (SOUTH DRAIN – APURA – ZANDERIJ – MOENGO – ALBINA), INCLUDING CONSTRUCTION OF THE BRIDGE OVER THE CORENTYNE RIVER | GU / SU / VE | USD 300,8 |
| 17 | HPP | IMPROVEMENT OF NAVIGATION CONDITIONS ON LA PLATA RIVER BASIN | AR / BO / BR / PA / UR | USD 854,8 |
| 18 | HPP | PARAGUAY – ARGENTINA – URUGUAY RAILWAY INTERCONNECTION | AR / PA / UR | USD 268,0 |
| 19 | HPP | REHABILITATION OF THE CHAMBERLAIN – FRAY BENTOS RAILWAY BRANCH LINE | UR | USD 100,0 |
| 20 | HPP | NUEVA PALMIRA BELTWAY AND PORT ACCESS ROADS NETWORK | UR | USD 8,0 |
| 21 | IOC | PASSENGER AND CARGO HUB AIRPORT FOR SOUTH AMERICA (VIRU VIRU – SANTA CRUZ INTERNATIONAL HUB AIRPORT) | BO | USD 20,0 |
| 22 | IOC | IMPROVEMENT OF ROAD CONNECTIVITY IN THE CENTRAL INTEROCEANIC HUB | BO / BR | USD 383,0 |
| 23 | IOC | INFANTE RIVAROLA – CAÑADA ORURO BORDER CROSSING | BO / PA | USD 2,0 |
| 24 | IOC | CENTRAL BIOCEANIC RAILWAY CORRIDOR (BOLIVIAN SECTION) | BO | USD 6,7 |
| 25 | MCC | NORTHEASTERN ARGENTINA GAS PIPELINE | AR / BO | USD 1.000,0 |

TABLE 4    API project details (cont.)

| # | HUB | API project name | Countries involved | Amount |
|---|---|---|---|---|
| 26 | MCC | CONSTRUCTION OF THE JAGUARÃO – RÍO BRANCO INTERNATIONAL BRIDGE | BR / UR | USD 65,0 |
| 27 | MCC | MULTIMODAL TRANSPORTATION IN THE LAGUNA MERÍN AND LAGOA DOS PATOS SYSTEM | BR / UR | USD 100,0 |
| 28 | MCC | MONTEVIDEO – CACEQUI RAILWAY CORRIDOR | BR / UR | USD 196,0 |
| 29 | MCC | OPTIMIZATION OF THE CRISTO REDENTOR BORDER CROSSING SYSTEM | AR / CH | USD 7,0 |
| 30 | MCC | AGUA NEGRA BINATIONAL TUNNEL | AR / CH | USD 850,0 |
| 31 | PBB | PORTO VELHO – PERUVIAN COAST CONNECTION | BR / PE | USD 119,0 |
|   |     |                                        | TOTAL   | USD 13,652.7 |

SOURCE: UNASUR, COSIPLAN, 2012

In 2011, UNASUR incorporated the IIRSA and created the South American Defense Council (Calixtre & Barros, 2010). By means of the Planning and Infrastructure Council (*Conselho em Infraestrutura e Planejamento*-COSIPLAN, formerly the IIRSA) it intended to foster the integration of energy, transportation, and communication. Of the 531 COSIPLAN projects, only 31 are on the Priority Infrastructure Projects agenda; 19 are being executed and 47 are at the pre-execution stage. As Table 4 shows, the Brazilian State participates in 11 of the 31 priority projects.

Although Brazilian companies are involved in most of the infrastructure works in the region, the BNDES is not the main financer of COSIPLAN projects; national governments, the Inter-American Development Bank and the Andean Development Corporation also finance the works. A considerable part of the BNDES outlay has been in direct funding for the Brazilian companies that other national governments have contracted. There has been a convergence of BNDES budget availability and the regional demand for investment in infrastructure that has enabled Brazilian companies to operate in those territories. Even so, the amount destined to those activities in foreign countries is not greater than the amount invested in Brazil itself (Carvalho, 2012).

### 1.3 Neo-developmentalism and Regional Politics

At the center of the theses about a supposed Brazilian imperialism or sub-imperialism there is a discussion on the nature of the various Brazilian governments' foreign policies and, given that in both the domestic and the foreign spheres those governments act as representatives of a class, it is actually a discussion about the Brazilian bourgeoisie's economic and political situation and its relations with the national State.

The concept of an internal bourgeoisie refers to a fraction of the dominant class which, in a dependent social formation, occupies an intermediate position between the purchasing bourgeoisie and the national bourgeoisie (Poulantzas, 1978). Traditionally 'national bourgeoisie' refers to one that has an autonomous accumulation of capital and organizes itself politically and ideologically in alliance with the people's classes in an anti-imperialist struggle. In the case of the 'Brazilian imperialism' theses, even though those authors do not state it explicitly, everything is presented as if Brazil had a national bourgeoisie that intended to occupy or dispute the United States' position in the region; as if there were an inter-imperialist dispute between Brazil and the United States and that bourgeoisie had organized itself politically to set a capitalist expansion in motion and dominate Latin America politically and economically. Lastly the purchasing bourgeoisie concept indicates that fraction of the bourgeoisie that does not have its own internal accumulation and so tends to perform as a simple intermediary of imperialist interests in the interior of a dependent social formation. Thus, the sub-imperialism thesis seems to suppose that the Brazilian bourgeoisie behaves as if it were a purchasing bourgeoisie.

Getting back to the internal bourgeoisie, it is a fraction that has not broken off from technological, financial and political dependence on imperialist capital, nor does it intend to do so. Even when there is an internationalization of Brazilian companies and the exportation of Brazilian products increases, the internal bourgeoisie remains submitted to the imperialist production system and political domination. It is not willing to confront imperialism as a national bourgeoisie would and is in fact, in the same way as the purchasing bourgeoisie, a simple intermediary of imperialist interests. It does have sporadic contradictions with imperialism, insofar as it intends to curb the latter and compete with it, but it fails to act in an organized way guided by a political project of its own and the intended conquest of the regional economy, as Zibechi would have it.

In short, the strengthening of the internal bourgeoisie and the support of the dominated classes contributed towards a new projection of the Brazilian State on the international scene; one which, even though it did not adopt an anti-imperialist policy, favored the preservation and advancement of progressist governments in Latin America.

## 2   People's Movements and Unionism in Relation to Regional Integration Processes in South America[3]

This section describes and analyzes Brazilian people's movements and unionism in the light of the regional integration processes during the period of Workers Party (PT) governments (2003–2016). The interest here is in gaining an understanding of how the people's organizations and leftist organizations that were united in the Campaign Against the Free Trade Area of the Americas (FTAA) performed in the ten years following the shelving of the proposal during the 2005 Americas Summit in Mar del Plata.

---

[3]  This section has been published as an article entitled "Popular movements and trade unions due to South American regional integration processes" (*Mural Internacional*, vol 8, n.2, 2017).

Despite the economic gains that the internal bourgeoisie enjoys from the MERCOSUR and all the other Brazilian government initiatives in the regional ambit, it is a fraction that cannot accept a regional integration process that brings with it profound political commitments and direct open conflict with imperialism such as the Bolivarian Alliance for the Peoples of Our America (*Aliança Bolivariana para os Povos de Nossa América*-ALBA). Consequently, that fraction was against Venezuela's joining the bloc and against strengthening political commitments such as the Competitive Adaptation Mechanism (*Mecanismo de Adaptação Competitiva*-MAC). That is because the Brazilian internal bourgeoisie is technologically and financially dependent on imperialism and has a national political-ideological dissolution that impedes it from forming an alliance with the people's classes in an anti-imperialist posture. Thus, in spite of depending on the State's actions for protection and for its very survival and ability to compete with foreign capital, which resulted in the existence of a regional economic bloc, that fraction of the dominant class configures itself as an internal bourgeoisie and not a national one. So, economic gains apart, it has no interest in a regional integration with strong political profile and a robust institutional framework.

Therefore, in moments of political crisis, that fraction is liable to ally itself with imperialist interests and those class fractions that are most dependent on foreign capital and to openly oppose regional initiatives that seek to obtain a greater margin for maneuver for the South American States when dealing with the United States. That is because the PT governments (Lula and Dilma), in addition to proposing a more conflictive stance for the Brazilian State in the international scenario, were also marked by their adoption of distributive social and economic policies. Thus, the Brazilian internal bourgeoisie does not accept an anti-imperialist alliance with the people's classes, quite the contrary, it allies itself with the imperialist forces and the purchasing bourgeoisie against those policies. That explains the pro-impeachment demonstrations in 2015 and 2016 which denounced the 'Bolivarian-ism' of Brazil's foreign policy and of the São Paulo Forum and declared itself against the Brazilian States' relations with the Cuban and Venezuelan States. Could it be then, that the creation of regional anti-imperialist articulations capable of constructing real, concrete processes of solidarity and struggle among the peoples is a role to be played by the people's movements and unionism?

The underlying idea here is that the classes of ordinary people do not have the power to directly influence the State's decisions on foreign policy matters but, in certain situations, they can produce pertinent effects on the foreign policy decision-making process; based on mobilization of the class or even through forming political alliances or fronts with the dominant class or class fractions, the people's classes may have their interests attended to by the State. That is because the capitalist State, albeit presenting itself as a State-nation and the representative of the supposed general interests of the populace, actually busies itself with organizing the interests of the power bloc, that is, of the classes and class fractions united under the hegemony of one of them. The fact of addressing the ordinary people's demands is done in the name of maintaining the 'unstable equilibrium of compromises', of impeding political crises that affect the long-term interests of the dominant classes in regard to the maintenance and reproduction of the capitalist mode of production. In that light, the people's classes can occupy three positions regarding State policy: opposition, class support in an alliance of classes or integrating a political front with some bourgeois fraction or other.

Thus, the national campaign against the Free Trade Area of the Americas (FTAA) agreement can be considered an important political mobilization of opposition to Brazilian foreign policy. During the Campaign process, albeit a joint articulation and action of people's classes with the fractions of the dominant class did not occur, the fact that the position of the people's classes converged with that of the agglutination of Brazil's internal bourgeoisie that became reunited in the Brazilian Business Coalition (*Coalizão Empresarial Brasileira*-CEB) led by the National Confederation of Industry (*Confederação Nacional da Indústria*-CNI) ended up producing an important effect that contributed to the agreement's being rejected and to the formation of a neo-developmentalist political front in which the internal bourgeoisie was the ruling force and for which the support of organized sectors of the people was of fundamental importance.

In the light of the above, it is interesting to investigate what happened to the Brazilian people's sectors in the ten years following the shelving of the FTAA proposal. Were they capable of constructing a regional integration process with their social power?

## 2.1   Brazilian People's Movements and Unionism and Regional Integration in the 1980s and 1990s

The Brazilian people's movements and unionism at the end of the 1970s and in the early 1980s were highly active in the struggles to re-democratize the country and they brought with them a commitment to regional integration. For the Landless Rural Workers Movement (*Movimento dos Trabalhadores Rurais Sem-Terra*-MST), the Unified Workers Central (*Central Única dos Trabalhadores*-CUT) and the Workers Party (*Partido dos Trabalhadores*-PT), the first space for international action was most certainly Latin America. In the first few years those organizations were strongly influenced by the revolutionary processes of Cuba (1959), Nicaragua (1979) and El Salvador (1981) and there were many exchanges of Brazilian militants with those countries, seeking political formation and closer links among the organizations. In addition to their geographic proximity, a reading of the international insertion of those social formations and the relations among the social classes, imperialism and the role of civil and military bureaucracies contributed to making Brazilian organizations draw closer to the revolutionary experiences of Latin America. From the theoretical standpoint, it was a question of revisiting the theses of the 3rd International and elaborating a Marxist reading of Latin America in the light of a revolutionary strategy.

Internationalism in Latin America is essentially anti-imperialist and accordingly defends regional integration as a means to fortifying the struggle for the sovereignty of the national States. Regional integration became a strong banner of the Brazilian left's organizations in the 1980s. During the Constituent Assembly of 1988, the performance of the Workers Party and especially of Luiz Inácio Lula da Silva helped to guarantee the approval of the sole paragraph of Article 4: "Sole paragraph. The Federative Republic of Brazil shall seek the economic, political, social and cultural integration of the peoples of Latin America, with a view to the formation of a Latin-American community of nations". That was the first time any Brazilian Constitution had made a commitment to regional integration (Dallari, 1994). At that time, the Brazilian and Argentinean States had already signed the Nuclear Cooperation Agreement and the Protocols for the Economic Cooperation and Integration Program (*Programa de Cooperação e Integração Econômica*-PICE). Those agreements paved the way for the signing, in 1991, of the Asuncion Treaty by the Brazilian, Argentinean, Uruguayan and Paraguayan States, creating the Common Market of the South (*Mercado Comum do Sul* – MERCOSUR) which later included the Venezuelan State but whose membership is currently suspended.

With the implantation of neoliberalism during the 1990s, the Brazilian unions and people's organizations created regional articulations with their peers in the neighboring countries, endeavoring to fortify resistance to the imperialist policies for the region. Outstanding among such articulations were the Latin American Coordination of Rural Organizations (*Coordenação Latino-americana das Organizações do Campo*-CLOC) and the *Via Campesina*, of the Coordination of Southern Cone Union Centrals (*Coordenação das Centrais Sindicais do Cone Sul*-CCSCS), of the Network of Latin American Women Transforming the Economy (*Rede de Mulheres Latino-americanas Transformando a Economia*-REMTE), of the Continental Social Alliance (*Aliança Social Continental*) and of the São Paulo Forum. Those entities played an important role in the struggle against the advance of neoliberalism in the region, especially in the fight against the Free Trade Area of the Americas (FTAA).

In the first two years of MERCOSUR's existence, 1991 and 1992, Brazilian unionism and people's movements took a stance against the initiative because they saw it as being merely commercial and aligned with the main neoliberal principals and the USA's Initiative for the Americas agenda. However, from 1992 on the Unified Workers Central (*Central Única dos Trabalhadores*-CUT) began to get involved in the questions that arose with the increasing implementation of the bloc, especially its impact on the relocation of industrial plants to exploit low wage, fiscal, and market access advantages. In that light, CUT, together with other union confederations in the region, endeavored to strengthen each country's social policies and to make a stand against the liberalization of trading. What actually interested unionism was not just guaranteeing social and labor rights threatened by the implantation of neoliberalism in the region, but to infuse MERCOSUR with a social and political character of regional integration. Accordingly, in 1994 the participation of the central organizations of union confederations in MERCOSUR's organizational structure was institutionalized, first in the Sub-working Groups and afterwards in the Social and Economic Consultative Forum (*Fórum Consultivo Econômico e Social*) created in 1996 (Mello & Silva, 2005). In 1997, the Peoples' Summits began which took place alongside the Summits of the Americas events (Meetings of Presidents to negotiate the FTAA) and so did the Hemisphere Meetings that brought together social and union movements in the region. In 2001 there was the first edition of the World Social Forum in the city of Porto Alegre, Brazil. The World Social Forum became the symbol of the so-called 'anti-globalization movements'. As a decade had already passed since the demise of the Union of Soviet Socialist Republics (USSR), the global left experienced a pragmatic crisis, given the absence of a reference and the ideological offensive of the defenders of neoliberalism like Francis Fujayama and his work 'The End of History and the Last Man'. The WSF meetings played the important role of bringing together various leftist organizations to debate the direction of international policies and to think about alternatives to the neoliberal globalization in course (Codas, 2007). It was even said that the WSF was the 'International of the 21st century' even though the great majority of the organizers and idealizers did not have a socialist orientation at all. The event was imbued with a strong spirit of identification insofar as its editions took place in the city of Porto Alegre where there was a rich ongoing experience of participative budgeting, led by a municipal administration linked to the Workers Party (PT).

The WSF brought together very different segments of the social, union and non-governmental organizations and in its 5th edition in 2005, it united 150 thousand people from the four continents. According to Ribeiro (2011) the World Social Forum was made up of the middle and academic classes with a strong participation of non-governmental organizations. Over the years, the International Committee faced critical debates on the low level of social mobilization and the absence of any space for political deliberations in spite of the fact that the 2002 edition in Porto Alegre had contributed to publicizing a great people's mobilization that had unified various social and political organizations in the region, namely, the fight against the Free Trade Area of the Americas (ALCA) (Codas, 2007).

The draft of the Continental Campaign against the FTAA was delineated at the Peoples' Summit (the so-called 'Counter-Summit') articulated by the Continental Social Alliance and the *Via Campesina*. Those organizations took advantage of the second edition of the World Social Forum to launch a continental campaign which held its national summits during the year 2002. The Brazilian national campaign against the FTAA unified a broad set of social movements, union movements and leftist parties in Brazil. There were 55 organizations altogether and outstanding among them were the Unified Workers Central (*Central Única dos Trabalhadores*-CUT), the Landless Rural Workers Movewmnt (*Movimento dos Trabalhadores Rurais Sem-Terra*-MST), the social assistance bodies of the National Conference of Brazilian Bishops (*Conferência Nacional dos Bispos do Brasil*-the CNBB), the People's Consultation (*Consulta Popular*), the World March of Women (*Marcha Mundial das Mulheres*-MMM), the United Socialist Workers Party (*Partido Socialista dos Trabalhadores Unificado*-PSTU) and sectors of the Workers Party (*Partido dos Trabalhadores*-PT). The concrete result of that campaign was a plebiscite whose methodology contemplated the offering of mass political qualification courses that addressed the political and economic impacts that the FTAA would have, the foundations and social consequences of neoliberalism, and the United States' role in the region. All kinds of educational material were produced for that work among the people such as folders, videos and pamphlets. The campaign was conducted by state and local committees all over the country and they held debates in schools, universities, neighborhoods, churches and on local radio and TV channels to mobilize the people and collect signatures. The plebiscite collected more than 10 million votes and 95% of them were against Brazil's entering the FTAA and against the 505 protocol that foresaw the ceding, to the United States, of a rocket-launching base in Alcântara, Maranhão (Silva, 2008).

In addition to fostering the unity of different sectors of the Brazilian left, the campaign against the FTAA in Brazil was a historical landmark because the country had been experiencing a decade of reduction in the struggles of the masses, of a powerful offensive against labor rights and of the criminalization of social movements, especially that of the Landless Rural Workers Movement (*Movimento dos Trabalhadores Rurais sem Terra*-MST). That mobilization not only represented a reaction against the neoliberal offensive, but it also identified the defense of regional integration as an important banner for the Brazilian people's organizations to raise and put into effect so that it would stop being merely a programmatic issue, as it had been in the 1980s. The people's sectors perceived MERCOSUR's political and economic importance and began to argue that the bloc should take on social and political profiles consistent with the interests of the classes of the ordinary people. With the progress of the FTAA and MERCOSUR-European Union negotiations and the Doha Round of the World Trade Organization (WTO), the bloc became an important political actor in regard to the Brazilian State's performance in the international scenario.

### 2.2   The People's Classes and Regional Integration during the PT Governments

In 2003, during the presidency of Luiz Inácio Lula da Silva, the Brazilian State adopted a dual strategy designed to debilitate the United States' proposal and obtain a consensual position of the South American states against the FTAA. To that end it sought to prioritize South American regional integration and proposed that the negotiation terms should become more flexible, the so-called 'light' FTAA proposal whereby the negotiations would be conducted in a more fragmented and sector-based manner. With a view to fortifying MERCOSUR, the Brazilian State drew closer to the Argentinean State and proposed initiatives to re-launch the bloc government by means of proposals that sought to enhance institutionality and reduce the asymmetries among the member states. The MERCOSUR Structural Convergence Fund was created in that spirit, as were the parliament, the Social Summits, and the specialized meetings such as the Family Agriculture Specialized Meeting. Efforts were also made to give a more social and political profile to the Meetings of South American Presidents that began in in the early years 2000, creating the South American Community of Nations (CASA) in 2004, which became the Union of South American Nations (UNASUR), in 2008.

However, the entities that had integrated the National Campaign Against the FTAA drifted apart and they formed groups with three different political stances, as listed below:

1) opposition to the government – headed by the Unified Workers Socialist Party (*Partido Socialista dos Trabalhadores Unificados*-PSTU), the Socialism and Liberty Party (*Partido Socialismo e Liberdade*-PSOL), and the Brazilian Communist Party (*Partido Comunista Brasileiro*-PCB).
2) government support base – formed by the Workers Party (PT) and the Unified Workers Central (CUT).
3) people's sectors giving critical support to the government – People's movements and political organizations that maintained autonomy in relation to the government while at the same time adopting a critical posture. They supported progressist policies such as the increase in social policies and the policy of enhancing the real value of the official minimum salary but were critical of policies of a neoliberal nature such as the public-private partnerships, the maintenance of a primary surplus and, above all, they denounced the failure to carry out structural reforms such as the agrarian, educational and urban reforms. In this group were the Landless Rural Workers Movement (*Movimento dos Trabalhadores Rurais Sem-Terra*-MST), the Movement of People Affected by Dams (*Movimento dos Atingidos por Barragens*-MAB), the World March of Women (*Marcha Mundial das Mulheres*-MMM), the People's Consultation (Consulta Popular) and the Young People's Uprising movement (*Levante Popular da Juventude*).

At first Group 1 was highly critical of the launching of the 'Light-FTAA' insofar as they considered that the State should abandon the negotiations with the United States altogether. After that they were against the State's decision to command the UN mission to Haiti in 2004. From 2009 to 2012 this groups criticism of the government's regional integration policy became ever more apparent. PSTU, PSOL and PCB militants openly criticized the relations that existed between Brazil's role in the leadership of MERCOSUR and UNASUR and the notable increase in exportation of manufactured goods and installation of Brazilian companies in neighboring territories; they characterized the process as being Brazilian 'imperialism' or 'sub-imperialism' (Berringer, 2013).

The other two groups supported the Lula government's set of foreign policies, especially the regional integration initiatives of MERCOSUR and UNASUR. They could count on the actions of the Brazilian Network of Integration for the Peoples (*Rede Brasileira de Integração para os Povos*-REBRIP) created in 2001 and which articulated people's movements and union entities endeavoring to influence the regional integration process and the international economic negotiations. In 2004 they took action against the negotiations between MERCOSUR and the European Union when the Landless Rural Workers Movement (MST) held a protest demonstration of about 100 militants in front of the Itamaraty building. In 2008 the CUT unionism created the Unions Confederation of the Americas (*Confederação Sindical das Américas*-CSA).

The difference between the two groups is very subtle as and can be detected in the emphasis placed on the People's Movements Articulation of the Bolivarian Alliance for the Peoples of Our America (*Articulação dos Movimentos Populares da Aliança Bolivariana para os Povos de Nossa América*-ALBA) and on the proposal for the Americas Development Platform (*Plataforma de Desenvolvimento para as Américas*-PLADA) put forward during the Hemisphere Meeting in 2015, as will be shown below.

During the 2009 World Social Forum held in Belem, the Social Movements Assembly decided to create the Articulation of the ALBA Social Movements enabling people's movements whose nation States had not adhered to the Bolivarian initiative to become part of the regional integration process, thereby turning it into an initiative of organized sectors of the ordinary people's classes which should boost solidarity and the struggles of resistance to imperialism. It meant that ALBA came to have three levels of organization; the national state level, the sub-national level of states or municipalities and the articulations of people's movements. In general, this last initiative sought to articulate the people's movements and leftist organizations in the fight against neoliberalism, and in favor of sovereignty and the defense of progressist governments. In Brazil, the MST, the World March of Women, the Brazilian Communist Party (PC do B) and the PT were the movements and parties that adhered to the articulation.

Actually, after the shelving of the FTAA in 2005 and with the creation of the Bolivarian Alternative for the Americas (ALBA), the analysis of the Brazilian people's movements, especially the MST, was that there were three extant regional integration processes: 1) the United States' neoliberal project which after the demise of the FTAA became dismembered into bilateral Free Trade Agreements with Chile, Colombia, Peru, Central America etc.; 2) the ALBA project of cooperation, complementarity and solidarity which brought together the Venezuelan, Cuban, Bolivian Ecuadorian and Nicaraguan States; and 3) the political-economic project headed by the Brazilian State by means of MERCOSUR and CASA/UNASUR. Little by little the analyses began to underscore how the MERCOSUR, UNASUR projects of the Community of Latin American and Caribbean States, (*Comunidade de Estados latino-americanos e Caribenhos*-CELAC) created in 2011, did not oppose the ALBA in any way. In fact, from the geopolitical point of view they were complementary because, together, they excluded the United States from Latin American political processes in the bid to obtain more room for international maneuver for the States and their peoples.

Ribeiro (2011), reports how, in 2010 when the World Social Forum FSM held a meeting to review its 10 years of existence, both João Pedro Stédile of the MST and Antônio Felício of the CUT, albeit they had reiterated the importance of the event's existence as a democratic space for debate and the ideological battle against neoliberalism, underscored the Forum's organizational and programmatic fragility as an instrument for constructing an international mass movement (Ribeiro, 2011, p.60). CUT, however, being part of the support base of the PT governments, remained in the orbit of the projects headed by the Brazilian State, that is, MERCOSUR and UNASUR, while the MST began to place more emphasis on the ALBA and other initiatives.

Two elements justify that position: 1) the relation between MERCOSUR and the generation of employment in Brazil; 2) the relations between that central union and the PT government. Considering that the central was already part of MERCOSUR's Social and Economic Forum and of its sub-working groups, after 2006 it also began to accompany the Social Summits and in 2015 it accompanied the elaboration of MERCOSUR's New Socio-Laboral Declaration and welcomed its approval at the last Social Summit and the Meeting of Heads of State (CUT, 2015). Based on the periodization of CUT's international policy that Hermes da Costa (2005) constructed, it can be stated that after the shelving of the FTAA project in 2005, CUT took a more offensive, more protagonist stance accompanying the foreign policy of Lula and Dilma and its quest for room to maneuver for the Brazilian State in the international power structure. In that regard, in 2010 the entity created the International Cooperation Institute with which it became a donor of resources for foreign partners, especially in countries with development indices lower than Brazil's. Furthermore, it should be underscored that it took the initiative in the defense of immigrants' rights and defended other progressist actions and questions in the international field. Other outstanding activities are those of the National Confederation Workers connected to Agriculture (*Confederação Nacional dos Trabalhadores da Agricultura*-CONTAG), of the Federation of Workers in Family Agriculture (*Federação dos Trabalhadores na Agricultura Familiar*-FETRAF) and of the REBRIP at MERCOSUR's Specialized Meeting of Family Agriculture (*Reunião Especializada da Agricultura Familiar*-REAF). Bulow and Carvalho (2014) state that those Brazilian organizations use the regional space as a trampoline to propagate domestic policies and ideas, to dispute political projects and to deepen the dialogue with other people's movements.

However, Botto (2014) argues that the Brazilian unionism's strategy in regard to social participation in the regional integration initiatives is limited to the institutional spaces, namely, the MERCOSUR Social Summit, a social participation sphere that is being created in UNASUR, and the Specialized Meetings.

Those are all formal spaces with little capacity to influence the South American regional integration decision-making process. In the same vein, Ramanzini Jr. and Farias (2014) call attention to the difference between participation and influence (power of decision). They consider that the latter is limited in the case of the bloc's Social Summits for they have become institutional events that fail to reflect any direct influence of the people's sectors on the State decisions. The seasonality and alternation of the participants impede the existence of a more profound process of articulation of the people's movements and union centrals in the member countries. Furthermore, the fact that the summits are organized, and the invitation sent out by the State that is in the (*pro-tempore*) presidency of MERCOSUR means that there is little autonomy for the people's movements. A good example of the low extent to which the Summits influence the decisions of the bloc's heads of State is that in various final declarations there was an appeal for the suspension of the MERCOSUR-Israel agreement, a topic that never came up at all in the meetings of the Bloc's heads of State. Another fact is the people's movements and union centrals' unawareness of the terms of negotiation of the agreement between MERCOSUR and the European Union, as the list of offers involved has been kept a close secret. The extract below, from the final declaration of the 2015 Summit confirms that:

MERCOSUR should not go ahead with the negotiations for a Free Trade agreement with the European Union, seeing that in the examples of the six association agreements that Europe has signed with Latin America, it is clear that the agreements impose unfair conditions in the trading relations and promote obligations that curb the development capacity of our States: public purchasing, protection of intellectual property rights, protection for investments, demand for the opening of industrial sectors that put our jobs at risk. No to the retrogression of the agricultural subsidies policies and the opening of markets in that sector. Negotiations with third parties must be sustained on the basis of equilibrium and be in agreement with regionally constructed strategic objectives. We denounce the lack of transparency and the secrecy that has been maintained in the negotiations of MERCOSUR and the European Union.

In 2008, the Brazilian State created the Social and Participative MERCOSUR Program (*Programa MERCOSUR Social e Participativo*-PMSP) intending to open a channel of dialogue with organized sectors of the people's classes about issues concerning the regional bloc. The program brought little progress, having functioned irregularly and without an Executive Department and it failed to guarantee periodicity or even its capability of exerting influence on the Common Market Council (Ramanzini & Fontes, 2014).

After that, CUT and the Brazilian Men and Women Workers Central (*Central de Trabalhadores e Trabalhadoras do Brasil*-CTB) have been accompanying the process of implementing UNASUR's sphere of social participation. The creation of that sphere is provided for in the 2008 constitutive charter; it started to be discussed by the Heads of State in 2012 and the 1st Social Participation Forum was held in Cochabamba in 2014. Later those Brazilian organizations decided to create a National Chapter to accompany every one of UNASUR's Social Participation Spheres such as the MERCOSUR Social Summits. It was hoped that unifying the national activities would boost the articulating capacity of those sectors, reduce the effort involved and ensure synchronization of the two regional integration projects. However, each country could only nominate 10 delegates which meant that it would be a space for articulation among leaders and not one for the construction of people's regional integration.

As previously explained, the MST opted to place little emphasis on MERCOSUR's institutional spaces and began to play a more forceful role in the continental articulations of urban and agrarian people's movements. Outstanding among the respective initiatives were: the Youth Camps, the Latin American courses held in the Florestan Fernandes National School, the brigades and events of solidarity with Venezuela, Paraguay, Ecuador and Bolivia and, especially, the construction of Alba's Social Movements Articulation. The general office of the articulation remained in Brazil from 2009 until 2016, coordinated by the MST. The commitments made at the first Assembly of the Continental Social Movements in 2013 under the aegis of Alba were:
- to promote regional unity and integration based on a model of an alternative, sustainable life of solidarity whereby the modes of production and reproduction are at the service of the peoples;
- to relaunch the struggle of the masses and the class struggles at the national, regional and continental levels that will enable us to curb and dismantle the projects of neoliberal capitalism;
- To weave effective peoples communication networks that enable us to face up to the battle of ideas and curb the manipulation of information by the big corporations and communication media.
- to make our political and ideological qualification processes more profound in order to strengthen our organizations and to make progress in processes of deliberate and consequential unity with the necessary transformations (Declaração da 1ª Assembleia dos Movimentos Populares pela ALBA, 2013).

In 2012, activists engaged in unionism, people's movements and non-governmental organization activists and, above all, progressist intellectuals formed the Reflections on International Relations Group (*Grupo de Reflexões Sobre Relações Internacionais*-GR-RI) with the dual objective of defending the so called 'New Foreign Policy' unfolded by the PT governments and pressuring for the creation of a National Foreign Policy Conference to achieve the democratization of the Brazilian foreign policy decision-making process chronically marked by the bureaucratic insulation of the Ministry of Foreign Affairs. In July 2013, the GR-RI held a big Foreign Policy Conference at the Federal University of the ABC to mark the 10 years of what they called the 'New Foreign Policy' and took the opportunity to hand over to then Minister of Foreign Affairs, Antonio Patriota, a formal demand for the creation of the National Foreign Policy Conference. During the second round of the presidential elections in 2014, the group acted vigorously, launching the book *Uma nova política externa: 2003–2013* (A New Foreign Policy) (Maringoni, et al., 2014), the result of interventions in the 2012 Conference, and promoting debates in universities. The GR-RI sought to underscore the geopolitical importance of President Dilma's reelection, especially in the light of the political crisis in Venezuela, the peace negotiations in Colombia and other issues. In 2013, given the political crisis Brazil was experiencing the group continued to observe and defend the regional integration policy, especially MERCOSUR, and it declared itself against the MERCOSUR-European Union Agreement. However, despite bringing together union, party and people's leaderships, the group did not have social mobilization capacity and maintained itself merely as a group of intellectuals and militants of the summits; the social bases, the people's movements and unionism were hardly involved in international analyses and articulations at all.

In 2015, through ALBA's Social Movements Articulation, the MST held an anti-imperialist event marking the 10 years since the demise of the FTAA, and it set in march a campaign for the withdrawal of Brazilian troops from Haiti. The union centrals also unfolded actions to remember the fight against the FTAA. Both the Brazilian people's movements and Brazilian unionism took part in the Hemisphere Meeting in Cuba. The objective of the meeting was to reflect on some of the dilemmas posed by regional integration 10 years after *Mar del Plata*, especially in view of the political crises in Venezuela and Brazil. The Union Confederation of the Americas presented the Americas Development Platform (*Plataforma de Desenvolvimento das Américas*-PLADA) which, as the text below makes clear, sought a policy of industrial development, generation of employment and gender equality:

> That is our vision of development, constructed based on our union option, reaffirming the pillars of decent work, the distribution of wealth, participative democracy, gender equality, regional integration prioritizing articulation in the international negotiations and the consolidation of common positions on issues of common interest and the exchanging of successful experiences among governments; social protection and

inclusion for all, intergenerational and environmental, thereby integrating the economic, social environmental and political dimensions. Development cannot be achieved without the full inclusion and participation of women and young people. All the components we present on this platform have gender equity and youth participation as transversal approaches and women and young people as protagonists and main actors to make sustainable development become a reality.
>   PLADA, p.9

During the meeting, the people's movements maintained a reticent posture in regard to the PLADA's insisting that what should be prioritized was to fight and resist the imperialist offensive in the region and support the Brazilian and Venezuelan governments, immersed in profound political crises. Thus it can be seen that despite the fact that the national and regional contexts demanded a resistance strategy and a policy for the people's movements in regard to the actions attacking progressist governments, national sovereignties and labor rights, there was no social force mobilized to defend a people's regional integration project capable of taking to the streets and with the capillarity needed for the social rooting of the defense of the unity of the South American peoples That seems to be the main challenge. Apart from that it does not seem to be contradictory to defend an industrializing project that generates employment with a struggle for autonomy/sovereignty and solidarity among the peoples.

That is why despite the 2015 Hemisphere Meeting's not obtaining programmatic consensus, there is no contradiction in the midst of the people's classes. There are different forms and ways for constructing regional integration processes and for analyzing priorities regarding the regional political conjunctures. The people's movements, especially the MST and the MMM, bear with them a commitment to the construction of solidarity and of the anti-imperialist struggle of the Latin American peoples' movements, whose strategy is concentrated in the Social Movements Articulation of ALBA, and in the strengthening of their own transnational networks. The CUT unionism is interested in defending jobs, expanding labor rights, and social, political and economic integration, which leads it to act more in the institutional ambits and those of the union networks and confederations.

CHAPTER 5

# Brazil under FHC and Lula

Unlike those analyses that address the dynamics among State institutions (Ministry of Foreign Affairs and the Executive), the influence of the government team or the government political party and the existence of a 'national interest' as if they were in some way homogeneous, this work has shown that there is actually a determinant relationship between the power bloc and foreign policy, in other words, between the politically hegemonic fraction and the State's position in the international power structure, at a given historical conjuncture.

These chapters have argued that foreign policy was an important instrument for both the orthodox neoliberalism that the FHC governments implanted and the neo-developmentalist platforms put into effect by the Lula and the Dilma administrations. The FHC governments drew closer to the imperialist States and adhered to a series of international disarmament regimes in their anxiety to obtain loans, attract investments and, in that way, ensure the consolidation of neoliberalism in Brazil. That context demonstrated how the hegemonic fraction in the power bloc, made up essentially of the national and international financial capital and the associated bourgeoisie, performed as a purchasing bourgeoisie insofar as it was closely bound to imperialist interests. Accordingly, the Brazilian State's stance in the international scenario at the time was one of passive submission.

Over the years, and especially after 1996, the negative effects of unilateral trade liberalization on industry together with the interest in maintaining and evolving MERCOSUR and curbing the threat represented by the FTAA negotiations, led the industrial bourgeoisie and agribusiness to agglutinate into a single bourgeois fraction which then pressured the State to adopt a posture strategically coherent with that fraction's interests. The political and ideological behavior of that bourgeois fraction fits very well with Nicos Poulantzas's definition of an internal bourgeoisie. Aggregating more sectors, it became the fraction with an ascendant trajectory in the course of the years 2000.

That was why, during the PT governments, the Brazilian State sought to draw closer to the dependent States and adopted postures that generated sporadic conflicts with imperialism, but which guaranteed the Brazilian State more room for maneuvering in the international power structure. That position was strategically coherent with the interests of Brazil's internal bourgeoisie even though, in some cases, it was not readily apparent. The more concrete results of the State's international performance for the internal bourgeoisie were protection for the internal market, the conquest of new markets for its exports and enhanced access to other territories for the installation of its companies.

For the State to fortify that bourgeois fraction it had to conquer greater capacity for action in the face of imperialism so that, at times, there was conflict between the two. However, despite the conflictive tone of the relations with the imperialist States, they were maintained. Accordingly, the Brazilian State's political stance in the international scenario must be considered one of conflictive subordination; that is, given the correlation of forces within the Brazilian social formation and the relations between the power bloc and imperialism, it can be clearly stated that the foreign policy of the Lula governments was neither independent nor anti-imperialist.

Neo-developmentalism, the political platform of the Lula governments, was, *grosso modo*, driven by the State. It financed national groups and companies enabling them to internationalize their activities, protected the internal market, conquered new markets, increased the purchasing power of the working class by making more credit available, stimulated consumption, generated employment and unfolded important social policies. Accordingly, whether they realized it or not, both the internal bourgeoisie and the people's classes came to support the neo-developmentalist platform, constituting what can be called a neo-developmentalist front.

There are many ways in which neo-developmentalism differs from orthodox neo-liberalism, and foreign policy was one of the most obvious aspects of that difference. That explains why it was the object of dispute between those sectors that defended the return of orthodox neo-liberalism and those that supported neo-developmentalism.

Lastly, it is important to underscore the contribution the Brazilian State's position in the international scenario made by enabling it to perform a major role in South America, especially in maintaining and strengthening progressist governments and in boosting the creation of political integration processes like those of UNASUR and CELAC.

Furthermore, the political processes of the 1990s and the years 2000 show that the people's classes can exert some influence on foreign policy albeit they are not the commanding force behind the policies that the national States adopt. During the actions of the anti-FTAA campaigns, the unity of the people's movements and unionism played an important role insofar as their convergence with the interests of the dominant class fraction, the internal bourgeoisie, effectively interrupted the negotiations. After that. the Brazilian State, during the PT administrations invested heavily in relaunching MERCOSUR, opening up participation channels for unionism and people's movements while at the same time creating a new regional political integration process, the UNASUR, which from the outset provided spaces for the so-called 'civil society'.

It must be acknowledged that those formal spaces that the national States created did not actually make it possible for the interests of the people's classes to drive the regional integration processes. For that to happen, it would be necessary to create initiatives to articulate the interests of the people's classes, creating social rooting for a people's regional integration of an anti-imperialist nature. To that end, there should be no dichotomy between solidarity/cooperation and development. The defense of people's employment and the anti-imperialist struggles are intertwined and must travel together. Unionism and people's movements can converge tactically in the effort to achieve regional integration.

It is also important to highlight that the position of the Brazilian State in South America was not imperialist or sub-imperialist. The role of the Brazilian State during the 'Pink Tide' was to ensure the enforcement of the Bolivarian state's policies and the pushing away of US intervention in the region.

In the coming pages the role of the middle-class sectors and the Brazilian bourgeoisie in Brazil's 2016 political crisis will be examined and how the changes in foreign policy took place during the Temer government.

CHAPTER 6

# Power Bloc and Foreign Policy in the Dilma, Temer and Bolsonaro Governments

## 1 The Dilma Government: Foreign Policy, Political Crisis and Power Bloc

The first woman ever to become president of Brazil, Dilma Rousseff, took office in 2011 after the two terms served by Luiz Inácio da Silva from 2003 to the end of 2010. He finished his second term of office with the highest approval rating for a president (over 80%) since the country was re-democratized in 1988. That was because, taking advantage of a favorable international conjuncture, the Lula governments' social economic, and foreign policies managed to achieve increased economic growth, income distribution, reduction of unemployment and an important protagonist role for the Brazilian State in the international scenario. During that period Brazil was host to three big international events: the World Soccer Cup, the Olympic Games and the visit of Pope Francis.

So how did the Dilma government perform? As she was Lula's successor, did she maintain the same international insertion strategy? What were the interests of classes and class fractions that the Dilma government's political platform represented? Why was there a political crisis and why was President Dilma impeached? What role did foreign policy play in the Brazilian political crisis? Those are the questions the coming pages will address.

The Dilma government experienced a political crisis that had many acts and ramifications. Analysts identify 2012 as its beginning, marked by the reaction to the economic policy the government had adopted (Singer, 2018). That was followed by the big demonstrations in the streets in June 2013, the so-called *Jornadas de Junho* (June Days). After that, in 2014 there was the fiercely disputed election campaign and, despite her victory in the elections, Dilma had later to face an impeachment process in the house of representatives and in 2016 she was defeated. The political crisis led to the breakup of the neo-developmentalist front composed of Brazil's internal bourgeoisie, and those segments of the people's classes that supported the PT governments. The orthodox neoliberal front, made up of the associated/purchasing bourgeoisie, imperialism and the upper middle class managed to attract the Brazilian internal bourgeoisie to its alliance and conducted the 2016 *Coup d'état* (Boito Jr., 2018).

Broadly speaking, the analyses of Singer (2018), Boito Jr. (2018) and Carvalho (2018) are in agreement when they consider that in the first two years of the first Dilma government (2011 and 2012) there was an effort to intensify the neo-developmentalist program, not only to curb the impacts of the international financial crisis on the Brazilian economy but also in an endeavor to consolidate the hegemony of the internal bourgeoisie in relation to the bourgeoisie associated to financial capital (Boito, 2018).That endeavor took the form of the political program that Guido Mantega elaborated which came to be known as the 'New Economic Matrix' and involved the following policies: reduction of interest rates and the bank spread,[1] reduction of the Selic tax rate from 12.5% to 7.5% in the period between August 2011 and October 2012; devaluation of the exchange rate of the real against the dollar from 1.25 to 2 reals over the period between August 2011 and mid-2013; increased credit subsidized by the BNDES; six-year prorogation of the Investment Sustainment Program (*Programa de Sustentação de Investimento*-PSI) created in 2009; enacting a Law determining an increase in tariffs on more than 100 imported items (Law 13.137/2015); reduction of taxes on imports for automobiles, building materials and household appliances; Provisional Measure 613 which provided for tax relief in the acquisition of materials for the Chemicals industry; tax relief on paysheet taxes for labor intensive sectors; a package of highway and railway concessions; reform of the electricity sector; control of capitals; obligatory use of local content by strategic sectors and Petrobras purchasing orders; a government purchasing policy directed at local production; and the Inovar Auto program. In addition, the policy of promoting real gains in the value of the minimum salary was maintained and the housing policy *Minha casa, minha vida* was expanded.

Despite all those policies, the economic results were not so good, and the government lost the support of the internal bourgeoisie, especially after 2015 (Valle, 2021). Actually, from 2013 on, the interest rates had begun to rise again; there were cuts in public investments and the restrictions on speculative capital were eased (Singer, 2018, p.53). The GDP dropped, oscillating from 4%

---

1 "[…] A margin charged by the private banks over and above the basic interest rate of the economy in credit operations. The measure was implemented by Bank of Brazil reducing the interest rate and expanding the limits for various lines of credit of the Bank of Brazil. Some days later, the Federal Savings Bank followed suit (*Caixa Econômica Federal*). Thus, using the public banks, the government forced the private bank competitors to reduce their own spreads. If they failed to do so, their participation in the market would reduce (Carvalho, 2018, p.74–75)".

growth in 2011, to 1.9% in 2012, 3% in 2013 and 0.5% in 2014. Carvalho (2018) believes that the 'FIESP Agenda' adopted in the early years had flawed principles that included low levels of public spending, non-reduction of the interest on the public debt and the non-alteration of the tax burden. The various concessions of tax relief drastically reduced the State's revenue while, at the same time, the social policies were maintained or expanded thereby generating a deficit which to some extent was what led to the adoption in 2015 of Joaquim Levy's fiscal adjustment policy. Singer (2018) argues that:

> The drop in profitability, the full employment with an increase in strikes, the perception of a new liberalizing international realignment and the ideological offensive stemming from financial capital may have consolidated a conviction among the industrialists that they were facing a project that wished to expand the State's radius of action, fix prices, regulate and control private activities, and that presented the eventual possibility of nationalizing strategic sectors. Fear unified them with the rest of the bourgeoisies in combatting the neo-developmentalist experience.
> SINGER, 2018, p.75

Boito Jr. (2018) argues that the main contradiction was not centered between the rentier coalition and the industrial coalition, as Singer believed, but instead the conflict between foreign capital and national capital was at the center of the Brazilian political dispute.[2] The Brazilian internal bourgeoisie,[3] he declared,

---

2  Poulantzas (1978) considers that in relation to foreign capital and imperialism, the bourgeoisie is divided into three fractions: the national bourgeoisie, the internal bourgeoisie and the purchasing bourgeoisie also called the associated bourgeoisie. The national bourgeoisie concentrates the economic accumulation within the (dependent) national social formation and is therefore interested in protectionist policies, in breaking off with imperialism and in alliances with people's classes. The internal bourgeoisie is one that emerges with the installation of a productive internationalization process and is therefore an intermediary between the other two. It is at one and the same time dependent on and a competitor of foreign capital which leads it to support political positions of selective conflicts with imperialism to guarantee its survival. The purchasing (associated) bourgeoisie is the fraction that is most dependent on foreign capital and accordingly performs as a mere transmission belt for imperialist interests in the heart of the social formation.
3  During the PT governments, the Brazilian internal bourgeoisie agglutinated around those neo-developmentalist policies designed to reform the then extant neoliberal policies. Such reform policies included selective protectionism, (government purchasing, BNDES financing, favoring local content, etc.), negotiated opening of trade markets, (access to markets for exports to the detriment of unilateral trade liberalization agreements proposed by the imperialist States) and stimulating and providing support for the internationalization of Brazilian companies. The fraction in question was made up of agribusiness, the

was led to support the orthodox neoliberal front made up of the associated bourgeoisie, imperialism and the upper middle class. The main reasons for this particular fraction to abandon the neo-developmentalism front were the distributive conflict, the considerable increase in the number of strikes in 2013 and that 95% of the victorious agreements and settlements guaranteed wage increases greater than inflation. To that author, however, what had led to the Brazilian political crisis was the orthodox neoliberal front's offensive against the 'New Economic Matrix', which the government endeavored to implement in 2011 and 2012, and the front used the fight against corruption as an instrument to mobilize the support of ordinary people. The offensive was able to count on the action of the upper middle class, especially civil servants in the legal system, in the Federal Police and in the Offices of the Public Prosecutors. Members of that sector had been affronted by the neo-developmentalist social policies and felt threatened by the increase in access to universities, the enhanced rights of domestic servants etc. as they are strongly attached to the values of meritocracy and social hierarchy. Confronted by the neoliberal offensive, the Dilma government decided to back off and in 2015 adopted a contractionary fiscal policy thereby aggravating the political process that led to the impeachment.

One should not minimize the fact that the political crisis also experienced outside influences especially by means of the *'Lava Jato'* (Car Wash) operation,[4] the Free Brazil Movement (*Movimento Brasil Livre*-MBL) and the call to Take to the Streets (*Vem pra rua*) (Baggio, 2016). It was an offensive against the economic policy and against the foreign policy that was being adopted by the PT governments which could have led the Brazilian State to alter its position in the international power structure especially with South America and the BRICS group. Furthermore, there was imperialism's interest in the pre-salt deposits regarding which the sharing regime and expectations of economic gains could lead the Brazilian state to change it position in the international power structure. According to Boito Jr., with the unfolding of the *Lava Jato*

---

manufacturing industry, the major construction companies, the mining industry etc. (Boito Jr., 2012; Berringer, 2015).

4  The Lava Jato operation began in 2014 and was supposed to investigate corruption and money-laundering crimes involving Petrobras, big Brazilian construction companies and the Workers Party. The processes were conducted by the then judge Sérgio Moura in the Federal Courts of Curitiba, capital of the State of Paraná. As has now been revealed by The Intercept, the legal processes were conducted with partiality and transgressions so that they were in fact an example of 'lawfare' (using the law for political, economic r commercial ends). The process led to the imprisonment of Marcelo Odebrecht, Luiz Inácio Lula da Silva and other important actors of neo-developmentalism.

operation, it became evident that "imperialism and the associated bourgeoisie had used corruption politically to destroy the hegemony that Brazil's internal bourgeoisie had acquired during the PT governments" (Boito Jr., 2018, p.260).

It can now be safely said that there was a collaboration agreement between the United States Department of Justice and the 'Lava Jato' (DOJ-EUA) (WikiLeaks, 2009; Boito Jr., 2018). That relationship was aimed at sharing information on bank accounts and offshores that companies had in the region to effectuate illegal payments. The US Foreign Corrupt Practices Act (FCPA) enables the Department of Justice to judge cases of corruption even when they have not been practiced in the United States; it is only necessary for the companies to be open capital companies with actions negotiated in the stock exchange as is the case with Petrobras (Viana, Maciel & Fishman, 2020). Thus, the task force of the *Lava Jato* operation performed as if it were an upper middle-class party,[5] which for moral reasons understood the fight against corruption to be at the center of the political struggle. That was because that social sector with its meritocratic ideology was and is against social ascension through the undue use of public resources or through the violation of the rules of bureaucratism. Bureaucratism is a form of organization of the capitalist State whereby the middle class is integrated to the State. In the case in question, the judges and prosecutors are part of the upper middle class due to their high schooling level, high incomes and the distinguished social position they occupy for doing intellectual work and performing a 'socially prestigious' function. Accordingly, they have a strong tendency to support, or be the leading forces of conservative, elitist movements (Boito Jr., 2018).

It must be borne in mind that the impeachment process and Lula's imprisonment in 2018, took place at an international conjuncture in profound transformation due to the intertwining of four pillars: 1) the US 2008 financial crisis which was followed by its eruption in Europe in 2011 when it began to have impacts on South America; 2) the ascension of the Chinese economy and the increased importation of manufactured goods and investments in the region; 3) the intensification of the United States' offensive against the Latin American

---

5  Poulantzas refers to the new petit bourgeoisie as the 'middle class', alluding to the position of the traditional petit bourgeoisie. It is a sector which, albeit not the owner of the means of production, undertakes intellectual work (or works in the services sector), has a high schooling level and high income (and can be the owner of shares or government bonds) and it occupies positions in the hierarchies of companies and factories (as managers, engineers, etc.). For that reason, the class's political-ideological position is, in most cases convergent with that of the bourgeoisie. It is a social stratum that, driven by fear of proletarianization, embraces the ideology of meritocracy and the myth of social ascension through education.

governments; 4) the emergence of extreme right political movements and governments such as Brexit in the United Kingdom and Erdogan in Turkey and the election of Donald Trump as president of the USA etc. That context affected the Brazilian State's domestic and foreign policies as will become clear in the paragraphs that follow.

With the establishment of the background portrayed above, it now is possible to pass on to the analysis of the Dilma administrations' foreign policy and the role it played in the 2016 political crisis. The text is divided into two parts. The first puts forward the central argument of the thesis that foreign and domestic, social and economic policies presented a certain degree of continuity in relation to those of the Lula governments, and in some cases, they were even intensified in the Dilma government, but the international context and the domestic political crisis led to inflections and a reduction of Brazil's protagonist role in the international scenario. Following that, in the second section, comes a reflection on the relationship between the political crisis and the foreign policy with an analysis of how the latter played an important role in the process that led to the president's deposition. The idea is to gain an understanding of what happened to the neo-developmentalist front and endeavor to explain the role of the street mobilizations and the political opposition, both of which acted in the name of the interests of the neoliberal front that directed the coup of 2016. The hypothesis being tested is that *the South-South policy displeased an important portion of the Brazilian upper middle class which was the driving force behind the coup and of Brazilian society's increasing permeability to 'neo-fascism',*[6] given that in addition to basing itself on a meritocracy ideology it is guided by 'Americanism', an ideology founded on the 'American way of life' and on the acceptance and/or defense of the Brazilian State's subordination to imperialism (Barros, 2018). Furthermore, given the changes in the international political economy and the intensification of the distributive conflicts, the *internal bourgeoisie broke away from the neo-developmentalist front and began to clamor for changes in the Brazilian State's international insertion.*

The next item characterizes the power bloc and the Dilma government's foreign policy.

### 1.1   Foreign Policy in the Dilma Governments

The analyses of the Dilma governments' foreign policy call attention to the harsh criticisms of the president herself, emphasizing her apparent disinterest in the area or her political inability to listen to, and negotiate with the business

---

6   For more on Brazilian neo-fascism see Boito Jr. (2018, 2020).

world (Cervo & Lessa, 2014; Cornetet, 2014). Cornetet (2014) shows that there was an alteration in the so-called 'Presidential diplomacy'[7] which was evident in the reduced number of President Dilma's international trips compared to those of Lula. Cervo and Lessa (2014) attribute the decline in the Brazilian State's international relations to Dilma's difficulty in "mobilizing Brazilian society and the State around foreign policy strategies" (Cervo & Lessa 2014, 104). Those authors suppose that the fact was due to the characteristics of the President herself insofar as she had reduced dialogue with the industrialists and with agribusiness. However, it must be argued here that those elements were not central to the initiation of a decline in the Brazilian State's international projection. What actually led to the reduction in the protagonist role in the international scenario was the impact of the international financial crisis, the new dynamics of international politics and, above all, the national political crisis.

The present analysis has some affinities but also delineates some differences with the neoclassic realism approach that Professor Maria Regina de Soares Lima (2018) has adopted. She argues that just like the Vargas government's 'Policy of Bargaining', the Jânio and Jango governments' 'Independent Foreign Policy' and Geisel's 'Responsible Pragmatism', the PT governments' foreign policy was a strategy that sought for autonomy in the international scenario. In that author's view the strategy was an exceptionality and not a continuation of the post-Cold War as other authors have suggested (Fonseca Jr, 1998; Vigevani & Cepaluni, 2011). For her, autonomy in foreign policy involves three elements: 1) contesting the international rules; 2) greater identification with 'third world' issues; and 3) adopting a rule-maker stance to the detriment of a passive acceptance of international regimes, that, is, being a rule-taker. Thus Lima elaborates a critique of the thesis of Itamaraty's bureaucratic insulation, that is to say, that the task of formulating and conducting the Brazilian State's international insertion falls is concentrated in the Ministry of Foreign Affairs and has a thread of continuity, determined by the country's diplomatic history and geographic insertion, and represented by the quest for international prestige as exemplified by Brazil's candidature for a seat on the UN security Council and other campaigns. In Lima's view, the prestige-orientated policies have always enjoyed the support of the Brazilian elites whereas autonomist policies

---

7   Danese (1999) coined the term 'presidential diplomacy' to indicate that the head of government had overshadowed the Ministry of Foreign Affairs in the formulation and execution of foreign policy. It is based on the premise that Itamaraty has power of decision in that area and thus the decisions come to be considered as being a State policy.

have ended up being suffocated by conservative forces, especially in 1964 and 2016, moments that led to brusque reorientations of Brazilian foreign policy.

The neoclassic realism that provides the framework for Lima's analysis is based on a combination of systemic factors of the international scenario with domestic factors. In that conception, the increase in internal material capacity leads to an increase in the State's ambitions and its projection in the international scenario. At the same time, it leads to changes in the balance of forces in international politics, opening up for the States possibilities of greater room for maneuver in the international sphere. That same author argues that foreign policy is a public policy and therefore it is subject to alterations that depend on the correlation of social forces and their influence on the government; her affirmation supports the idea of the agency of foreign policy. In that light, it is an area that is subject to the political and ideological orientations of the governments and of the political coalitions that can support or veto them. Thus, the PT governments' foreign policy must have "displeased the economic elites, corporate associations and conservative political sectors" (Lima, 2018, p.50).

There is no doubt that, as Lima's analysis affirms, there is an umbilical relation between the domestic environment and the international scenario, and that alterations to foreign policy are subject to the correlation of forces at the respective historical conjuncture. Nevertheless, the approach in this present work diverges, insofar as it sets priority on the interests of classes and class fractions. The focus is not on party political coalitions or the relations among parties, the legislative branch, the executive branch and elites consensus. The focus of interest is on the relations between the bourgeoisie, the State, foreign capital and the interests of imperialism. To that end empirical research was conducted in the documents, declarations and interviews of those entities that represent the interests of the Brazilian internal bourgeoisie.

The approach here is centered on the relations between the power block and foreign policy and how economic and social policies are determined by interests of the hegemonic class fraction in the power bloc. Thus, it would have been the changes in hegemony within the power bloc that contributed to altering foreign policy after the 2016 impeachment. The aim here is to analyze the Brazilian State's political stance in the international political conjuncture bearing in mind the international and domestic conflicts that traverse and conform the social conflicts among classes and class fractions. It must be said that the power bloc is not exclusively defined by the internal classes and class fractions of the national social formation but also depends on and is influenced and determined by foreign capital and its relations with the State and the internal class fractions. The influence of foreign capital and imperialism on the power bloc dynamics is all the greater in a dependent social formation.

Proceeding to the analysis itself, right after Dilma took office a series of uprisings erupted in Arab countries; a phenomenon that became known as the 'Arab spring'. Furthermore, in a visit to the United States in February of 2011, the then Minister of Foreign Affairs, Antonio Patriota, during a collective interview alongside US Secretary of State Hillary Clinton, said that the Brazilian State was worried about the situation in Libya. That apparently unimportant fact revealed the new status the Brazilian State had achieved in the course of the first decade of the years 2000. After all it was the first occasion on which the United States expressed its proposition regarding the political protests and demonstrations in the Middle East after the wave of political agitation that began in Tunisia and Egypt and then broke out in Syria and Libya. It was therefore the representative of the Brazilian State that made the first pronouncement from inside the White House to the international community.

At the time, Hillary Clinton and Antonio Patriota were making the preparations for Barack Obama's visit to Brazil. That visit of the US president gave the impression that the Brazilian State was seeking greater proximity with the United States after the sporadic moments of friction that had occurred during the Lula governments such as the opposition to the installation of US military bases in Colombia, the negotiation of the Nuclear Agreement with Iran and Brazil's stance in regard to the *Coup d'état* in Honduras etc. (Pecequillo, 2014).

Another notable moment was when, at the United Nations, Brazil voted in favor of the investigation of supposed human rights violations in Iran and the condemnation of the stoning of Sakineh Ashtiani. Those two actions were seen as indicating an inflection in the defense of human rights, something that, up until then, Brazilian diplomacy had never prioritized. In a subtle way the Brazilian State also condemned the violence of the Syrian State against people's protests in that country and it also agreed to take command of the Maritime Task Force of the United Nations Interim Force in Lebanon (UNIFIL). Those facts were concentrated in the early part of the Dilma administration and some analysts and journalists vulgarly interpreted them as representing a change of orientation in relation to the foreign policy of the Lula governments. However, the priority set on regional integration and the BRICS was maintained and moments of sporadic friction with the USA also continued to occur. Those aspects characterize a continuation of the conflictive subordination condition in regard to imperialism.

During the time it had a seat on the Security Council as a non-permanent member, Brazil abstained from voting on the control of Libyan airspace and expressed its critical view of the concept 'Responsibility to Protect', proposing an alternative, namely 'Responsibility while Protecting'. Furthermore, during her speech at the United Nations, Dilma expressed criticism of the restrictive orthodox neoliberal policies that the developed countries were adopting as a means to getting out of the financial crisis. There was also participation of the Brazilian State in the 3rd BRIC summit which decided in favor of incorporating South Africa thereby transforming the group into BRICS.

Regarding South America, the Brazilian State participated in the creation of the Community of Latin American and Caribbean States (CELAC) which replaced the older Rio Group. Another outstanding fact was the appointment of Brazil's former minister of foreign affairs, Samuel Pinheiro Guimarães, to the post of MERCOSUR's High General Representative with a view to constructing, among other things, the Citizenship Statute applicable to all member States. An effort was also made to institute the Condor Archive with the aim of guaranteeing the memorial of and ensuring justice for all those imprisoned and tortured during the military dictatorships that had cooperated with one another, backed by the USA, in the infamous Operation Condor. There was also the creation of the South American School of Defense Studies (*Escola Sulamericana de Estudos de Defesa*-ESUDE) linked to UNASUR. Those initiatives were all in alignment with the preceding government's actions designed to strengthen regional integration and they expanded the agenda to embrace political and social issues to the detriment of an exclusive focus on economic ones. It was in fact a model of multidimensional regionalism (Granato, 2015), far different from the open regionalism proposal of the 1990s whereby neoliberal alignment guided the region's economic opening up and the attempted insertion in the so-called 'globalization'.

In regard to economic integration, the Brazilian State made progress with the zero tariff agreements with the Alliance for the Pacific States (the Peruvian, Chilean and Colombian States). MERCOSUR also signed an agreement with the Palestinian Authority (2011). In October 2015, the Brazilian State and the Colombian State signed an Investment Facilitation Agreement and an Automotive Agreement and committed to reducing tariffs within the framework of Economic Complementation Agreement n° 59 covering steel and textiles products and indicating a future expansion to include plastic products.

Despite all those agreements, however, the Balance of Trade which since 2001 had always shown surpluses, presented falls and consolidated changes in the portfolio of Brazilian exports and their destinations in the light of the Chinese economy's growth, year after year. Furthermore, the crisis in Argentina and the increase in the importation of Chinese goods in South America had a strong impact on the Brazilian economy, especially on industry with its production destined mainly for the domestic and regional markets. Both factors highlighted, once more, two questions: 1) MERCOSUR's internal difficulty in consolidating a free trade area because of the increase in Argentina's safeguards;

2) domestic sector pressures for new trade agreements, especially for progress in the MERCOSUR-European Union negotiations, as a way to counterbalance regional losses and difficulties and from fear of the country's possible 'isolation' given the advance of the WTO-plus mega-agreements.

Meanwhile, some events in 2012 put Brazil once again at the center of the International political scene. They were the Rio +20 Conference and the nomination of Brazilian diplomat Roberto Azevêdo as President of the WTO. There was also the signing of a Strategic Global Partnership between the Brazilian and Chinese states that altered the level of technological exchanges between the two countries. Other outstanding events were Brazil's vote in favor of the recognition of the Palestinian State as a member of UNESCO and observer member of the UN, and the Brazilian State's volunteering to mediate the conflict between the Israeli and Palestinian States.

Still in 2012, in August, the diplomatic relations of the Brazilian State with Bolivian State were shaken by the transportation of Bolivian senator Roger Pinto Molina from the Brazilian embassy in La Paz to the frontier of Brazil in a diplomatic corps vehicle duly accredited with the Bolivian government. However, it was done without the issue of a safe-conduct pass by the Bolivian State or the authorization of the Brazilian government.[8]

Shortly after that came the *Coup d'état* in Paraguay that deposed President Fernando Lugo in 48 hours, without the right to defend himself. UNASUR endeavored to act as a mediator of the crisis, as it had done in Ecuador and Bolivian State in 2008, but it was unsuccessful. To exert pressure, it decided to use the Ushuaia Protocol (Democratic Clause) and suspended Paraguay from MERCOSUR (Soares, 2016). That opened the way for the incorporation of the Venezuelan State to the Bloc as its ingress had been pendant on a decision of the Paraguayan congress. Thus, a crisis situation was created in MERCOSUR that also affected Brazil. Right after those events, Minister Antonio Patriota was dismissed from his post at Itamaraty. The main factors causing the fall of Patriota were the Molina incident and the MERCOSUR-Paraguay-Venezuela issue.

---

8  Senator Molina was head of the opposition in the Bolivian Senate. On May 28, 2012, he sought asylum in the Brazilian Embassy in La Paz alleging that he was the victim of political persecution on the part of the Bolivian government which accused him of various crimes against the economy of the State calculated to be to the amount of 1.7 million US dollars. There were also a further 20 legal accusations most of them for contempt of court orders. On June 8, 2012, the Brazilian government granted the senator diplomatic asylum and he then requested territorial asylum in Brazil which could only be concluded without the risk of his being captured after the Bolivian government had issued a safe-conduct pass for his internal passage. Up until the moment when he was transferred to Brazilian territory, the senator had spent 455 days of asylum in the Brazilian Embassy in La Paz.

In 2013 there was the denunciation of a supposed overpricing in Petrobras's purchase of a refinery in Pasadena, Texas when Dilma had been Minister of the Civil Office of the Presidency in the Lula governments. That process eventually led to the 'Lava-Jato' operation and culminated in the 2016 coup and Lula's imprisonment in 2018. 2013 was also the year when Wikileaks revealed that the United States had been spying on President Dilma's messages and those of the president of Petrobras; facts that shook the bilateral relations between the United States and the Brazilian State and led to the cancelling of an official visit Dilma was scheduled to make to the USA. It was an event that aroused a public debate on the importance of bilateral relations.

In 2014, alongside German Chancellor Angela Merkel, the Brazilian State managed to get a resolution on international privacy protection in the digital media passed at the UN. That same year, a CELAC meeting was held in Cuba. On that occasion the port of Mariel, a work that had received a lot of BNDES financing was launched. Many sectors of the upper middle class criticized that financing, setting in motion a process criticizing the Dilma government's foreign policy in general. When the electoral dispute was beginning, there were many events that highlighted Brazilian foreign policy. Among them, the World Cup held in Brazil, the 4th BRICS Summit, held in Fortaleza and during which the New Development Bank and the BRICS Contingency Reserve Agreement (*Acordo de Contingente de Reservas*-ACR) were launched. Following that there was the meeting between BRICS and UNASUR. The President also participated in the MERCOSUR Summit in Caracas when the Special South American Cooperation Zone was created involving MERCOSUR, the Petrocaribe states and the Bolivarian Alternative for the Americas (*Alternativa Bolivariana para as Américas*-ALBA).

According to Vasconcelos (2020) the creation of the ACR[9] and the NDB[10] addressed the demands of the member states and was designed to enable the construction of a new international financial architecture. The new BRICS

---

9   The ACR would be a kind of Monetary Fund of the NBD'. It has reserves to the amount of 100 billion US dollars deposited by the BRICS member countries. It could be used at times of liquidity crises or balance of payments pressures. However, to have the right to access 70% of ACR resources, the country in question had to have an IMF agreement in force otherwise access would be limited to 30% of the total.

10  The NDP deposits were to be directed to private or public initiative to finance sustainable development, and infrastructure projects in: renewable energy, transportation, basic sanitation and irrigation, The loans are granted on presentation of projects. Although it was created by the five BRICS member States, the NBD statutes provide for loans to other dependent States and also provide for the adherence of new members in the medium and long-term, provided they are members of the UNO.

institutions also represented a process of conflictive subordination in relation to the Bretton Woods institutions insofar as they did not break off from them, but neither did they passively associate to them. That author underscores how the creation of the NDB, the volumes of investment in infrastructure, were linked to the interests of Brazil's internal bourgeoisie. The Brazilian State's role in that process guaranteed the post of Vice-president of the Bank for Paulo Nogueira Batista Jr.

Another event worth mentioning was the diplomatic conflict with the State of Israel in the face of that State's new offensive against the Gaza Strip. The Brazilian Government called back its ambassador from Tel Aviv for consultations and issued a declaration condemning the actions of the State of Israel which, in turn, displayed its irritation by referring to the Brazilian State as a 'diplomatic dwarf'. Furthermore, the Brazilian State did not position itself in regard to the 2014 conflict in the Ukraine when the United States and the European Union endeavored to stigmatize the process that led to the fall of the president of that country. It was after his refusal to sign an agreement with the European Union that generated a series of social protests involving separatist groups and pro-Russian groups eventually resulting in Russia's annexation of the Crimea. President Dilma came out in defense of the principle of non-intervention in domestic affairs, a position revealing a point of conflict with the positions of the USA and the EU. The Brazilian State adopted a similar stance in regard to the Islamic State and the war in Syria. In that year too, the United Nations Stabilisation Mission in Haiti (MINUSTAH) completed ten years of existence under Brazilian command and accordingly the balance of the mission and its termination came up for debate.

Generally speaking, the expectations surrounding the pre-salt deposits and the maturation of the neo-developmentalist program called for investments in national defense and security. Those elements seem to have received due attention from the government insofar as there was an expected launching of a nuclear-powered submarine in cooperation with France, and there were agreements signed with Russia, China and Japan in the areas of missiles, satellites and other technologies and the conclusion of the purchase of Swedish Gripen fighter planes which involved a technology transfer program that had been the object of debate and negotiation between the two governments during the Lula governments. Another point was the ratification of Act 12.705/2012 that allowed for the ingress of women in the military qualification courses of the Brazilian Army.

To sum up, it can be said that the first Dilma government's foreign policy (2011–2014) followed the same strategy as the Lula governments and maintained the status of conflictive subordination in regard to imperialism, especially in the South American regional policy and in its relations with the Chinese State and the BRICS. That was all linked to the interests of the internal bourgeoisie and those sectors of the people's classes that were part of the neo-developmentalist front. Nevertheless, support for the government began to wane; foreign policy came under criticism and was taxed with being isolationism, Bolivarianism, ideologization etc. and those criticisms were related to the consequences of the economic crisis that was beginning to have an impact on the Brazilian economy. They were also strongly present in the street protests and demonstrations in 2015 and in the declarations of political leaders during the impeachment process.

### 1.2 The Power Bloc, the Political Crisis and Foreign Policy[11]

It is hard to identify the exact moment at which a political crisis begins but it is possible to put a series of facts and elements together that can help to piece together the puzzle that culminated in the impeachment of President Dilma Rousseff in 2016. It was the intertwining of internal and external interests around certain essential factors, namely: the economic crisis and the maintenance of the income distribution policies, the protests of June 2013, the National Truth Commission and the 'Lava-Jato' operation.

The political crisis can be considered as having been triggered and unfolded by the contradictions between two political fronts: the orthodox neoliberal front and the neo-developmentalist one (Boito Jr., 2016). The neoliberal front is made up of imperialism and that fraction of the bourgeoisie imbricated with it (the purchasing or associated bourgeoisie) and by the upper middle class (especially legal system operators, civil servants, services sector workers and autonomous professionals such as lawyers, doctors and others), whereas the neo-developmentalist front was made up of the internal bourgeoisie and sectors of the people's classes such as unionized workers, rural workers and part of the marginalized masses (Boito Jr., 2016).

The first Dilma government's efforts to boost industry with measures such as reducing the bank spreads and the interest rates, together with tax relief, reducing the Tax on Industrialized Products generated a vigorous reaction from the purchasing bourgeoisie and imperialism who felt highly threatened. In a bid to curb that reaction, the government adopted fiscal austerity measures such as cuts in government spending and reduction in the financing policy of the BNDES but that was at the very moment Brazil was feeling the effects of the

---

11    Parts of this text have been published in articles, see: Berringer, 2017; Berringer & Forlini, 2018.

international financial crisis that came in the wake of generalized deceleration of economic growth. Then began a period of fragmentation of the internal bourgeoisie and accordingly, of the neo-developmentalist front, leading that fraction to ally itself with the neoliberal front and the coup-plotting sectors (the media, judiciary, etc.). In addition to the economic slowdown, the increasing number of strikes and the continuation of the policy for enhancing the real value of the minimum wage all strongly influenced the change in the support base of the PT government; the internal bourgeoisie had never wholeheartedly supported the income distribution policies of the neo-developmentalist program and so, when the GDP began to decline, its objection to the policies became much stronger (Boito Jr., 2016). Among the motives that led it to break away from the neo-developmentalist front and join the neoliberal front in supporting the coup were its support for the labor reform and the social insurance reform and other anti-worker agendas that they favored.

The question that arises here is whether the alliance between the internal bourgeoisie and the pro-coup sectors persisted after the Coup. In that case the fraction would have stopped being a productive bourgeoisie and become an importing and rentier one (SINGER, 2018). In other words, the internal bourgeoisie would have become a purchasing or associated bourgeoisie. Or could there have been a fragmentation inside the fraction, leading sectors like the agribusiness sector to integrate the purchasing bourgeoisie together with financial capital and defending a return to the passive subordination of the Brazilian State to imperialism. However, the industrial bourgeoisie continued with its moderate neoliberal agenda, that is with neo-developmentalism with its implicit selective protectionism (defense of the government purchasing and local content policy, rejection of unilateral trade opening agreements, etc.) and the defense of the search for territories and markets for the exportation of goods and capital. To address those questions, it is necessary to continue analyzing the documents and positionings of the representatives of the internal bourgeoisie over the years. It is also important to consider the impact of the Lava Jato operation on the destruction of the big Brazilian construction corporations.

In the aspect of foreign policy, inside the political crisis there was an observable inflection after 2012 when a conjunction of factors led the internal bourgeoisie to question the support they had been giving to the 'bold and active' (*altiva e ativa*) foreign policy that Celso Amorim had delineated. The factors were: 1) a drop in the GDP value; 2) an increase in trade barriers imposed by Argentina in view of the economic and political crisis it was going through and the need to protect its own industries; 3) the imperialist offensive stimulating the formation of the Alliance for the Pacific as a way of disputing the formation of MERCOSUR and UNASUR and curbing China's role; 4) the *Coup d'état* in Paraguay that had triggered the crisis of that period of the 'progressist' or 'neo-developmentalist' (reformist) governments in the region; 5) Venezuela's admission to the MERCOSUR and the worsening of the political crisis in that country; and 6) the increased importation of Chinese goods in the region disputing markets with the Brazilian internal bourgeoisie. This last factor was, to some extent, a new one given that ever since the 2008 crisis China had come to occupy a new position in the international political economy and had become the main exporter of manufactured goods to Latin America and the main importer of commodities produced in the region.

In addition to its involvement in the new trading dynamics, after 2020, China also became a major investor in the energy and infrastructure sectors in Brazil (Schutte, 2020b). The two States officially recognized the Brazil-China Business Council (*Conselho Empresarial Brasil-China*-CEBC) in 2015. The CEBC strives to further the interests of sectors of the Brazilian internal bourgeoisie, and it acknowledges that so far Brazil-China relations have been concentrated more in investments than in trade and especially investments in the energy, electronics and automotive sectors (CEBC, 2016). In a document it published in 2016, the CEBC appraised Chinese investments in 2014–2015 in the light of China's new position in the global economy, stating that:

> Naturally, Brazil is part of this new phase of Chinese investments – whether because it is included in the operations of big multinationals or for its characteristics, given the country's present circumstances, or for the investment opportunities, especially in infrastructure and the attraction represented by the natural resource offer, highly concentrated in foodstuffs.
> 
> CEBC, 2016, p.7

In the same vein, the CNI declares itself in favor of direct foreign investments that the People's Republic of China makes in Brazil. The Confederation's Director of Industrial Development, Carlos Abijaodi, explains that: "Industry's China agenda has three points: increase the access of Brazilian products to Chinese markets, foster Chinese investment in strategic projects in Brazil and maintain the extant trade defense instruments" (CNI, 2016). Thus, it can safely be inferred that even though some sectors of Brazil's internal bourgeoisie call on the Brazilian State for protection in regard to importation of Chinese goods, there is more generalized agreement regarding: Chinese large-scale investments, especially in infrastructure, and the question of access to

Chinese markets for Brazilian exports, especially basic products[12] (Berringer & Belasques, 2020).

What a part of the internal bourgeoisie questioned most was the regional policy. Venezuela's admission to MERCOSUR triggered the rejection of the PT governments' foreign policy by the Brazilian internal bourgeoisie. The Chavez and Maduro governments' political stance in regard to imperialism became the target of harsh criticism from the oppositionist and mediatic sectors in Brazil. It gave rise to the criticism of the ideologization, party politicization and Bolivarianism of the PT governments' foreign policy and those accusations ended up being assimilated by a considerable part of the internal bourgeoisie during the process of the 2016 *Coup d'état* (Berringer, 2017, p. 26). That all goes to show how the internal bourgeoisie could not accept an anti-imperialist position and feared that MERCOSUR would be 'contaminated' by the position of the Venezuelan State.

Furthermore, the progress obtained in the negotiations of mega international agreements, namely, The Trans-Pacific Treaty (*Tratado Trans-pacífico*-TPP), The Investments Treaty (*Tratado de Investimentos*-TISA) and the Transatlantic Treaty (*Tratado Transatlântico*-TTA) seemed to sustain the idea that the Brazilian State was leading the country into international isolation. In one of its documents the CNI declared that:

> Brazil cannot ignore the advent of a new 'wave' of preferential [trade] negotiations whose origin can be traced to the crisis of multilateralism, to the search for a response to the requirements of the international value chains and to the perception of the risks of disloyal competition linked to the emergence of new competitors.
> CNI, 2014, p.11

That position is similar to the one the internal bourgeoisie adopted in the 1990s when it decided to support neoliberal governments for fear of being left out of the so-called 'globalization' or 'new international order'. It is essentially associated to that class fraction's political/ideological political weakness.

That change of position in relation to the regionalism model defended by the internal bourgeoisie can be traced in the FIESP documents during the crisis period. In 2012, demonstrating consonance with the progress of UNASUR, the entity organized a seminar on regional infrastructure which resulted in the

---

12   The analyses of Sino-Brazilian relations were extracted from an article published with Bruna Belasques in the *Carta Internacional Review* (2020).

publication of a book on the theme. In November 2015, it organized another seminar but this time on productive integration in South America. Those initiatives reflect the entity's enthusiasm for the COSIPLAN projects. However, in the FIESP, CNI and ICONE documents of 2012, 2013 and 2014, there are manifestations of growing discontent in regard to MERCOSUR. They began to criticize the imperfections in the bloc's implantation of a free trade zone and, at the same time, to attack the Customs Union and call for the abandonment of that commitment in order to guarantee the Brazilian State greater freedom in the international arena. They questioned costs and the implications that the bloc had come to represent for Brazilian foreign policy supposing that it was an obstacle to the adherence of others to bilateral agreements. The following is an excerpt from a CNI document:

> MERCOSUR is important for the Brazilian manufacturing industry but the state of paralysis that its main decision-making spheres are in and the growing divergences between the associates suggest that it is time to review the integration model. The preferential trade agreements should provide instruments to facilitate the flow of merchandise, goods and services and offer legal security and predictability. That is what Brazilian companies need to operate more efficiently in MERCOSUR and invest in constituting value chains, led by Brazil. That will not be possible unless the bloc completes and updates its free trade agenda. That must be the priority.
> CNI, 2014, p.12

The MERCOSUR-EU agreement is emblematic in the way it reveals how changes in the internal bourgeoisie's positioning took place in 2013 when the political and economic crises became more profound. In addition to MERCOSUR's having been one of the pillars of the PT governments' foreign policy, there was the notable fact of a clear opposition between agribusiness and industry that became apparent in the early rounds of the trade agreement negotiations between the two blocs during the period 1999 to 2004. Agribusiness saw positive points in the agreement and was therefore more demanding whereas industry feared losing market space with the advent of EU products and was accordingly more resistant to the agreement. In that context, the leaders in the creation of the Brazilian Business Coalition (CEB), CNI and FIESP, played preponderant roles in curbing the acceptance of an agreement that was at once unequal and burdensome for Brazilian industry. The performance of CEB/CNI reflected the position of an internal bourgeoisie that was, in some respects, discontented with the neoliberal policies of the 1990s especially in regard to the unilateral opening of markets imposed by the imperialist States. Thus, many industrial sectors within the CEB expressed their concern with the FTAA and the MERCOSUR-EU agreement (Berringer, 2015). Those sectors mostly involved with exportation such as textiles, footwear and steel sectors were favorable to the agreements, whereas machinery and equipment, cellulose and paper, chemicals and electro-electronics sectors demonstrated greater opposition (Oliveira, 2003). So, it can be said that historically, FIESP/CNI and the machinery and equipment sector have resisted the agreement.

FIESP and CNI maintained that posture through to 2010 when the negotiations were resumed. A technical study conducted by FIESP & ICONE (2012, p.58–61), stated that gains for industry would be relatively small compared to those of the agricultural sector and that the latter depended on the European abandonment of its protectionism for its own agriculture. Furthermore, the balance of trade would definitely be unfavorable for Brazil, especially in the sectors of manufactured goods, machinery, equipment and chemicals. However, in a complete turnaround, the documents of FIESP (2013) and CNI (2014), in the midst of the Brazilian political crisis, began to demand priority for the finalization of the negotiations.

The MERCOSUR-European Union Agreement is an immediate foreign policy priority and must be finalized by the beginning of 2015. The agreement can also be effectuated, on the part of MERCOSUR at different velocities by means of differentiated tariff relief schedules and lists with a view to a future normative convergence among bloc members (FIESP, 2014, p.4).

It must be reiterated that the change in position occurred after the Paraguayan State's suspension from MERCOSUR and the Venezuelan State's entry. Those acts further exacerbated the rejection of the regionalism model the PT governments had been constructing. The opposition interpreted the concomitancy of the suspension of the Paraguayan State and the entry of the Venezuelan State as a maneuver on the part of the Brazilian State's designed to favor the Hugo Chaves government. It then went on to a campaign of denunciations alleging that the political aspects were superimposing on the bloc's economic interests. According to Ferraz 2021, p. 69–70):

> CNI director Carlos Abijaodi, in harmony with FIESP wrote that the stagnation of trade and the business community's accentuated disbelief in the bloc had been aggravated by "the institutional problems experienced with the suspension of Paraguay, with the unpredictability of the Venezuelan administration and with the effects of Argentina's economic context". The Confederation also published that MERCOSUR had "turned to the social and political themes, leaving the fundamental questions for

the companies to be able to operate in suspension" (CNI 2014, 70 p.22). In addition, Abijaodi was emphatic in affirming that Brazil was interested in a MERCOSUR "that prioritizes an economic agenda and leaves political themes in second place".

CNI, 2014

It should be remembered that Brazil was removed from the European General Preferences System in 2014 thereby losing an important tariff reduction privilege (FIESP, 2014) and that the Brazilian State had to face a WTO panel in regard to its Inovar Auto program showing that there was a Japanese and European offensive in course against Brazilian neo-developmentalism.

Nevertheless, a more in-depth analysis, coupled with a survey of the positions of the sector associations shows that there were contradictions within the internal bourgeoisie itself. In 2013, the same year that FIESP and CNI publications began to express support for the agreement, the Machinery and Equipment Association (*Associação de Máquinas e Equipamentos*-ABIMAQ) evinced its concern with the direction the negotiations were taking. The Association stressed how difficult it was to compete with German products and stressed the fact that the negotiations embrace the government purchasing sector, one that is highly important to national industry, especially to those industries associated to Petrobras (Berringer &Forlini, 2018).[13]

In view of all the above, it is clear that the internal bourgeoisie's position oscillated regarding MERCOSUR and the extra-bloc agreements and that oscillating posture was linked to the fraction's political-ideological stance in regard to imperialism. As it was technologically and financially dependent on foreign capital, the internal bourgeoisie had little interest in a regionalism model that might take on an anti-imperialist profile. Thus, at the moment of national political crisis and a simultaneous strong imperialist offensive against neo-developmentalist and progressist governments in the region, the sectors that led the *Coup d'état* focused on strongly criticizing Brazilian foreign policy in the hands of the PT governments and on clamoring for closer alignment with the imperialist States. So, the Brazilian internal bourgeoisie allied itself with the purchasing bourgeoisie (financial capital) and with imperialism for, even though it was the major beneficiary multi-dimensional regionalism, it could not accept the idea of acquiring a profile of affronting the United States and

---

13   The analysis of ABIMAQ's position in relation to the MERCOSUR-EU agreement has been taken from an article the author published together with Luana Forlini in the *Conjuntura Austral Review* (UFRGS) in 2018.

neither was it in favor of an alliance with governments with vigorous income redistribution policies like the Venezuelan State at the time.

Thus, there was a connection between the accusations of the 'ideologization' of Brazilian foreign policy that appeared in the innumerable editorials of Rubens Barbosa, FIESP's director of its Foreign Trade Council, in the Estado de São Paulo newspaper, and in the street demonstrations that expressed opposition to the 'Bolivarianism' of MERCOSUR.

Another point to bear in mind is that in the 1950s and 1960s, the Brazilian internal bourgeoisie, given its financial and technological dependence, had preferred to ally itself with imperialism rather than place its bets on an alliance with people's classes and with neighboring States that would have given Brazil greater autonomy in the international sphere. That confirms the hypothesis that it was a fraction that could not be classified as a national bourgeoisie with a political project of its own and disposed to ally with people's sectors, and indicates why it allied itself with the campaign promoting MERCOSUR flexibility and adherence to extra-bloc agreements even though that course was of greater interest to the Agribusiness sector insofar as it was associated to the quest for access to markets in Europe and the United States. In short, the integration project closest to the internal bourgeoisie's ideology is a free trade zone, with liberty for direct investment, without any political commitments and with a low level of institutionality. It can be seen that the multidimensional MERCOSUR (commercial, social and political), albeit guaranteeing the interests of a fraction of the dominant class, is a composition of the interests of the internal bourgeoisie, those of the people's classes, of part of the diplomacy and of organized sectors of the left (social movements and union centrals) and that, once the crisis of the neo-developmentalist front began, the integration process entered on a new process (Berringer, 2021).

Multidimensional regionalism[14] began to show signs of fatigue too great to allow any return to the open regionalism that had been adopted in the 1990s when MERCOSUR was created. It is a model that mainly seeks for opening of trade in the region with a view to achieving 'insertion' in the global economy and therefore it defends an economic regional integration with an eye to insertion in the so-called global value chains' but without any endogenous political or social commitments. That being the case, the defense of the conclusion of the MERCOSUR-European Union negotiations re-emerges all the more forcefully.

---

14  The idea of multidimensional regionalism is linked to the incorporation of social and political themes to MERCOSUR and UNASUR. The outstanding feature of the latter is the creation of the South American Defense Council.

The BRICS also experienced an inflection, and various coalitions and forums took on different formats. According to Vasconcelos (2020), starting from 2016, with the changes of government in Brazil, South Africa and the United States, there was a notable change in the regulatory agenda and in the political position of the BRICS; the assertive, conflictive agenda was abandoned and a phase of accommodation in regard to the international financial system and international security policy began. The Brazilian State continued to participate in the meetings of the group but with a much lower profile.

It must be said that the Brazilian upper middle class played an important role in that process. Together with the press and fractions of the neoliberal front, it worked against the PT governments. According to Cavalcante and Arias (2019), of the participants in the street demonstrations clamoring for the president's impeachment and claiming national identity for themselves using T-shirts of the Brazilian Football Confederation. Three quarters of them had or were in higher education, two thirds had salaries of more than five times the minimum salary and most of them were white. Ostensibly the main reason for that sector's mobilization was the fight against corruption but actually there was an easily detectable discomfort among them with the social ascension of the people's classes that been benefitted by the policies generating employment, greater access to universities, and other policies that enabled those classes to frequent, airports, restaurants, shopping malls which had formerly been preponderantly social spaces of the upper middle classes. That was in addition to the policy of quotas for the university entrance of black people and for approval in competitive public entrance exams, which affronted their ideas of a meritocracy. There was also the regularization of employment in domestic service which made the service o servants that the upper middle class was accustomed to much more expensive.

That explains the appearance of placards in the street demonstrations bearing phrases like 'Brazil is not Cuba', 'Down with Bolivarianism', 'Let's go to Miami', 'Brazil must not become a Venezuela', 'Down with the São Paulo Forum', etc. It can be seen then that after the distributive issue, foreign policy was an important element of the 2016 crisis. That social stratum's base is meritocratic ideology and so the anti-corruption agenda was also mobilized by 'Americanism', that is, the ideas of progressivism, consumerism based on the 'average American'. In the end it means taking a nation that has prospered as an ideal and one that should serve as a model for the Americas. *The hypothesis here is that in addition to its defense of meritocracy and morals, the Brazilian upper middle class has historically defended the subordination of the Brazilian State to imperialism via the ideology of the 'American way of life'.* Starting in the 1940s, the USA disseminated Americanism as a State policy within its broader 'Big

Stick' policy. The use of cinema, propaganda, investments in cultural actions and educational exchanges was closely linked to that strategy; it was one of ideological cooptation of social sectors to ensure the maintenance of the USA's political and economic dominance in Latin America (Tota, 2000). That is why the social stratum in question rejects any bonds of identity with Latin America and rejects policies enhancing proximity with it, preferring instead subordination of the State to imperialism (Barros, 2018).[15] That is exactly how it was at the times of the crises in the 1950s and 1960s.

During the second Vargas government, the main representatives of the upper middle class, the National Democratic Union party (*União Democrática Nacional*-UDN) and Carlos Lacerda, conducted a vigorous propaganda campaign against the proposal of then president of Argentina Juan Domingo Perón for the formation of an Argentina, Brazil Chile Pact (*Pacto ABC*) as a third 'way' for the region to adopt in the face of the Cold War. In Brazil, the case evolved to become a call for impeachment in the middle of the political crisis that led Vargas to commit suicide. That was added to an anti-people stance and the fear of the support of, or alliance with 'unionist' governments; a fear shared by Brazil's internal bourgeoisie and its upper middle class. In 1964 there were various demonstrations and protests in the streets against the Independent Foreign Policy, especially against the decoration of Che Guevara, against the defense Cuba's self-determination and even against the relations with the USSR. It is thus clear that the class nature of the coups d'état in the 20th century were reproduced in the 2016 coup against the workers. The upper middle class was the driving force of the process.

## 2   The Temer Government and the Return to Passive Subordination[16]

In the Temer government, once the Coup had been consolidated, foreign policy was one of the fist areas where changes were made. Senator José Serra (PSDB) headed the Ministry of Foreign Affairs and took it on himself to 'purge

---

15   This part of the text is supported on the course conclusion paper of Larissa Barros whom the author tutored in 2018 and which is being worked on in depth and improved as part of her Master's degree course in International Relations at the ABC Federal University, again under the author's tutorship.

16   This section has been written with my colleague Cristina Reis. It was published as a chapter called "Inserção externa decadente e estrutura produtiva dependente" in the book *O Brasil Pós-Recessão das origens da crise às perspectivas e desafios futuros* (1 ed. Santo André: Edufabc, 2021, v.1). The book was organized by the Brazilian Keynes Association.

the PEB (Brazilian Foreign Policy) of ideology'. Brazil adopted a new posture in regard to the Venezuelan State, to the trade agreements (especially the MERCOSUR-European Union agreement) and to regional integration. It also altered the regime for the oil deposits auctions and the extant sharing regime. The Brazilian State's insertion in the international scenario went right back to one of passive subordination to imperialism. There was greater alignment with the USA and efforts were made to dismantle political commitments with the dependent States, especially the Latin American ones. Some of the Temer government's acts illustrate the foreign policy changes very clearly, namely: the new role of the Brazilian State in South America; the drawing closer to the United States; the Brazilian candidature for OECD membership and the progress with the negations of the MERCOSUR-EU agreement.

That process further exacerbated the Brazilian State's decadence on the international political scene and its productive, technological and financial dependence. That was due to the transformations in the global political economy in the decade following the 2008 international financial crisis and Brazil's national political crisis. It has resulted in the conservative modernization reforms agenda after the 2016 judicial-parliamentary Coup. It must be said that those questions also arose because of the limitations of neo-developmentalism, mainly the non-effectuation of structural changes in the productive matrix and property rights in the country, related to the absence of any profound political, administrative, fiscal or agrarian reforms; that is, neo-developmentalism's difficulty in adopting an industrial policy and in carrying out the country's major structural reforms.

Against the background of that historical moment the next subsection investigates the evolution of the country's productive and commercial structures with a focus on industry and assessing Brazil's role in the global value chains in the regional and international geopolitical context of inter-State financial and technological competition. After that comes a subsection endeavoring to associate production's structural performance with the evolution of the interests of Brazil's internal bourgeoisie and investigate how the internal political crisis altered the country's international insertion in the global economy considering the impacts of the return to open regionalism (CEPAL, 2000) and the direction of the international agreements under discussion during the Temer government. The questions addressed are: a) Did Brazil become economically more vulnerable? b) What impact did the foreign policy change have on development possibilities as a whole and in the medium and short terms? The answers will be sought for by means of an analysis using structural macroeconomic theoretical approach from the perspective of demand and an effort is made to understand the fractioning of classes inside the Brazilian social formation and its relation to foreign capital from the theoretical perspective of Nicos Poulantzas.

**2.1** *Brazil's Trade and Production Structures Compared with the World*
In the first quarter of 2018, the four-month accumulated growth rate of the GDP at market price values was 1%, the first positive rate since the first quarter of 2015 having been down to – 4.2% during the period of Dilma Rousseff's impeachment. On the demand side, families' consumption grew by 1% while imports and exports achieved the figures of 5% and 5.2%, respectively, in 2017. On the other hand, government consumption fell by 0.6% and Gross Fixed Capital Formation (GFCF) suffered a drop pf 1.8% registering the lowest percentage of the GDP value this century, 15.6%; in 2013 it was 21%.

Given that the GFCF represents the economy's productive investment then clearly the Temer government got off to a very bad start. Whenever the principal variable for the dynamism of income/revenue falls to such low levels compared with the international ones, then, according to Keynesian economics, the prospects of sustained development are very slim especially if there is no stimulation from government or external markets. Considering the measures that were adopted such as curbing government spending and signaling greater opening of the markets, the possibility of development, that is, economic growth accompanied by a rise in living standards and inclusive redistribution of income, becomes even more remote. At the heart of that explanation lie the productive and technological relations that generate employment of fundamental importance for the maintenance of consumption and investment, and closely bound up with quality, in terms of productivity and the added value of the economic activities the country carries out, especially industry, considering the laws of Kaldo to be actual (Kaldor 1966, Marconi et al., 2016).

In the aspect of the added value offer, according to the IBGE, in 2017 the added value in industry did not vary (0.0%), for the extractive industry it increased 4.3% while for construction if fell 5% (helping to pull down the GFCF) and for the transformation industry there was a rise of 1.7%. In the case of agribusiness, however, there was a rise of 13% (mainly pushed up by soy and maize harvests) and for services 0.3%. Thus, according the IBGE, in 2017 the transformation industry registered its lowest participation in the GDP since 1950, just 11.8%. Although the last quarter figures for 2017 indicated a positive evolution, the figures for early 2018 showed oscillations, indicating the persistence of uncertainty in that sector and it was not expected to recover from the economic crisis losses in 2018 and 2019.

The industrialization process that Brazil experienced in the course of post-war period made its industry large, diversified and resilient insofar as it continued to be expressive even after the processes of economic liberalization in the 1990s and the exchange rate valuation in the years 2000. According to UNIDO, in 2016 Brazil had the 7th largest transformation industry in the world (calculated using constant added value in 2010 dollars) participating in the group of the top 15 producers worldwide in most divisions of industry except office equipment, computers, accounting and pharmaceuticals. Nevertheless, in 2005, Brazil only had a 2.8% participation of the added value of the world's transformation industry (VII) and by 2016 it had fallen to 1.8%. a drop of 25% in the *per capita* VII (from USD 1341 to USD 1080) associated to its low growth rate in the period 2005 to 2010. The average growth rate over that period was 1.6% a year, the lowest rate among the developing and emergent economies for which the average was 7.7% and for the world as a whole, 2.4%. It went down by 3.3% a year in dollars between 2010 and 2016, compared to an expansion of 5.3% in the emergent and developing economies and 2.8% in the world at large. A sector-by-sector analysis of UNIDO data for the GDP and VII in the year 2017 reveals industry with a new energy showing growth of 3.5% mainly ensured by the developed economies, whereas for Brazil the VII was 2.5%. On the other hand, while the Brazilian GDP in dollars grew more than the world average in the period 2005–2010 it remained practically stagnant in the period 2010–2016 at an average annual rate of 0.4%.

The fact that Brazil has managed to keep itself in seventh place in the world manufacturing ratings in spite of the crisis is proof of its resilience in regard to the weak recovery rate of the global economy, an average of less than 3% since the international crisis. UNIDO itself has made it clear that the prolongations of the effects of that crisis on industry through to recent years was largely due to the effects on international trade and investments of Donald Trump's election in the USA and of BREXIT, together with the reversal in commodities prices, which had a severe impact on developing countries in Latin America and Africa, on Russia and on other countries. During those years the participation of labor in the composition of the transformation industry's added value[17] dropped in the case of most of the analyzed countries for the period 2004 to 2014 but in Brazil, it went up from 20% to 26%; even so it was far lower than the percentage for the developed countries and for Turkey, or at a similar level to other developing countries like Malaysia and Russia. That increase was mainly brought about by metal products, equipment and machinery, textiles, automotive, other transportation equipment and food industries.

---

17   Composed on the one hand of wages and remuneration of work which takes into account the total cost of the work paid directly to remunerate labor, and on the other hand the capital depreciation and operational surplus (IEDI, 2017, based on UNIDO, 2017).

However, watching the forest from above once cannot see what is going on in its shade. In addition to examining the performance of the divisions of industry which tend to concentrate on goods with low or medium technological intensity, like intermediaries and beverages/foodstuffs,[18] it is necessary to analyze the quality of the activities which will be reflected in the internal and external performance of the domestic industries' markets. What can be seen, basically, is that since 2011 there has been a two-way movement of loss of competitiveness of Brazilian exports and greater penetration of imports in Brazil's internal markets with a trade deficit for industrial products and a return to raw products in the Brazilian export portfolio. In that of 2011 the foreign added value of Brazilian exports, the main indicator behind the global value chains, according to TIVA, (WTO/OECD), was 11%, far from that of the other emerging and developing countries. The mean imported participation in the exportation of Brazilian manufactured goods was 15% with the higher figures being registered for coke, refined oil and nuclear fuel (21.3%), electronic and optical equipment (19.85%), transportation equipment (19.5%), rubber and plastic (17.4%), non-metallic mineral products (16.7%), machinery and equipment (16.2%) and electrical instruments (16%). Those indicators show that certain industries involving high or medium-high levels of technology, are increasingly counting on more importations for the production of their products than other countries. That could be a sign of enhanced efficiency in terms of the relative costs of the chains, but it also implies in enhanced porosity of the internal chains, affecting employment, investment in production and revenue.

Furthermore, MDIC data show that, since 2010, trading in Brazil has been relying more on exporting raw materials from extractive industry or products with low levels of technological intensity and the counterpart to that has been the importation of manufactured goods, especially those with medium to high technological intensity which has led to burgeoning trade deficits, the lowest one having been in 2014. However, with the advent of the economic crisis, both

---

18  Considering the sectors, IEDI 2007 shows that the sectors for which Brazil obtained the most notable positions were leather, leather products and footwear (4th position) coke, refined crude oil and nuclear fuels (4th position), foodstuffs (5th position), beverages (6th position), and paper and paper products (6th position). In regard to the internal distribution by sectors those with the greatest participation in the Brazilian transformation industry in 2015 were foodstuffs and beverages (21%), chemical products (12%) coke, refined crude oil, and nuclear fuels (10%), automotive vehicles, full trucks and semi-trucks (8%) and machinery and equipment (7%). The first two sectors increased their participation in comparison with 2005 while the third decreased it. In the case of coke and refined crude oil, as well as in basic metals, the reduction in prices explains the significant retraction of their participation in the total added value of the transformation industry.

imports and exports registered negative values for various quarters in 2015 and 2016 (compared to the same quarters of the previous year) but in 2017 resumed growth resulted in the biggest surplus in the history of Brazil, 67 billion USD (FOB) in 2017, according to the IEDI (2018). That surplus occurred in products other than manufactured goods and was backed by a certain recomposing of commodities prices, especially oil and metals, and on the agricultural super-harvest which raised the sales volumes of raw and semi-manufactured products, such as soy oil, unrefined sugar, etc. Thus, natural resource-intensive products like those of agriculture, forestry, fishing and extractive industries together with low technology industries with products like recycled ones; wood, wood products and cellulose; foodstuffs, beverages and tobacco; textiles, leather and footwear, were responsible for 63% of Brazilian exports in 2017, practically the same percentage as in 2014 (64%). The transformation industry's total participation in 2017 was 61%, having been 59% in 2014. In turn, 90% of imports value in 2017 was associated to manufactured goods as compared to 86% in 2014. Lastly, despite having improved in comparison with 2016, exportation levels remained lower than those of the 2011 to 2014 period and so did importation levels.

Considering Brazil's trading partners and based on data of the MDIC and the Atlas of Complexity, in 2017 the USA continued to be the main destination of Brazilian exports especially in the markets for high to medium-high technology industrial products while, generally speaking, China is the main importer, importing manufactured goods with low technological intensity and products based on natural resources. However, China is also the principal origin of Brazilian imports with a predominance of manufactured goods with medium to low technological intensity. It is worth mentioning that Argentina was the destination for 30% of Brazilian exports of products with medium-high technological intensity and so it continues to be an important trading partner although it once was even more so. Indeed, Brazil's trading balance with South America continues to be positive while at the same time it is a net absorber of products derived from natural resources.

The tendencies of the profile of the trading structure related to the economic crisis and understood in the broad scenario of growth in international markets driven by the developed countries and the new digital technology paradigms indicate that their dependent nature has been reinforced. Brazil inserts itself in the global value chains and in the international division of labor fundamentally as a supplier of raw materials and foodstuffs on the one hand and a consumer of products to be absorbed by its internal market on the other. As technology importers with a balance of US$ 4.6 billion in 2017 in intellectual property-use services in 2017 (IMF data) the Brazilian industries with high technological intensity are less represented in the internal productive structure and the international markets than the others with the single important exception of Embraer whose privatization the Temer government consolidated. As for trading partners, the USA seems to be consolidating a profile of convenient exchanges for those multinational industries and services that operate in Brazil, relegating the activities with less added value to last place. China, in turn, performs as the main demand for raw materials and foodstuffs and also as a supplier of manufactured goods and is expected to increment its dispute to add value to the Brazilian industrial chains vis-à-vis the USA.

The consequence of the vulnerability of the dependent productive and trading structures in the economic crisis was that the unemployment rate in Brazil practically doubled in two years from 7.2% in the first quarter of 2014 to 13.1% in the same quarter of 2018. Furthermore, the number of formally employed people (with a labor contract) continued to drop in 2018 signaling the deterioration of the labor market; a consequence of the crisis and of the Temer government's economic policy and labor reform bill approved during his term in office.

### 2.2  The Brazilian State's Re-embracing of Passive Subordination

The reorientation of Brazil's foreign policy during the Temer government, referred to above as decadent, was in fact a return to the passive subordination of the Brazilian State to imperialism. The decadence is glaringly displayed in the following movements: 1) sidling up to the United States and the renegotiation of the MERCOSUR-European Union Agreement; 2) the dismantling of the regional integration policy, turning the MERCOSUR into a mere trading and economic integration process (reinstating open regionalism as the model for regional integration), and paralyzing the internal dynamics of UNASUR with the suspension of the State's participation in that initiative together with in the Argentinean, Paraguayan, Chilean, Peruvian and Colombian States for questions of alignment with or opposition to the Venezuelan State; 3) draining the BRICS of political content especially in regard the new strategy of international relations with China now seen more as an investor especially in strategic resources and public companies than as ally in the south cooperation alongside the multilateral institutions; 4) terminating the South-South cooperation policies such as the policy to combat hunger in the African States; 5) emitting notable signs of subordination and reversing the direction of the former bold foreign policy by, among other things, presenting its candidature for membership of the OECD and adherence to the additional protocol of the Nuclear Arms Non-Proliferation Treaty, the joint training exercises of United States and

Brazilian armed forces, the renegotiation of an American base in Alcântara in Maranhão and others.

The political front that the Temer government of the day headed was a neo-liberal front made up of the import purchasing bourgeoisie, the upper middle class,[19] and sectors of the internal bourgeoisie that had decided to break away from the neo-developmentalist front and ally with the coup-promoting sectors (Boito Jr., 2016). In addition to the attacks on workers' rights through the Labor and Social Insurance Reforms, there is a policy in course of making Brazil's technological, productive, and financial dependence even more profound with the notable examples of the abandonment of the sharing regime for the pre-salt deposits, the end of the local content policy, the reduction of BNDES resources, the rounds of privatization of the electricity sector, of ports and of airports, and the discarding of environmental criteria in public tendering processes, etc. The Brazilian political crisis that led to the 2016 *Coup d'état* had its beginnings in 2012 according to Singer (2018) when president Dilma endeavored to consolidate neo-developmentalism, diminishing the bank spread and the interest rate and at the same time reducing the growth in government spending and revenues involved in providing industrial subsidies and tax reliefs (Orair & Gobetti, 2017) thereby provoking GDP growth deceleration in a Brazil that was still reeling from the effects of the international financial crisis. After the 2013 street demonstrations and protests that mobilized a growing portion of the Brazilian population in favor of conservative agendas and led by the FIESP and the FEBRABAN, there was an entanglement of the economic crisis and the internal political crisis. The crises had overlapped counter-movements in the contemporary political economy dynamics ever since the 2008 economic crisis with the strengthening of the Chinese economy and the Russian State, the intensification of international conflicts with the invasion of Syria, the disputes in the South China Sea, the approval of United Kingdom's exit from the European Union and so on and which, after Trump's election in the USA, were the sign for the imperialist states to take power once more resulting in a

---

19   The Upper Middle class represented the greater part of the public that came out on the streets or beat on saucepans from the windows of their apartments, to call for the impeachment of President Dilma and it also corresponds to the judiciary, the Offices of the Public Prosecutors and the Federal Police who were important actors in the Lava Jato operation and the coup of 2016. In Brazil that sector is typified by its high schooling level and high income and is concentrated in sectors of the state services and other State apparats. Among the professions involved are: journalists, doctors, lawyers, directors of big companies, judges, prosecutors etc. A distinctive element of that commonly conservative and reactionary social stratum is its belief in meritocracy. Regarding the respective debate, see: Saes, 1985b; Boito Jr., 2016.

powerful offensive against Latin America. That retaking of power was marked by a scenario of paradigmatic change in technology whereby the 4.0 industry and the advanced manufacturing sector promised to revolutionize the production of the extant sectors and open spaces for a series of product, process and market innovations. It is not by chance that world's machinery and equipment industry has been growing vigorously, led by the United States, Germany and Japan. Parallel to that the dollar has enhanced its value and the United States are going to seek to establish a new foreign policy placing their bets on an old recipe: protecting intellectual property rights, opening emergent markets, privileged access to sources of raw materials and natural resources and foodstuffs, energy security and enhanced competition with rival States including the emergent BRICS States.

Given that context, the United States considered it highly important, on the one hand, to stifle the Brazilian State's leadership and protagonist role in the region by following the old recipe of establishing political and economic dependence of the Brazilian State and gaining in exchange its performance as a dismantler of regional articulation and an unthreatening neighborhood and, on the other, to break up the strategic alliance of the BRICS which as a bloc had gained some ground in international geopolitics in the period immediately following the international financial crisis. As mentioned earlier, the PT governments had formed partnerships with BRICS States and South American States in an effort to reduce the United States' influence on Brazil albeit without ever actually achieving that aim. The neo-developmentalist front had been most coherent during the period 2003 to 2011 when the Brazilian economy had been achieving positive economic results that had even led Brazil to be considered 'an emerging power' alongside the other BRICS countries. The south-south policy brought with it an enormous increase in the Brazilian State's room for maneuver in the face of imperialism. That was visible in the regional role the Brazilian State played with the creation of Union of South American Countries, its role in bringing together the BRICS group, and in using its Development Bank and Structural Reserves Arrangement to strengthen an alternative to the financial institutions of the Bretton Woods regime, such as the World Bank and the International Monetary Fund (Berringer, 2015). Those relations of the Brazilian State worried the US so much that President Dilma's government was the target of US spying exemplified by the tapping of ministers, diplomats and advisors' telephones by the US intelligence agency in 2014 and 2015, as WikiLeaks revealed.

However, from 2012 on there was an observable decline in the boldness of Brazil's stance in its international relations and an intensification of its productive, technological economic and financial dependence in the face of foreign capital. As there had been no structural changes in production or technology in Brazil in the preceding period, the fall in the prices of commodities after 2012/2013 was the first efficient blow struck against Brazil's balance of payments dynamics and its plans for the expansion of Petrobras. At the same time the blow jeopardized the economies of various other peripheral countries, including Venezuela and Russia. Then came the 'Lava-Jato' operation, which some writers state was sustained by United States resources and in its interests (Nassif, 2016), and it selectively detected corruption scandals that hit some the largest Brazilian companies active in other countries including Petrobras. The 2016 *Coup* ended up facilitating the access of US capital to the pre-salt deposits, to government purchases and to the internal market, guaranteeing greater gains for US companies as well as obtaining greater control over Brazilian government policy.

In that regard, a closer examination of the financial dynamics of productive and technological dependence reveals the decadence of Brazil's external insertion which in spite of its coming from outside to inside and difficult to curb was readily accepted by the Temer government and the neoliberal front instead of being curbed as it had been, at least to some extent, by the PT governments and the neo-developmentalist front. In Brazil, historically among the main receivers of Direct Foreign Investment, there was a drop of 9% in the inflows according to UNCTAD (2017). Investments in equity also fell by the same percentage especially due to the decline in the services sector considering the Brazilian crisis. The DFI in financial services suffered de-investment in 2016 since the Bradesco group purchased HSBC's assets in Brazil and in general the inter-companies DFI for Brazilian affiliates fell by 39%. In parallel to that, and also in 2016, there were increased DFI in equity in the areas of metal ore extraction, automotive vehicles (+50%), and in other sectors which basically took place through mergers and acquisitions. These grew from US$ 2 billion in 2015 to US$9 billion the most notable being the mega-agreements involving strategic resources especially in the electricity sector with the China Three Gorges Corporation (China) and Statoil ASA (Norway). Putting it another way, DFI outflows from Brazil dropped from 3 billion US dollars in 2015 to a situation of de-investment of 12 billion US dollars in 2016, including in F&A on the part of the Brazilian multinationals operating abroad. Reverse investment debts doubled, half of them being debts in the international capitals market of the Petrobras affiliate, Petrobras Global Finance BV (Holland). UNCTAD presents the main liberalizations for the sale of Brazilian assets that were destined to result in a new influx of capitals in 2017 but that actually jeopardized development and sovereignty; they were associated to oil, commercial aviation and other strategic areas. Insofar as it has relinquished power and wealth in productive, technological and financial terms, the decadence of Brazil's position in international politics has become increasingly clear and that unfortunately may have very negative consequences in the medium and long terms for inclusive development.

### 2.3  Decadent External Insertion and Dependent Productive Structure

Since the 2016 coup, Brazil has deepened its productive structural dependence and that has made it more economically vulnerable. Furthermore, the change in foreign policy to adopt a more decadent stance in internal relations has also deteriorated the possibility for development in the medium and long terms. It can be concluded that the weakening of a multilateral regionalism that pursued political, social and productive integration (Granato, 2015) and the advent of a greater proximity to the United States and the European Union, has affected the role of the Brazilian State in Latin America, blocking the possibility of its obtaining greater room for maneuver in its international insertion. The challenge to achieve that became more acute in the face of the progressive decadence of the industrial productive sector and the country's economic crisis. Adding to that the dependence on trade, knowledge and capital flows of the global value chains, the result has been an ambiguous action of the interests of the internal bourgeoisie in foreign and domestic political relations. Vacillating between the neo-developmentalist and neoliberal projects, but always anti – worker and opposed to any anti-imperialist policies, industry supported the 2016 coup and now finds itself at a crossroads that is decisive for its autonomy and for Brazil's sovereign development. The neo-developmentalist front's decision to passively align itself with imperialism, fostering and allowing the decadence of Brazil's external insertion could not have any other repercussion than the exacerbation of social inequalities A different pathway for international insertion would be to take neo-developmentalism up again with productive development planning specifically directed at reducing social inequality (Reis, 2018). Thus, the State must not exempt itself from its allocative and distributive attributions, nor of its sovereignty in regard to the country's strategic resources and in the discussions of 'new themes' in the international trade negotiations on: investments, services, intellectual property (and technology transfer), and labor and environmental clauses. Therefore, the orientation for foreign policy must be the south-south relations, especially in the regional framework and the BRICS Group with a view to constructing a political coalition capable of fighting against neoliberalism.

## 2.4 'Weak Meat'[20]

The national and international conjunctures bring up polemics, reflections and debates that are highly important for understanding Brazil's international insertion and the characteristics of the Brazilian bourgeoisie. Prior to Donald Trump's election and the approval of Brexit, among the Marxist intellectuals there were some who argued that neoliberalism was based on a productive, economic and financial globalization that had created a transnational bourgeoisie (Robinson, 2017), being driven by a transnational state under construction or an elite international consensus. The big multinational corporations and the agents of financial capital (pension funds, insurers, etc.), they said, were the principal actors of contemporary capitalism, undermining the existence of national and/or internal bourgeoisies. Along those lines of reasoning Brazil had had integrated itself to United States imperialism in a subordinate manner and the Brazilian industrial and services bourgeoisies had dissipated or become associated to foreign capital.

Such interpretations were the fruit of debates in Brazilian sociology in the 1970s involving André Gunder Frank, Rui Mauro Marini, Jacob Gorender, Fernando Henrique Cardoso, Enzo Faletto, etc. At the time the interest was in gleaning an understanding of the character and position of the Brazilian industrial bourgeoisie in regard to imperialism. Brazilian intellectuality and leftist organizations who were fighting against the military dictatorship pored over the critique of the thesis of the 3rd international defended by the Brazilian Communist Party prior to the 1964 coup. They diverged from the contraposition to the possibility that the Brazilian bourgeoisie was a national one: they were disposed to construct an anti-imperialist alliance with the people's classes as a stage in the revolutionary process. It is not by chance that, given the similarities in the class nature of the 2016 coup with that of 1964. The polemic has returned and intensified even further after the Federal Police's *Carne Fraca* (literally 'weak meat') operation denouncing irregular adulteration practices in the major Brazilian meat packing plants.

The questions that arise are: Are they national companies or multinational ones? Could that police operation contribute to the dispute of classes and class factions for markets and political-economic and ideological positions in the global economy and on the domestic political scene? Has the neoliberal crisis exacerbated the contradictions among the bourgeoisies and national States

---

20  Text published at: https://outraspalavras.net/sem-categoria/carne-fraca-na-politica-economica-e-na-pf/.

thereby showing that capitalism has not constructed a globally integrated bourgeoisie?

Lenin (1999), referring to capitalism at the beginning of the 20th century stated that the creation of trusts and holding, despite the centralization and concentration of capital did not eliminate the dispute among capitalists and between the States. The logic of capitalist accumulation presupposes that, for the profit rate to be maintained, there must be a permanent competition within and among industrialists, sectors and the big corporations. As the State organizes the interests of the dominant classes and class fractions so, in the international sphere, the dispute among capitals transforms itself into a dispute among States. That thesis is still capable of clarifying many aspects despite all the changes that have taken place in world capitalism. In that regard, the trading and investment agreements reflect a dispute among the States for access to markets and for privileges and guarantees for direct foreign investments. Thus, despite the financialization of the economies and the high degree of deregulation of capital flows, it still cannot be said that the bourgeoisies have either dissipated or integrated. The formation of value chains on an international scale does not eliminate the existence of 'selective conflicts' between the capital that is accumulated internally and foreign capital (Gonrender, 1981).

The Brazilian internal bourgeoisie, whether the industrial one of the services one, is financially and technologically dependent on foreign capital and for that reason cannot be considered a national bourgeoisie. However, perhaps it is not a bourgeoisie integrated to imperialism the way the purchasing (financial capital) bourgeoisie is. It maintains a *sui generis* stance insofar as to survive, it depends on the protection of the Brazilian State. It needs the State to have an international position that is not mere following of United States policy and which, without being anti-imperialist, preserves a certain degree of autonomy in the face of the States of the North. That is the position considered here to be conflictive subordination to imperialism; it means not cutting the ties, given its dependence, but imposing limits and conditions for competition and survival in the face of foreign capital.

In the case of the big meatpacking corporations created with the support of BNDES financing during the Lula governments, it is important to underscore that this industrial activity and especially the associated trading have always been run by foreign capital. The creation of big companies with national capital was only possible with State support. So even if they are part of a monopolizing process of the internal market and of Brazilian exportation of meat and poultry, they are the fruit of competition with foreign capital and part of a process and endeavor to alter the Brazilian economy's position in the international scenario. Although they are not the fruit of an alliance with people's classes, nevertheless the creation of employment they represented met the immediate needs and demands of many Brazilian men and women workers who integrated a neo-developmentalist front (Boito Jr., 2012).

On that point, putting forward the idea that those companies are part of the Brazilian internal bourgeoisie is not a case of trying to defend the undefendable; adulterating meat is a crime and so is corruption. However, it is important to call attention to what that Federal Police operation could be indicative of or at least to the political and economic moment at which it was launched, or can anyone believe that it was a new process? ... that the international packing house corporations that operated for a century in Brazil did not have the same practice?

It is also unacceptable to fall back on a mechanistic vision which would be: which is the corporation anxious to enter in Brazil to replace those that were denounced by the Federal Police operation? ... or which meat-producing country would be interested in dismantling the sector in Brazil? The international reflexes that have already appeared indicate that here will be sanctions and obstacles set to the exportation of Brazilian meat and that the European Union now has one more motive for not presenting a list of offers for the MERCOSUR-European Union negotiations. Even if the agreement were to be extremely negative it would be better, if possible, to denounce the practices of the imperialist States in these agreements than to suffer such a setback. In reality, that agreement seeks the promotion and protection of European foreign investments in the region, access to government purchasing deals and an increase in its exportation of industrialized products without any counterpart offer given that the European Union's Common Agricultural Policy, presupposes the defense of its food sovereignty, that is, of agricultural protectionism.

Understanding that disputes among bourgeoisies and among States persist and tend to intensify is part of the analysis of national and international political scenes. It is important to unveil the interests of classes and class fractions that underlie the political practices of the various actors and state and international apparats. The dynamics and the conjuncture being faced are new but without any big alterations in the political structures themselves or in the international division of labor. However, everything goes to show that there will be even more economic protection on the part of the United Kingdom and the United States, and that re-industrialization has become an urgent necessity to emerge from the international financial crisis that has lasted since 2008. Brazil seems to be marching in the opposite direction, adopting a stance of passive submission to imperialism and debilitating its own internal bourgeoisie. What stage, what international position is Brazil heading back to? That is the point! That is the question! Behold the interests!

## 3    The Bolsonaro Government and Its Explicit Passive Subordination to Imperialism: The Neofascist Alliance[21]

This section presents an analysis of the Bolsonaro government's foreign policy. The hypothesis is that the government's policy is neoliberal and therefore represents the interests of the foreign capital and the associated bourgeoisie to the detriment of the internal bourgeoisie which the governments of the PT favored (Boito Jr., 2018). That representation of a class also determines that the Brazilian State's international insertion is one of passive subordination to imperialism. It is a position that is clearly apparent in the alliance between Trump and Bolsonaro based on the neofascist ideology known as 'anti-globalism' and, in view of that, the passive subordination became explicit in the first two years of Bolsonaro's presidency. After Biden was elected, the Brazilian State reverted to a more cautious position or less explicit position with the emergence of conflicts in the environmental area and the changes in the USA's foreign and economic policies.

The preceding sections argue that there was a relation of determination between the changes in the Brazilian State's performance in the international scenario and the new dynamics of the power bloc, namely the strengthening of the internal bourgeoisie (a fraction made up of the transformation industry, big construction corporations, mining corporations and agribusiness) within the power bloc, which had displaced the onetime uncontested hegemony of the purchasing bourgeoisie (financial capital) in the 1990s. The effect of the new power bloc on foreign policy was to lead it to transit from a political stance in the international conjuncture of passive subordination to imperialism to one of conflictive subordination. Thus, there was no actual rupturing of the relations with the imperialist States, but the Brazilian State did manage to achieve an important space for maneuver, and with that it set priority on the non-acceptance of unilateral trade opening imposed by the dominant States and on conquering markets for the exportation of national products and the installation of Brazilian companies. To that end it counted on the support of

---

21  This text has been based on chapters of books and texts produced by the United States Work Group of the Brazilian International Insertion and Foreign Policy Observatory (Observatório da Política Externa e Inserção Internacional do Brasil-Opeb.org). The two chapters of the book are: Berringer, T.; Soprijo, G.; Barros, L. O; Carneiro, G.; Souza, L. M. Nacionalismo às avessas In: *As bases da política externa bolsonarista.*(1 ed.Santo André: EdufAbc, 2021, v.1, p.139–152); Berringer, T.; Soprijo, G.; Amparo, Gabrielly; Texeira, A. P. F. Relações Brasil-EUA e a pandemia In: *A política externa de Bolsonaro na pandemia.* (1 ed.São Paulo: Friederich Ebert Stiftunng, 2021, v.1, p.71–80).

the BNDES and other national agencies, boosting regional integration, creating and participating in international coalitions and drawing closer to the peripheral/dependent States. The outstanding fruits of that performance were the MERCOSUR, UNASUR, the IBAS Forum, the BRICS group and the Brazil-South Africa and Brazil-Middle East relations etc.

Even though the internal bourgeoisie had been the major beneficiary of that foreign policy, during the political crisis that led to President Dilma's impeachment, there was harsh criticism from the opposition of the Brazilian State's international performance that ended up producing street protests and demonstrations and manifestations of the representative entities such as the CNI and the FIESP. They alleged that the government's foreign policy was ideologized and was furthering Bolivarianism in Brazil and in the region which would eventually have isolated Brazil politically and ideologically.

In that aspect, the Brazilian State's international insertion during the Temer and Bolsonaro governments became one of passive subordination to the United States. Regionally, that submission materialized as the 'war' against Venezuela. That is perhaps the best illustration of the strategic significance of submission from the United States' point of view: to have the Brazilian State in its favor and perhaps be able to use the Brazilian State as its instrument to combat the Bolivarian governments. None of that changed in the Temer government or Bolsonaro governments, not even with the advent of the Joe Biden presidency in the USA (2021).

As has already been stated, the distancing from the neighboring States especially from the Venezuelan State was the central point of Brazilian Foreign Policy after the 2016 coup. Thus, apart from the changes in the profile of the MERCOSUR, the Brazilian state participated in the creation of the Lima Group (responsible for opposing the Nicolas Maduro government) and became a member of the Pro-Sul Forum. Furthermore, there was a reduction in Brazil's cooperation with South Africa, an attempt to sell Embraer to the Boeing Corporation, and changes were made in the Pre-salt tendering processes questioning the extant sharing model. The diagnosis proposed in this text is that Brazilian foreign policy transited from conflictive subordination to passive subordination with the passage from the Dilma administration to the Bolsonaro administration and in the latter government that submission has become absolutely explicit given the ideological alliance around the antiglobalism agenda of the Trump and Bolsonaro governments.

The choice of diplomat Ernesto Araújo to head the Ministry of Foreign Affairs was one of the clearest expressions of the political-ideological line adopted for Brazilian foreign policy in 2019. Araújo had published an article that was considered polemical even by Itamaraty's most conservative and liberal sectors.

In *Trump e o Ocidente* (Trump and the Occident) (Araújo, 2017) he proposes that alignment with the Trump government is based on the 'occidental' and 'pan-nationalist' ideology, which is endowed with a civilizing nature, guided by values defending 'God, faith and family'. That pro-occident ideology presents a specific notion of Brazilian nationalism that emphasizes the existence of a common history forged in the classical civilizations of Greece and Rome and with Judaic-Christian roots and the ideology's unifying feature is a vision of the homeland ('Patria') as an indissociable union of liberty, family history and belief. Thus, according to Araújo's logic, being 'pro-occident' means acknowledging a supposed common past that links Brazilians with the United States and with Europe. It also presumes the existence of a national interest that seeks almost unconditional alignment with those States, especially the United States of America, and resists any kind of globalist influence. Jair Bolsonaro boasts of being Brazil's first non-anti-American president in decades.

That alliance of the Trump and Bolsonaro governments seems to have been based on the idea of 'anti-globalism'. It has configured itself as a conservative, obscurantist and anti-communist alliance attacking the international political defense of human rights, multilateralism and the environment. It therefore ran contrary to the set of international trade, human rights, migration and environment regimes of the UN and WTO framework agreements of the 1990s and the years 2000 (the so-called globalism). It also embraced a crusade against 'Bolivarian communism' and Chinese communism. According to them the international regimes and organizations restricted the sovereignty of States in the name of the construction of an international civil society. Thus, it can best be classified as a neofascist transnational network (Netto, Charchur & Calvancante, 2020).

That ideological alignment with the Trump government centered on the idea of conservative and xenophobic Christian Occidentalism is actually a neo-fascist nationalism. Brazilian foreign policy of radicalized liberalism, the explicit subordination to the United States in line with the WTO Agreement on Safeguards, and the onerous concession of the pre-salt deposits are all expressions of a political program whose strategic meaning is explicit passive subordination to the Trump Government. The policy differs most from that of the Temer government in the political discourses which present the aspect of subordination far more explicitly and in the alliance with those neofascist governments that oppose globalism. It is neofascist nationalism because, ideologically, its nationalist and racist discourse excludes a part of the population, preaching the cult of violence against the non-bourgeois classes of ordinary people, Negroes, feminists, indigenous peoples and the LBGTQIA+ population.

The analysis now continues based on Nicos Poulantzas's Marxist theory, in this case, as set out in the book *Fascism and Dictatorship* (2020). In it the author argues that fascism is a type of State of exception resulting from a series of crises, namely, the crisis in the power bloc, the crisis in the political parties, the ideological crisis and the crisis of representativity. It is also an offensive against the working class. Fascism relies on the driving force of the new petit bourgeoisie or of the upper middle class which is the sector that most closely identifies itself with the ideology of a justification for violence, with racism, obscurantism and anti-intellectualism, with nationalism, militarism, defense of the family and the fetichism of the State. To Poulantzas, it is not a historic phenomenon that can only be recognized as existing in Germany and Italy in the period between the two World Wars. Furthermore, it must be analyzed as a political process with stages that begins with the fascism germinating in society at large, the existence of social movements, and then goes on to exist in a government or a political party and lastly, depending on whether those social forces advance or not, a fascist regime, that is a dictatorship, installs itself. Thus, in the case of Brazil it cannot yet be considered that there is a fascist dictatorship (Boito Jr., 2021).

### 3.1 Foreign Policies of the Bolsonaro Government and the Trump Government: The Neofascist Alliance

In his election victory speech delivered from his home, Bolsonaro said:

> We are going to free Brazil and Itamaraty from international relations with an ideological bias that they have been submitted to in recent years. Brazil will no longer be squeezed by the more developed nations. We will seek for bilateral relations with countries that can aggregate economic and technological value to Brazilian products. We will recover international respect for our beloved Brazil.
>
> PODER 360, 2018

In keeping with that speech, foreign policy came well to the fore in the Bolsonaro government. The Brazilian State's main actions in the international scenario have been the attempt to move the Brazilian embassy in Israel from Tel Aviv to Jerusalem, the Brazilian voting at the UN on the Palestinian question and gender issues, Brazil's defense at the OAS of maintaining the embargo on trading with Cuba (the first time in 50 years that the Brazilian Stated has voted in favor of the embargo), Brazil's withdrawal from the Migrations Pact, Brazil's declining to host the climate conferences and the public declarations of the president, his sons and even the Minister of foreign affairs of veneration for the United States (they formally saluted the American flag on July 4th, American Independence Day), and the accusation that China had actually fabricated the Covid Virus.

Brazil-USA relations were top priority on the government team's agenda and that was made explicit by President Bolsonaro's visits to the United States in March 2019 and March 2020. It was underscored by the visit to Brazil of US Secretary of State Mike Pompeo and US National Security Advisor Robert O'Brien in 2020 under the aegis of the so-called Prosperity Agenda. During that set of meetings, the topics under discussion were: the war against Venezuela, the Technological Safeguards Agreement, associated to the USA's use of the Alcântara Base in Maranhão, Brazil's request for the USA to support its candidature for OECD membership, and the visit of the president, six ministers and one of the president's sons to the Central Intelligence Agency. That was the first time any Brazilian president had made an official visit to the agency so that, apart from the agreement against corruption, which was part of the Prosperity Agenda, it seems to have been something of another piece in the Lawfare chequerboard of the 'Lava-Jato' operation and the relations between the Brazilian civil bureaucracy, especially the judiciary, and the United States.

The Brazilian State's candidature for admission to the OECD is closely bound to the Bolsonaro government's stance of passive subordination. Membership of the 'Club of the Rich' is seen by its defenders as a kind of 'Seal of Quality' that would guarantee security for foreign investors. The group represents the interests of the imperialist bourgeoisies of the member States which do not limit themselves to Trading and Investments but are also involved in the following areas: Agriculture, Fishing, Health, Science and Technology, Corporate Governance, Environment, Chemical Products, Insurance and Social Security, Territorial Development and others (Azzi, 2020). In addition to all the above, the Bolsonaro government has signaled that administrative and fiscal reforms would probably be added to that list.

In that framework, full membership would have important consequences for Brazil given that OECD decisions have to be accepted by its members as 'building blocks'. In regard to the financial sphere and capital flows, the OECD has a further set of Liberalization codices to which the countries must submit including, for example, the Code of Liberalization of Movement of Capitals which also includes the liberalization of investment flows (Azzi, 2020, p.67).

In addition, the price for US support for Brazil included the request to abandon its Special and Differentiated Treatment in the WTO which implies considerable losses of trade and political engagement. Furthermore, as Brazil already has the status of 'key partner', (non-founding member with strong engagement) it is hard to see the need for that. Azzi (2020) correctly calls it 'subordination by adherence'.

That agenda has enjoyed the support of Brazil's industrial bourgeoisie. According to the CNI (2021b, p.14):

> Brazil's access to the OECD is a priority on the Brazilian industry agenda. Alignment with OECD standards and future entry into the organization will provide juridical security, predictability, competitiveness and consequently economic growth for Brazil.

To become.part of the organization, Brazil needs to adhere to its legal instruments. Currently we are part of 41% of the total, some of which are obligatory such as the Liberalization Codes. The last pending item for the approval of Brazilian adherence is the approval of Draft Bill 5387/19, the so-called Exchange Bill.

In the sequence of the neoliberal program were the conclusion of the MERCOSUR-European Union agreement and the revision/review of the MERCOSUR Common External Tariff. The conclusion of the MERCOSUR-European Union agreement in July 2019, after 20 years of negotiations came as a surprise. The agreement was only finalized because of the new political conjuncture in a Europe cornered by Trumpism which had taken the transatlantic agreement off the agenda, and by the Chinese State's One Belt One Road initiative (later the Belt and Road Initiative) which was getting near to its frontiers. Those new situations, together with BREXIT, led the European Union to formulate a more strategic policy, drawing up agreements with Japan and Canada (Schutte, 2020a). The agreement with MERCOSUR foresees not only trading provisions but also rules regarding government purchasing, investments and intellectual property. In the trading aspect, agricultural products, MERCOSUR's main line of exportation, were restricted to quotas. Meat for example which in 2004 claimed a quota of 300 thousand tons was restricted to 99.9 thousand tons. Chicken was allocated 90 thousand of the 180 thousand tons the MERCOSUR had hoped for. The trading in agricultural products had always been an obstacle to progress in the negotiations given that the European common policy is a food security clause. The European Union, in turn managed to reduce considerably the importation tariff on automobiles (scheduled to be down to zero in 15 years) and has shown a lively interest in the machinery and equipment sector and chemical products. According to (Schutte, 2020a), the Brazilian steel sector was the only one that opposed the agreement.

Another important aspect to consider is the trade in services in which the Brazilian deficit is around 70%. In 2016, for example, importation of devices was to the value of 23 million dollars and exportation, 5 billion. The European Union is the leading investor in productive assets in Brazil. In the years 2020, the amount invested represented 65% of the total DFI in Brazil. With the slacking of the regulations provided for in the agreement, Brazil will probably become a land of mere assembly plants like Mexico (Schutte, 2020a).

As for government purchasing, the EU is clearly interested in the public tendering processes in the areas of infrastructure and health, sectors that have always been protected by the Brazilian State and so the work of the 'Lava-Jato' in destroying the big Brazilian construction corporations makes the construction sector a no man's land for foreign capital to enter.

The trouble is that the European Union believed it could influence the MERCOSUR's labor and environmental agendas, but the Bolsonaro government has an agenda precisely the opposite of what the Europeans expected, especially in regard to environmental issues and that has been the main stumbling block for the ratification of the agreement in Brussels.

Regarding MERCOSUR, besides the neutralization of its social and political commitments, the Bolsonaro government has endeavored to reduce the Common External Tariff (CET) and bend the rules of the Customs Union to consolidate the open regionalism model that is already being implemented in the bloc. The initial proposal was for a 50% reduction of the CET distributed as follows: 0–12% for raw materials; 12 to 16% for capital goods; and 18 to 20% for consumer goods. The final agreement was for a reduction of 10% in the above aliquots because there was resistance to the original proposal stemming from the Brazilian internal bourgeoisie and the Argentinean State, with the latter's resistance probably having been determined by the interests of that State's internal bourgeoisie too (Botão, 2021).

The National Confederation of Industry (2021a) declared that the Customs Union guarantees the bargaining power of the MERCOSUR member countries in negotiations with other nations and economic blocs and reducing that power would only accelerate the deindustrialization process and cause a drop in Brazilian exports to MERCOSUR. FIESP, too, is against the tariff reform as it considers that the reduction would be harmful to Brazilian industry (FIESP, 2019). The National Agriculture and Livestock Confederation (*Confederação Nacional da Agricultura e Pecuária*) also came out in favor of maintaining the tariff at a high level to bar the entrance of imported products and in that way control the supply side and market prices (Botão, 2021).

The greatest inflection in the change from the PT governments to the Bolsonaro government was in the regional policy. The Brazilian State's support for the war against Nicolas Maduro in Venezuela is an outstanding aspect. That was given not only through Brazil's participation in the Forum for the Progress and Integration of South America, an initiative of Argentinean president Sebastiã Piñera and Colombian president Ivan Duque with the participation of Argentina and Peru (who withdrew from it in 2021 under the presidencies of Fernandez and Pedro de Castillo respectively) of Brazil, Guyana, Ecuador and Paraguay. The initiative, following the political orientation of the Lima Group, focused on liberalizing trade and isolating Venezuela in the region. It did not prosper but although the invasion of Venezuela has not occurred there has been a vigorous destabilization of that country that has caused a massive migratory outflux to Colombia and Brazil. In the face of it, in Brazil, Operation Welcome (*Operação Acolhida*) was constructed in the State of Roraima with the intention of establishing relations between the Brazilian State and the Venezuelans who have arrived in Brazil.

In September 2020, US Secretary of State, Mike Pompeo accompanied by the Brazilian Foreign Affairs minister Ernesto Araujo, visiting the state of Roraima stated that the people of Venezuela are a threat to the Maduro government, and they need the support of Brazil and the United States. He made severe criticism of the Nicolas Maduro government even going so far as to call Maduro a drug trafficker. It must be remembered that during the 2019 *Coup d'état* in Bolivia the Brazilian State declared its support for the self-declared President Jeanine Áñez, breaking a long Brazilian foreign policy tradition of non-intervention in internal issues. Another incident that called attention was Bolsonaro's failure to congratulate the newly elected president of Argentina, Alberto Fernández, in 2020.

The most glaring example of passive subordination to imperialism was the signing of the Technological Safeguards Agreement that ceded the use of the Alcântara Base in Maranhão to the USA. That agreement affronts territorial sovereignty and heightens Brazil's technological dependence. It involves even more offensive clauses than Protocol 505 at the time of the FHC government. In regard to sovereignty, it determines that Brazilian authorities may not have access to the base, may not exercise control over the entrance of equipment and it restricts the use of revenue from the cession of the base for investment in aero-space technology. The agreement is highly illustrative of how the USA puts pressure on the Brazilian State to ensure its continuing dependence. The USA obliged the Brazilian State to review its access to 5G technology with the Chinese Huawei corporation by threatening to desist from the Technological Safeguards agreement.

The Prosperity Agenda involves three themes: trade facilitation, good regulatory practices and cooperation in combating corruption. Those agreements were signed on October 19, 2020, on the occasion of the visit to Brazil of the USA's National Security Advisor Robert O'Brien. The agenda included meetings with members of the government and with businessmen in Brasília and São Paulo. The signing took place at a time when the Brazil-United States trade index was at its lowest for 11 years having dropped by 25% in 2020 due to the effects of the Coronavirus pandemic (AMCHAM, 2020).

In regard to facilitating trade, the agreement provides for the abolition of some non-tariff trade barriers in bilateral trade and included the simplification or extinction of bureaucratic procedures (BRASIL, 2020). In the case of good regulatory practices, the agreement establishes internationally recognized processes, systems, tools and methods for improving the quality of regulation in the State's economic practices. The agreement is the first one with binding clauses that Brazil has ever signed on that aspect. The protocol follows the Bolsonaro government's line insofar as its platform is neoliberalism. Accordingly, the declared objective is the opening of trading and the attraction of foreign investment as formally set out in Act n° 13.874 dated September 20, 2019. The agreement determines the implementation of government practices designed to improve the quality of regulation through greater transparency, objective analyses, accountability and predictability with a view to facilitating international trade, investment and economic growth thereby contributing to each country's capacity to attain its public policy objectives, including those of health, security and environment policies.

The third theme concerns ant-corruption matters. It reaffirms Brazil and the United States' legislative obligations insofar as they have both multilaterally committed to a series of international conventions on corruption. The agreement expands the actions provided for in the criminal sphere by encompassing the private sector and civil society in the anticorruption agenda. It foresees procedures for selecting and training government employees in the two countries and establishes that public action and programs be carried out that foster intolerance of corruption.

Trump and Bolsonaro exhibited strong synergy in regard to the Covid-19 pandemic. In March 2020, when the World Health Organization (WHO) declared the existence of the Covid-19 pandemic, President Bolsonaro and an entourage embarked in a Brazilian Airforce aircraft for an official visit to the United States even though scheduled visits to Hungary and Poland had been cancelled alleging the high risk of Covid infection. On the agenda for discussion at the meeting of the two presidents was the formation of a strategic alliance between the two States. There were hopes that a bilateral trade and cooperation agreement in the areas of military research and development might come out of the trip. However, what most called attention were the declarations of the two presidents, disdaining the pandemic and its possible economic, social and public health impacts. In the course of the three-day trip Bolsonaro came out with declarations such as: "The coronavirus is not so great, much of what is said about the crisis is just fantasy and it is better that the price of oil should fall than go up". In the same vein, Donald Trump alleged that his government was "doing a great job" in containing the virus and predicted that in the USA the number of cases, which at the time was around 500, would go down to zero in a short time. Neither Bolsonaro nor the people that accompanied him thought there was much risk of being infected during the visit. On their return to Brazil, however, 23 members of the entourage were confirmed as being infected with Covid´19, including Augusto Heleno (Minister-Head of the Office of Institutional Security), Bento Albuquerque (Minister of Mines and Energy), Marcos Troyjo (Foreign Trade Secretary at the Ministry of the Economy) among others. So, it was quite clear that the White House was not paying attention to public health issues. The Brazilian president and his entourage were actually a threat to the USA.

Shortly after that visit, the United States began to accuse the Chinese State of having created the virus in a laboratory. Those accusations were reverberated by the Brazilian minister of foreign affairs, Ernesto Araújo and by the president's son Eduardo Bolsonaro, chairman of the Foreign Relations Committee of the Brazilian House of Representatives. That led the Chinese ambassador to Brazil to demand an apology from the Brazilian government. In the US and Brazil, the two presidents began to accuse the media and the opposition of wanting to create social panic and with no scientific backing whatever defended the use of Hydroxychloroquine in the combating, prevention and medication of Covid-19.

In short, the Trump and Bolsonaro governments joined their 'anti-Chinese communism' with their anti-science obscurantism and their anti-multilateralism (the role of the WTO) during the Covid pandemic thereby heavily underscoring the Bolsonaro government's explicit passive subordination to imperialism and its neofascist character.

### 3.2  A New Stage in Brazil-USA Relations: The Biden Government

The alliance between the Trump and Bolsonaro governments made its presence felt in the 2020 elections in the USA. Candidate at the time, Joe Biden declared that he was concerned about the environmental devastation in Brazil and that if elected he would propose international governance of the Amazon Forest and raise 20 billion dollars to that end. Thus, Bolsonaro was reluctant to recognize Biden's victory and on November 10 he even threatened the USA, saying:

> A short while ago we saw a big candidate for Head of State declare that if we don't put out the fires in Amazon, he will raise trade barriers against Brazil. So how can we face up to all that? Diplomacy alone won't do it, will it Ernesto? When the spittle runs out there must be powder, otherwise it doesn't work.
> EL PAIS, 2020

Influenced by the Brazilian ambassador in Washington, Nestor Forster, who sent a message backing the allegations of fraud in the US elections (Folha de São Paulo, 2020), the Brazilian government did not acknowledge Biden's victory and Bolsonaro even declared support for the invasion of the Capitol on July 4th. Following that the Brazilian minister of foreign affairs, Ernesto Araújo, declared that the government would not change its posture for Biden and expected mutual understanding from him (O Globo, 2021). However, once Biden had taken office the discourse of some members of the Brazilian government began to change. Former Environment Minister Ricardo Salles and Ernesto Araújo, for example, participated in a videoconference with John Kerry (American emissary for climate affairs) to intensify cooperation and dialogue on controlling deforestation and climate change (Folha de São Paulo, 2021a).

Again, after it had been clearly shown how the Brazilian government had jeopardized the delivery of vaccines from China due to the posture of figures in its upper echelons and the minister of health, the Brazilian Congress and civil servants of the ministry pressured for the removal of Araújo form his post, alleging bad administration of Brazilian foreign policy in the midst of a pandemic. That was the first sign of an adjustment of its stance in regard Biden's election on the part of the Brazilian government.

In May 2021 when he was called to testify before a parliamentary committee of inquiry regarding Covid, Ernesto Araújo denied any alignment with the USA during his period as minister, and declared that he would never accede to a treaty that was exclusively of interest to the USA. He alleged that the Trump government had offered to donate 2 million pills of Hydroxychloroquine and insisted that he had not been pressured at any time to veto the purchase of the Sputnik V vaccine even when he was confronted by an official report of the United States Department of Health and Human Services indicating that the Trump government had 'persuaded' Bolsonaro not to purchase the Russian vaccine.

The USA also made changes. Strong Trump ally, Todd Chapman, ambassador to Brazil announced that he was going to retire and leave Brazil within 30 days (Dias & Coletta, 2021). Chapman, who was an important articulator of the relations between Bolsonaro and Trump, received the Brazilian president for a lunch to commemorate US Independence Day, the 4th of July, and drew close to Bolsonaro's son Edward. With Biden's election victory, the situation changed, and Democrat advisors considered that Todd did not have a suitable profile for the new government and so the change of ambassador came from a decision in Washington. After Chapman's retirement Douglas Koneff stepped in as the USA's interim ambassador to Brazil.

Thus, it can be said that the Joe Biden presidency coupled with the COVID CPI brought about a change in Brazilian foreign policy. The new US government provoked an alteration in the Bolsonaro government's foreign policy leading to new administration of the Ministry of Foreign Affairs and the replacement of the United States' ambassador to Brazil. The fact that Carlos Alberto Franco França came to head the Ministry of Foreign Affairs did not mean there was no more subordination, instead it became less blatant, and the discourse adopted became more cautious and pragmatic especially in regard to the anti-globalist agenda. For example, the new minister expressed his interest in mobilizing Brazil's diplomatic missions for the confrontation of Covid-19 with the search for vaccines and he underscored the importance of the Brazil-China partnership for obtaining them. Apart from that, the conflict in regard to the environment is a neuralgic point in Brazil-US bilateral relations.

Joe Biden reinserted the USA in the Paris Agreement and called for a Climate Summit (an international meeting to address environmental problems in terms of global cooperation). Meanwhile, the Brazilian government continued its policy of deforestation, decreed budget cuts for the Ministry of the Environment and failed to put forward any proposals to control the fires in the Amazon Forest. That provoked a reaction from the American Congress. Senator for Hawaii, Brian Schatz, presented a draft bill designed to restrict any raw materials originating from illegally deforested areas to gain access to United States' markets and the creation of a consultative committee to monitor the supply of products to the USA (Dias, 2021b). That Bill could affect Brazilian meat exports given that part of its production is in illegally occupied lands. The conflict surfaced when an integrant of the American State Department declared that Brazil would only receive financial help from the global community, as Biden had promised during the presidential debates in 2020, if it demonstrated effective results of real action taken in 2021 to curb illegal deforestation "and not waiting five or ten years or making commitments for the year 2050" (Dias, 2021c).

The tone of Jair Bolsonaro's speech at the Climate Summit was moderate and deceitful. He promised to put Brazil "in the vanguard of facing up to global warming" (Folha de São Paulo, 2021b) and to double government spending on inspection/surveillance. The international community did not seem to be very credulous, especially since the day after the event he cut 240 million reals from the 2021 budget that were supposed to go to the Ministry of the Environment thereby clearly breaking his own promise. Those cuts affected programs for combating deforestation and for environmental protection conducted by the Brazilian Institute of the Environment and Renewable Natural Resources (IBAMA) and the Chico Mendes Institute for Biodiversity Conservation (*Instituto Chico Mendes de Biodiversidade*) (Teófilo & Medeiros, 2021).

In regard to the economy, the Biden government's new economic policy is very different from the Brazilian neoliberalism. Biden defends an increase in government investments, a fiscal reform with the taxing of great fortunes, an employment generating policy and a policy of sustainability. Brazil is experiencing a massive increase in unemployment and the return of hunger, an intensification of the de-industrialization process, the privatization of strategic sectors and a huge increase in environmental deforestation and devastation. Despite the Bolsonaro government's avowed objective of attracting foreign capital, in 2020 Brazil experienced a drop of 62% in the flow of Direct Foreign Investment (*Investimento Estrangeiro Direto*-IED). Among the other countries of the region, Brazil had one of the worst performances and received the lowest flow of investment in twenty years (approximately US$ 25 billion).[22] The balance of trade (Figure 6) retuned a positive balance of de 24 billion dollars in 2019, 43 billion dollars in 2020, and 16.1 billion dollars in 2021.

In 2020, industrialized products answered for 92% of Brazilian imports while agricultural and extractive industry products represented 45% of Brazilian exports.[23] That is indicative of a deindustrialization process in course and the return to an exportation portfolio of raw products. According to the Focus review, the estimated GDP growth was 5.18%. The General Price Index – Market (*Índice Geral de Preços – Mercado*-IGP-M) an index that measures the general prices practiced in the economy, closed at 18.33% and the IPCA which measures the price for the final consumer at 6.07%.[24] The unemployment rate registered a record high of 14.7% in the first quarter of 2021. In the same period of 2020, it was 12.2%.[25] That shows how closely dependence, subjugation and

---

22   UNCTAD data.
23   Data obtained at https://comexstat.mdic.gov.br/.
24   Banco central do Brasil. Relatório Focus. Available at: https://www.bcb.gov.br/content/focus/focus/R20210702.pdf.
25   https://valorinveste.globo.com/mercados/brasil-e-politica/noticia/2021/05/27/taxa-de-desemprego-no-19brasil-bate-recorde-no-primeiro-trimestre.ghtml https://opeb.org/2021/05/07/100-dias-de-governo-biden-as-relacoes-brasil-eua-e-a-vacinacao-contra-covid/20 https://opeb.org/2021/06/13/eua-e-brasil-a-nova-diplomacia-das-vacinas/21

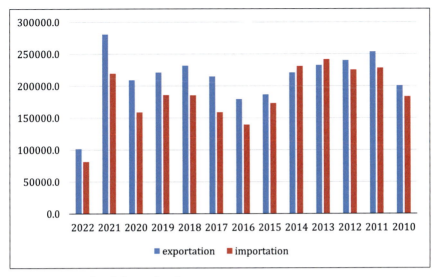

FIGURE 6   Brazilian balance of trade 2010–2022
SOURCE: MINISTRY OF THE ECONOMY (2022)

inequality interlace with Brazilian neofascism, and that foreign policy is an important facet of that process.

---

https://www.cnnbrasil.com.br/saude/2021/06/23/estados-unidos-anunciam-a-doacao-de-3-milhoes-de-doses-de-vacinas-para-o-brasil.

# References

Allison, Grahan. "Modelos conceituais e a crise dos mísseis de Cuba". in Braillard, Philippe (org.) *Teoria das Relações Internacionais*. Lisboa: Fundação Calouste Gulbenkian, 1990.

Almeida, Lúcio Flávio R. *Ideologia nacional e nacionalismo*. São Paulo: Educ, 1995.

Althusser, Louis. A querela do humanismo. in *Revista Crítica Marxista*. Nº 9, São Paulo: Ed Xamã, 1999.

Amaral, Oswaldo E. O Conceito de bloco no poder e o estudo das relações internacionais. In: *Cadernos Cemarx*, nº4. Campinas: Unicamp, IFCH: publicação do Centro de Estudos Marxistas (CEMARX) do Instituto de Filosofia e Ciências Humanas da Universidade Estadual de Campinas, 2007.

AMCHAM. Comércio entre Brasil e Estados Unidos atinge a pior marca em 11 anos, 2020. Available at: <https://www.amcham.com.br/noticias/comercio-exterior/comercio-entre-brasil-e-estados-unidos-atinge-a-pior-marca-em-11-anos-aponta-monitor-da-amcham> Consulted on: December 09, 2020.

Amin, S. *Oltre il capitalismo senile*. Milão: Punto Rosso, 2002.

Amorim, Celso. *Conversas com jovens diplomatas*. São Paulo: Benvirá, 2011.

Amorim Neto, Octavio. *De Dutra a Lula: a condução dos determinantes da política externa brasileira*. Rio de Janeiro: Elsevier, 2011.

Araújo, Ernesto Henrique Fraga. Trump e o Ocidente. In: *Cadernos de Política Exterior*. Brasília: FUNAG, Ano III, nº6, 2º semestre de 2017.

Ardissone, Carlos Maurício Pires e Albuquerque. *Percepções e ações do empresariado industrial brasileiro no contexto do Mercosul*. Dissertação de mestrado apresenta ao Instituto de Pesquisa em Relações Internacionais da PUC-RJ, Rio de Janeiro, 1999.

Azevedo, Débora Bithiah. *Acordos para promoção e proteção recíproca de investimentos assinados pelo Brasil*. Biblioteca Digital da Câmara dos Deputados, Estudo Maio, 2001.

Azevêdo, Roberto Carvalho. Reflexões sobre o contencioso do algodão entre o Brasil e os Estados Unidos; in. *Política Externa*, vol 19, nº2. São Paulo: Editora Paz e terra, 2010.

Azzi, Diego. Subordinação pela adesão: pleito do Brasil a membro pleno da OCDE. in Berringer, T. Schutte, G. Maringoni, G. (orgs). *As bases da política externa bolsonarista*. Santo Andre: Editora Ufabc, 2020.

Baggio, Kátia. Gerab. Conexões ultraliberais nas Américas: o think tank norte-americano Atlas Network e suas vinculações com organizações latino-americanas. Anais do XII Encontro Internacional da ANPHLAC. 2016.

Bandeira, Luis Alberto Muniz. *As relações perigosas: Brasil-Estados Unidos (Collor a Lula, 1990–2004)*. Rio de Janeiro: Editora Civilização Brasileira, 2004.

Bandeira, Luis Alberto Muniz. O Brasil e a América do Sul. in *Relações Internacionais do Brasil: temas e agendas*. São Paulo: Saraiva, 2006.

Barros, Larrisa. *Golpes de Estado, política externa e a classe média no Brasil: apontamentos sobre 2016*. Trabalho de Conclusão de Curso do Bacharelado de Relações Internacionais da UFABC, 2018.

Bastos, Pedro Paulo Zaluth. A economia política da integração da América do Sul no mundo pós-crise. Observatório da economia global. Textos avulsos, nº10, abril 2012a.

Bastos, Pedro Paulo Zaluth. A economia política do novo desenvolvimentismo e do social-desenvolvimentismo. In: *Economia e Sociedade*, Campinas, vol. 21, nº especial, 2012b.

Bastos, Pedro Paulo Zaluth & Hiratuka, Célio. A política externa econômica do governo Dilma: comércio, cooperação e dependência. *Texto para Discussão* nº360, Instituto de Economia da Unicamp, 2017.

Becard, Danielly Silva Ramos. O que esperar das relações Brasil-China. in *Revista de Sociologia e Política*, Curitiba, Vol. 19, número suplementar, novembro 2011, pp. 31–44.

Berringer, Tatiana. A tese do imperialismo brasileiro em questão. in *Crítica Marxista*, nº36. São Paulo: Editora Unesp, 2013.

Berringer, Tatiana. *A burguesia brasileira e a política externa nos governos FHC e Lula*. Curitiba: Editora Appris, 2015.

Berringer, Tatiana. A burguesia interna brasileira e a integração regional da América do Sul (1991–2016). *OIKOS* (Rio de Janeiro), v. 16, p. 15–29, 2017.

Berringer, Tatiana. The Neodevelopmentalist Front and MERCOSUR under the PT Governments: The Rise and Fall of Multidimensional Regionalism. *Latin American Perspectives*, v. 3, p. 111–127, 2021.

Berringer, Tatiana & Belasques, B. As relações Brasil-China nos governos Lula e Dilma. in *Carta Internacional*, v.15, p.151–173, 2020.

Berringer, Tatiana & Forlini, Luana. Crise oolítica e Mudança na política externa no Governo Temer: contradições no seio da burguesia interna brasileira. in *Revista Conjuntura Austral: Journal of Global South*, Porto Alegre, p.5–19, 2018.

Bezerra, Vicente Amaral. *Participação de grupos empresariais em negociações comerciais: o caso das negociações entre Mercosul e União Europeia (2001–2004)*. Dissertação de mestrado apresentada ao Centro de Pesquisa e Pós-Graduação sobre as Américas. Brasília, UNB, 2008.

Bianchi, Alvaro. *Um ministério dos industriais: A Federação das Indústrias do Estado de São Paulo na crise das décadas de 1980 e 1990*. Campinas: Editora da Unicamp, 2010.

Bobbio, Norberto. Existe uma doutrina marxista do Estado? In: Bobbio, Norberto et al. *O Marxismo e o Estado*. Rio de Janeiro: Graal, 1979.

Bobbio, Norberto. As relações internacionais e o marxismo. in *Ensaios escolhidos*. São Paulo: C. H. Cardim, 1988. p.109–126.

Boito Jr., Armando. *Política neoliberal e sindicalismo no Brasil*. São Paulo: Editora Xamã, 1999.

Boito Jr., Armando. *Estado, política e classes sociais*. São Paulo: Editora Unesp, 2007.

Boito Jr., Armando. Governos Lula: a nova burguesia nacional no poder. IN Boito Jr., Armando & Galvão, Andréia. *Política e classes sociais no Brasil nos anos 2000*. São Paulo: Editora Alameda, 2012.

Boito Jr., Armando. A nova burguesia nacional no poder. In Boito Jr., Armando; Galvão, Andréia (orgs.). *Política e classes sociais no Brasil dos anos 2000*. São Paulo: Alameda Editorial, pp. 69–106, 2012.

Boito Jr., Armando. A crise política do neodesenvolvimentismo e a instabilidade política da democracia. *Crítica Marxista*, nº42, 2016.

Boito Jr., Armando. *Reforma e Crise Política no Brasil: os Conflitos de Classe nos Governos do PT. 1ª edição*. São Paulo: Editora UNICAMP/Editora UNESP, 2018.

Boito Jr., Armando. O caminho brasileiro para o fascismo. *Caderno CRH (UFBA)*, v. 34, 2021.

Boito Jr., Armando & Marcellino, Paula. Decline in Unionism? An Analysis of the New Wave of Strikes in Brazil. *Latin American Perspectives*, Issue. 178, Vol. 38, No. 5, September 2011.

Boito Jr., Armando & Rojas, Gonzalo. *Estado e burguesia no Brasil e na Argentina: os governos Lula da Silva e Nestor Kirschner*. Comunicação apresentada no VI Encontro da ABCP, 2008.

Bonomo, Diego Zancan. *A mobilização empresarial para a Tríplice Negociação Comercial: ALCA, Mercosul-União Europeia e OMC (1994–2004)*. Dissertação de mestrado apresentada ao Programa de Pós-graduação em Relações Internacionais San Tiago Dantas (PUC-Sp), São Paulo, 2006.

Botão, Gustavo. A burguesia interna e a reforma da Tarifa Externa Comum do Mercosul. (Mimeo) 2021.

Botto, Mercedes. La transnacionalizacion del capital y las nuevas formas de activismo político. La experiencia de las centrales del Cono Sur. in *Pensamiento Proprio*, nº40, ano 19. Buenos Aires, CRIES, 2014.

Bracey, Djuan. O Brasil e as operações de manutenção de paz da ONU: Timor Leste e Haiti. in *Contexto Internacional*, vol 33, nº2, jul/dez 2011.

Bresser-Pereira, Luis Carlos. O novo desenvolvimentismo e a ortodoxia convencional. In: *São Paulo em Perspectiva*, v. 20, nº3, 2006.

Bresser-Pereira, Luis Carlos. A taxa de câmbio no centro da teoria do desenvolvimento. in *Estudos avançados*. Vol. 26, nº75, 2012.

Bugiato, Caio. *O papel do BNDES na expansão dos negócios da burguesia interna brasileira*. Caderno de resumo das comunicações – UFPR: Curitiba. VIII Workshop empresas, empresários e sociedade, 2012.

Bullow, Marisa Von & Carvalho, Priscila Delgado de. Entre o nacional e o transnacional: o caso das organizações da agricultura familiar no Mercosul. in Gohn, Maria da Glória & Bringel, Breno M. *Movimentos sociais na era global*. 2ª edição. Petrópolis: Editora Vozes, 2014.

Calixtre, André & Barros, Pedro da Silva. Além da circunstância: caminhos da integração sul-americana, do Mercosul à Unasul. in *Brasil em desenvolvimento*. Parte III, IPEA, 2010.

Callinicos, Alex. Does capitalism need a state system? *Cambridge review of international affairs*. Volume 20, n° 4, dez/2007.

Cardoso, Fernando Henrique & Faletto, Enzo. *Dependência e desenvolvimento na América Latina: ensaio de interpretação sociológica*. 6ª edição. Rio de Janeiro: Zahar Editores, 1981.

Carr, E. H. *Vinte anos de crise*: uma introdução aos estudos de relações internacionais. Brasília: Editora da Universidade de Brasília e IPRI, 2001.

Carvalho, Clarissa. *O protagonismo do BNDES no financiamento da infra-estrutura sul-americana durante o governo Lula: interface entre os interesses domésticos e a política externa*. I Seminário Nacional de Pós-graduação em Relações Internacionais promovido pela Associação Brasileira de Relações Internacionais, Brasília, 2012.

Carvalho, Laura. *Valsa brasileira: do boom ao caos econômico*. São Paulo: Todavia, 2018.

Carvalho, Maria Izabel. Estruturas domésticas e grupos de interesse: a formação da posição brasileira para Seattle. In: *Contexto Internacional*, Rio de Janeiro, vol 25, n°2, 2003, pp 363–401.

Carvalho, Maria Izabel. Condicionantes internacionais e domésticos: O Brasil e o G-20 nas negociações agrícolas da Rodada Doha. *Dados – Revista de Ciências Sociais*, vol 53, n°2, 2010, pp. 405–455.

Casarões, Guilherme Stolle Paixão. O papel do Itamaraty na definição da política externa brasileira do governo Collor de Mello. *Revista Brasileira de Política Internacional*, vol 55, n°1, 2012, pp. 135–153.

Casarões, Guilherme Stolle Paixão. *As três camadas da política externa do governo Collor: poder, legitimidade e dissonância*. Dissertação (Mestrado em Relações Internacionais) Programa San Tiago Dantas, Unicamp, 2011.

Cason, Jefrey & Power, Timothy. Presidencailizacion, pluralization and the rollback of Itamaraty: explaining change in Brazilian foreign policy making in Cardoso-Lula era. In: *International Political Science Review*, Vol 30, n°2, 2009, pp 117–140.

Cavalcante, Sávio. Estado, capital estrangeiro e burguesia interna no setor de telecomunicações nos governos FHC e Lula. in Boito Jr., Armando & Galvão, Andréia. *Política e classes sociais no Brasil nos anos 2000*. São Paulo: Editora Alameda, 2012.

Cavalcante, Sávio & Arias, Santiane. A divisão da classe média na crise política brasileira (2013–2016). in Bouffartigue, Paul; Boito, Armando; Galvão, Andréia; Béroud, Sophie. *O Brasil e a França na mundialização neoliberal: mudanças políticas e contestações sociais*. São Paulo: Alameda, 2019.

CEPAL. Regionalismo aberto na América Latina e no Caribe. In Bielchowisky, Ricardo (org.). *Cinquenta anos de pensamento da CEPAL*. Vol 2. Rio de Janeiro: Editora Record, pp. 937–958, 2000.

CEPAL. Foreign Direct Investment in Latin America and the Caribbean, *Boletim Informativo*, 2011.

Cervo, Amado Luiz & Bueno, Clodoaldo. *História da política exterior do Brasil*. 3ªedição. Brasília: Editora UnB, 2008.

Cervo, Amado Luiz & Lessa, Antônio Carlos. O declínio: inserção internacional do Brasil (2011–2014). *Rev. Bras. Polít. Int*, Brasília, v. 57, n. 2, p. 133–151, Dez, 2014.

Codas, Gustavo. Retalhos para uma história dos movimentos contra a globalização neoliberal. in Frati, Mila (org.) *Curso de formação em política internacional*. – São Paulo: Editora Fundação Perseu Abramo, 2007.

Cornetet, João Marcelo Conte. A Política Externa De Dilma Rousseff: Contenção Na Continuidade. *Conjuntura Austral*, Porto Alegre, v. 5, n. 24, p.111–150, 2014.

Costa, Hermes Augusto. O sindicalismo, a política internacional e a CUT. *Lua Nova*, CEDEC, v. 64, p. 129–152, 2005.

Cruz, Sebastião C. Velasco. *Estado e economia em tempo de crise – política industrial e transição política no Brasil nos anos 80*. Rio de Janeiro: Relume Dumará; Campinas: Editora Universidade de Campinas, 1997.

Cruz, Sebastião C. Velasco. Ideias do poder: dependência e globalização em F. H. Cardoso. *Estudos avançados*, nº13, vol. 37, 1999.

Cruz, Sebastião C. Velasco. Opções estratégicas. O papel do Brasil no sistema internacional. Lua Nova. Revista de Cultura e Política, v. 53, n.1, p. 135–158, 2001.

Cruz, Sebastião C. Velasco. Novo rumo à política externa. in *Revista Teoria e Debate*. Fundação Perseu Abramo. Nº55, set/ou/Nov/2003.

Cruz, Sebastião C. Velasco. *O Brasil no mundo: ensaios de análise política e prospectiva*. São Paulo: Editora Unesp – Programa San Tiago Dantas de Pós-graduação em Relações Internacionais, 2010.

Cruz, Sebastião C. Velasco. A política externa e a sucessão. in *A nova política externa brasileira (2003–2013): Balanço e perspectivas*. São Paulo: Instituto de Estudos Contemporâneos e Cooperação Internacional, 2013.

Cruz, Sebastião & Silva, Érica. *A atuação do empresariado brasileiro no governo Lula: o posicionamento da CNI sobre questões internacionais*. Dissertação de mestrado apresentada ao Departamento de Ciência Política da USP, São Paulo, 2011.

Dallari, Pedro. *Constituição e Relações Exteriores do Brasil*. São Paulo: Editora Saraiva, 1994.

Danese, S. Diplomacia presidencial. Rio de Janeiro: Topbooks, 1999.

Diniz, Eli & Boschi, Renato R. Lideranças empresariais e problemas da estratégia liberal no Brasil. Trabalho apresentado no seminário internacional "Estratégias liberais de refundação, dilemas contemporâneos do desenvolvimento", IUPERJ/CLACSO/ISA, Rio de Janeiro, 19–21 de agosto de 1992. Apresentado também no XVI Encontro Anual da ANPOCS, em Caxambu (MG),de 20 a 23 outubro de 1992.

Diniz, Eli. Empresariado industrial, representação de interesses e ação política: trajetória histórica e novas configurações. *Política e Sociedade*. Vol 9, n°17, Outubro, 2010. Pp.101–139.

Dumenil, Gerard; Levy, Dominique. O imperialismo na era neoliberal. *Revista Crítica Marxista*, n° 18. Rio de Janeiro: Revan, p.11–36, 2004.

Farias, Francisco. *Estado e classes dominantes no Brasil (1930–1964)*. Tese (doutorado em Ciência Política), Unicamp, 2010.

Felício, João Antônio. Uma visão a partir do movimento sindical. in Jakobsen, Kjeld (org). *A nova política externa*. São Paulo: Fundação Perseu Abramo, 2010.

Ferraz, Kayque. Burguesias, Estado e regionalismo: uma análise do Mercosul. Dissertação de mestrado defendida no Programa de Relações Internacionais da UFABC, 2021.

Figueira, Ariane Roder. Rupturas e continuidades no padrão organizacional e decisório do Ministério das Relações Exteriores. *Revista Brasileira de Política Internacional*. n°53, 2010.

Fine, Ben & Saad, Alfredo. (2017) "Thirteen Things You Need to Know About Neoliberalism". *Critical Sociology*, Volume: 43 issue: 4–5, page(s): 685–706.

Fiori, José Luís. A globalização e a novíssima dependência. *Em busca do dissenso perdido: ensaios críticos sobre a festejada crítica do Estado*. Rio de Janeiro, Insight, 1995.

Fiori, José Luis. *Brasil e América do Sul: o desafio da inserção internacional soberana*. Brasília, DF: CEPAL. Escritório no Brasil/IPEA, 2011.

Fonseca Jr., Gerson. *A legitimidade e outras questões internacionais*. Rio de Janeiro, paz e Terra, 1998.

Fontes, Virgínia. *O Brasil e o capital-imperialismo: teoria e história*. Rio de Janeiro: Escola Politécnica de Saúde de São Joaquim Venâncio, Universidade Federal do Rio de Janeiro, 2010.

Fuser, Igor. Integração energética na América do Sul: um debate político. in *Anuário da Integração de América Latina y el gran Caribe*, 2010.

Fuser, Igor. *Conflitos e contratos — A Petrobrás, o nacionalismo boliviano e a interdependência do gás natural (2002–2010)*. Tese de doutorado apresentada ao Departamento de Ciência Política da USP, 2011.

Galvão, Andreia. A reconfiguração do movimento sindical nos governos Lula. in Boito Jr., Armando & Galvão, Andréia. *Política e classes sociais no Brasil nos anos 2000*. São Paulo: Editora Alameda, 2012.

Goldemberg, José. O TNP e o protocolo adicional. in *Política Externa*. Editora Paz e Terra, São Paulo, 2010.

Gomes, Julia. *Indústria da Construção naval e o neoliberalismo no Brasil: primeiras aproximações*. Mimeo. 2013.

Gorender, Jacob. A burguesia brasileira. São Paulo: Editora brasiliense, 1981.

Gramsci, Antônio. *Cadernos do Cárcere*: Maquiavel – Notas sobre o Estado e a política. Vol 3. Tradução: Luís Sérgio Henriques, Marco Aurélio Nogueira e Carlos Nelson Coutinho. Rio de Janeiro: Editora Civilização Brasileira, 2000.

Granato, Leonardo. *Brasil, Argentina e os rumos da integração: O Mercosul e a Unasul*. Curitiba: Appris, 2015.

Halliday, Fred. *Rethinking International Relations*. London: Macmillan. 1994.

Hermann, Charles. Changing course: When governments choose to redirect foreign policy. *International Studies Quartely*, n°32, 1990.

Herz, Monica. Abordagem cognitiva. in *Contexto Internacional*. Rio de Janeiro: PUC-RJ, v. 16, Jan 1994.

Hirata, Francine & Oliveira, Nathália. Os movimento sem-teto de São Paulo no contexto neoliberal. in Boito Jr., Armando & Galvão, Andréia. *Política e classes sociais no Brasil nos anos 2000*. São Paulo: Editora Alameda, 2012.

Hiratuka, Célio (orgs). *Internacionalização e desenvolvimento da indústria no Brasil*. São Paulo, Editora Unesp, 2003.

Hirst, Monica & Pinheiro, Letícia. A política externa do Brasil em dois tempos. *Revista Brasileira de Política Internacional*, n°38, 1995.

Hirst, Monica; Lima, Maria Regina de Soares & Pinheiro, Letícia. *A política externa brasileira em tempos de novos horizontes e desafios*. Análise de Conjuntura, Observatório Político Sul-americano, n°12, dez 2010.

Honório, Karen dos Santos. *O significado da Iniciativa para a Integração da Infraestrutura Regional Sul-americana (IIRSA) no regionalismo sul-americano (2000-2012): um estudo sobre a iniciativa e a participação do Brasil*. Dissertação (mestrado pelo Programa de Pós-graduação em Relações Internacionais) San Tiago Dantas, 2013.

Hudson, Valerie & Vore, Chistopher S. Foreign policy analysis yesterday, today and tomorrow. in *Mershon International Studies Review*, Vol 39, n°2, 1995.

Iglesias, Wagner. O empresariado do agronegócio no Brasil: ação coletiva e formas de atuação política — as batalhas do açúcar e do algodão na OMC. Revista de Sociologia e Política, Curitiba, n°28, 2007.

Iglesias, Rodrigo & Costa, Katarina. *O investimento direto brasileiro na África*. CINDES, Rio de Janeiro, 2011.

IPEA (2011a). *Comunicados do IPEA n°86* – Relações comerciais e de investimentos do Brasil com os demais países do BRICS.

IPEA (2011b). *Comunicados do IPEA n°121* – As relações do Mercosul com Estados Unidos e China ante o deslocamento do centro dinâmico mundial.

Jakobsen, Kjeld & Martins, Renato. *ALCA: quem ganha e quem perde com o livre comércio das Américas*. 2ªed. São Paulo: Fundação Perseu Abramo, 2004.

Kaldor, Nicholas. 1966. Causes of the Slow Rate of Economic Growth in the United Kingdom. IN: Kaldor, N., *Further Essays on Economic Theory*. New York: Holmes & Meier.

Kautsky, Karl. O imperialismo e a guerra. *Revista História e luta de classes*. Ano 4, edição, nº5, Abril 2008.

Keohane, Robert O & Nye, Joseph Jr. *Transnational Relations and world politics*. 2º edição. Massachusetts: Harvard University Press, 1973.

Kocher, Bernardo. Os Brics no governo Lula. in Freixo, Adriano et al (orgs). *Política externa brasileira na era Lula*. Rio de Janeiro: Apicuri, 2011.

Kovarick, Lucio. 1975. *Capitalismo e marginalidade na América Latina*. Rio de Janeiro: Paz e Terra.

Lenin, Vladimir I. *Imperialism: the highest stage of capitalism*. Australia, Resistance Books 1999.

Lima, Marina Regina Soares de. *Ejes analíticos y conflicto de paradigmas e la política exterior brasileña*. América Latina/Internacional, Volumen 1, nº2. Argentina: Flacso, 1994.

Lima, Marina Regina Soares de. Autonomia, não-indiferença e pragmatismo: vetores conceituais da política exterior. *Revista Brasileira de Comércio Exterior*. Rio: Funcex, 2006.

Lima, Marina Regina Soares de. A agência da política externa brasileira: uma análise preliminar. In: Desiderá Neto, W; Florencio, S.B.L.; Ramazini Jr., H.; Silva Filho, E.B. (org.). *Política Externa Brasileira em debate: dimensões e estratégias de inserção no pós-crise de 2008*. Brasília: FUNAG, IPEA, 2018.

Lima, Marina Regina Soares de & Hirst, Mônica. Brazil as an intermediate state and regional power: action, choice and responsabilities. in *International Affairs*, vol. 82, nº1, 2006, pp. 21–40.

Linklater, Andrew. *Beyond realism and marxism*: critical theory and international relations. London: McMillan Press, 2001b.

Lohnbauer, Cristian. A inserção internacional do Brasil e papel das associações de empresas exportadoras. in *Política Externa*, vol. 19, nº2, 2010, pp.69–80.

Luce, Mathias. *O subimperialismo brasileiro revisitado: a política de integração regional do governo Lula*. (2003–2007). 136f. Dissertação (Mestrado em Relações Internacionais)-Instituto de Filosofia e Ciências Humanas, Universidade Federal do Rio Grande do Sul, Porto Alegre, 2007.

Marconi, N.; Reis, C. F. B.; Araujo, E. C. 2016. Manufacturing and economic development: The actuality of Kaldor's first and second laws. *Structural Change and Economic Dynamics*, v. 37, p. 75, 2016.

Maringoni, Gilberto; Schutte, Giorgio Romano & Berron, Gonzalo. *2003-2013: uma nova política externa*. Tubarão: Editora Copiart, 2014.

Marini, Ruy Mauro. *Subdesarollo e revolución*. México, 1974.

Marini, Ruy Mauro. "La acumulación capitalista mundial y el subimperialismo". *Cuadernos Políticos* nº12, México, 1977.

Martuscelli, Danilo. A burguesia mundial em questão. In: *Revista Crítica Marxista*, nº30, 2010.

Martuscelli, Danilo. A transição neoliberal para o neoliberalismo e a crise do Governo Collor. in Boito Jr., Armando & Galvão, Andréia (orgs). *Política e classes sociais no Brasil nos anos 2000*. São Paulo: Editora Alameda 2012.

Mathias, Meire. Sob o prisma dos interesses: a política externa brasileira e a Confederação Nacional da Indústria. Tese de doutorado apresentada ao Departamento de Ciência Política da Unicamp, Campinas, 2011.

Mello, Flávia de Campos. *Regionalismo e inserção internacional: continuidade e transformação da política externa brasileira nos anos 90*. Tese (Doutorado em Ciência Política) USP, 2000.

Mello, Flávia de Campos. *O Brasil e o multilateralismo contemporâneo*. Texto para discussão 1628. IPEA, 2011.

Mello, Flávia de Campos & Silva, Leonardo. Trabalhadores do Mercosul: uni-vos. A construção de uma voz coletiva contra-hegemônica: quando o dissenso é "por-se de acordo com, a propósito". in Santos, Boaventura de Souza (org.). *Trabalhar o mundo: os caminhos do novo internacionalismo operário*. Rio de Janeiro: Civilização Brasileira, 2005.

Melo, Fátima. Uma visão a partir do movimento social. in Jakobsen, Kjeld (org). *A nova política externa*. São Paulo: Fundação Perseu Abramo, 2010.

Menezes, Roberto G. A política externa brasileiras sob o signo do neoliberalismo. Dissertação (Mestrado em Ciência Política), Unicamp, 2006.

Mesquita, Lucas. *Itamaraty, partidos políticos e política externa brasileira: a institucionalização de projetos partidários nos governos FHC e Lula*. Dissertação de mestrado apresentada ao Departamento de Ciência Política da Unicamp, 2013.

Messari, Nizar. O Brasil e o mundo árabe. in Altemani, Henrique & Lessa, Antônio Carlos (org). *Relações Internacionais do Brasil: temas e agendas*. São Paulo: Saraiva, 2006.

Miliband, Ralph. *O Estado na sociedade capitalista*. Rio de Janeiro: Zahar, 1972.

Miyamoto, Shiguenoli. A política externa do governo Lula: aspirações e dificuldades. *Revista Ideias*, n°3, Campinas, 2°semestre 2011.

Morgenthau, Hans. *Politic among nations: the struggle for power and peace*. New York: Alfred A. Knopf, 1948.

Netto, Michel Nicolau; Chaguri, Mariana Miggiolaro; Cavalcante, Sávio Machado. The struggle for the nation: the rise of the far right and the war on diversity in Brazil. In: *Conservatism and Authoritarianism in Brazil: Histories, Politics, and Cultures*, Columbia University, Fevereiro, 2020.

Novoa, L F. O Brasil e seu "desdobramento": o papel central do BNDES na expansão das empresas transnacionais brasileiras na América do Sul. In: *Transnacionais Brasileiras: um debate necessário*. São Paulo: Expressão Popular, 2009.

Nun, José. 2001. *Marginalidad y exclusión social*. México, Fondo de Cultura Economica.

Oliveira, Amâncio Jorge. O governo do PT e a Alca: política externa e pragmatismo. *Estudos avançados*, 17, 48, 2003.

Oliveira, Amâncio Jorge & Pfeifer, Alberto. *O empresariado e a política exterior do Brasil*. in Altemani, Henrique & Lessa, Antônio Carlos (org). *Relações Internacionais do Brasil: temas e agendas*. São Paulo: Saraiva, 2006.

Oliveira, Henrique Altemani. Brasil e China: uma nova aliança não escrita? in *Revista Brasileira de Política Internacional*, 53 (2), 2010 pp.88–106.

Onuki, Janina. O Brasil e a construção do Mercosul. In: *Relações Internacionais do Brasil: temas e agendas*. São Paulo: Saraiva, 2006.

Onuki, Janina & Oliveira, Amâncio Jorge. Grupos de pressão e a política comercial brasileira: a atuação na arena legislativa. Núcleo de Estudos sobre o Congresso: Papéis Legislativos, n°8, dez, 2007.

Orair, Rodrigo; Gobetti, Sergio. 2017. Brazilian fiscal policy in perspective: from expansion to austerity. Working paper n. 160 Institute for Applied Economic Research (IPEA) and International Policy Centre for Inclusive Growth (IPC-IG), Brasilia, Agosto.

Pecequillo, Cristina. A política externa do Brasil no século XXI: os eixos combinados de cooperação horizontal e vertical. In: *Revista Brasileira de Política Internacional*, n°51, 2008.

Pecequillo, Cristina. As relações Brasil-Estados Unidos no governo Dilma Rousseff. *Revista Conjuntura Austral*, UFRGS, 2014.

Pereira, Celso de Tarso; Costa, Valéria Mendes & Araujo, Leandro Rocha. 100 casos na OMC: a experiência brasileira em solução de controvérsias. in *Política Externa*, Vol.20, n°4, 2012.

Pimenta, José Luiz. O *Brasil e o regime internacional de investimentos*. Mimeo. 2010.

Pimenta, José Luiz. *Coalizões internacionais e o G-20: aspectos da liderança brasileira na Rodada Doha de Desenvolvimento da OMC*. Dissertação (Mestrado Relações Internacionais), USP, 2012.

Pinheiro, Letícia. Traídos pelo desejo: um ensaio sobre a teoria e a prática da política externa brasileira contemporânea. In: *Contexto Internacional*, vol. 22, n °2, 2000.

Pinto, Eduardo Costa. *Bloco no poder e governo Lula: grupos econômicos, política econômica e novo eixo sino-americano*. Tese (Doutorado em Economia) Universidade Federal do Rio de Janeiro, 2010.

Poulantzas, Nicos. The Problem of the capitalist State. in *New Left Review*, n°58, Vol, 1, 1969.

Poulantzas, Nicos. *Political power and Social class*. London: Verso, 1975.

Poulantzas, Nicos. *The crises of dictatorships: Portugal, Greece, Spain*. London: Humanities Press 1976.

Poulantzas, Nicos. *Classes in Contemporary Capitalism*. London: Verso, 1978.

Poulantzas, Nicos. *Fascismo e Ditadura: a III Internacional face ao fascismo*. Florianópolis: Editora Enunciado, 2020.

Pul, Kess van der. *Transnational class formation and states forms*. in Gill & Mittelman (editors), Innovation and transformation in International Studies. United Kingdom: Cambridge University Press, 1997.

Putnam, Robert D. Diplomacy and Domestic Politics: The Logic of Two-Level Games. in *International Organization*, Vol. 42, No. 3. (Summer, 1988), pp. 427–460.

Ramanzini Jr., Haroldo. O Brasil e as negociações do sistema Gatt/OMC: uma análise da Rodada Uruguai e Rodada Doha. Tese (Doutorado em Ciência Política), USP, 2012.

Ramanzini Jr., Haroldo & Farias, Rogério de Souza. Missão impossível: Mercosul, participação social e politica externa no Brasil. in *Pensamiento Proprio*, n°40, ano 19. Buenos Aires, CRIES, 2014.

Reis, Cristina Fróes de Borja Reis. 2018. *O que Significa Melhorar a Inserção do Brasil nas Cadeias Globais de Valor?* Radar, n. 58, IPEA, abril.

Ribeiro, Santiane Arias.Tese de doutoramento. O perfil de classe média do movimento altermundialista: o caso da ATTAC. Campinas, SP, 2011.

Ricupero, Rubens. Charles de Gaulle. in *Novos Estudos*. São Paulo: CEBRAP, n°87, julho 2010.

Robinson, Willian. Debate on the New Global Capitalism: Transnational Capitalist Class, Transnational State Apparatuses, and Global Crisis, *International Critical Thought*, 2017, 7:2, 171–189.

Rosenberg, Justin. *The empire of civil society: a critique of the realist theory of international relations*. New York/London: Verso, 2001.

Ruiz, Briceño. La UNASUR: Continum o nuevo inicio del regionalismo sudamericano? in *Anuário da Integração de América Latina y el gran Caribe*, 2010.

Sabbatini, Rodrigo. Mercosul e a internacionalização comercial do Brasil in Laplane, Mariano; Coutinho, Luciano & Hiratuka, Célio (orgs). *Internacionalização e desenvolvimento da indústria no Brasil*. São Paulo, Editora Unesp, 2003.

Saes, Décio Azevedo Marques de. A formação do Estado burguês no Brasil. Rio de Janeiro: Paz e terra, 1985a.

Saes, Décio Azevedo Marques de. Classe média e sistema político no Brasil. São Paulo: T. A Queiroz, 1985b

Saes, Décio Azevedo Marques de. *República do Capital*. Boitempo Editoral: São Paulo, 2001.

Saes, Décio Azevedo Marques de. Modelos políticos latino-americanos na nova fase de dependência. in Francis, Nogueira; Rizzoto, Maria. *Políticas sociais e desenvolvimento: América Latina e Brasil*. 1ªedição. São Paulo: Editora Xamã, 2007, Vol 1, pp. 155–172.

Sallum Jr., Brasílio. Hegemonia liberal, desenvolvimentismo e populismo. *Nueva Sociedad*, N°217, septiembre-octubre, 2008.

Sallum Jr., Brasílio. Governo Collor: o reformismo neoliberal e a nova orientação da política externa brasileira. In: *Dados – Revista de Ciências Sociais*, Rio de Janeiro, n°2, 2011.

Santana, Helton. Os grupos de interesse e a ALCA. *Contexto Internacional*. Rio de Janeiro: PUC-RJ, n°23, vol 1, Jan-Jun 2001.

Saraiva, José Sombra. The new Africa and Brazil in Lula era: the rebirth of brazilian atlantic policy. in *Revista Brasileira de Política Internacional*. Vol 53. Edição Especial, 2010.

Saraiva, Miriam Gomes. A América do Sul na política externa do governo Lula: ideias e mudanças. in Freixo, Adriano et al.(orgs). *A política externa brasileira na era Lula*. Rio de Janeiro: Apicuri, 2011.

Sarti, Fernando. Crises e perspectivas do Mercosul. in Laplane, Mariano; Coutinho, Luciano & Hiratuka, Célio (orgs). *Internacionalização e desenvolvimento da indústria no Brasil*. São Paulo, Editora UNESP, 2003.

Sarti, Fernando & Laplane, Mariano. O investimento direto estrangeiro e a internacionalização da economia brasileira nos anos 90. in Laplane, Mariano; Coutinho, Luciano & Hiratuka, Célio (orgs). *Internacionalização e desenvolvimento da indústria no Brasil*. São Paulo, Editora UNESP, 2003.

Schutte, Giorgio Romano. *Neodesenvolvimentismo e a busca de uma nova inserção internacional*. 1732 Texto para discussão. Rio de Janeiro: IPEA, Abril de 2012.

Schutte, Giorgio Romano. Acordo União Europeia-Mercosul: falsas promessas de crescimento e sustentabilidade. in Berringer, T. Schutte, G. Maringoni, G. (orgs). *As bases da política externa bolsonarista*. Santo Andre: Editora UFABC, 2020a.

Schutte, Giorgio Romano. *Oásis para o capital: solo fértil para a "corrida de ouro". A dinâmica dos investimentos produtivos chineses*. Curitiba: Editora Appris, 2020b.

Secco, Lincoln. *História do PT: 1978–2010*. Cotia, SP: Ateliê Editorial, 2011.

Serbin, Andrés. Atuando sozinho? Governos, sociedade civil e regionalismo na América do Sul. *Lua Nova*, São Paulo: CEDEC, N°90, 2013, pp. 297–327.

Silva, André Luiz Reis. O Brasil diante da globalização: a política externa do governo Fernando Henrique Cardoso (1995–2002). In: *Carta Internacional*, Associação Brasileira de Relações Internacionais, Vol 7, n°1, Jun 2012. Pp. 20–34.

Silva, Suylan de Almeida. *"Ganhamos a batalha, mas não a guerra": a visão da Campanha Nacional contra a Alca sobre a não assinatura do Acordo*. Tese de doutorado, Departamento de Sociologia da Universidade de Brasília, 2008.

Singer, André. *Os sentidos do lulismo*. São Paulo: Companhia das Letras, 2012.

Singer, André. *O lulismo em crise: um quebra-cabeça do período Dilma (2011–2016)*. São Paulo: Cia das letras, 2018.

Soares, Arthur Murta. Paraguai 2012: o papel do Brasil e a ação da Unasul. Dissertação (Mestrado em San Tiago Dantas) – Universidade Estadual Paulista, 2016.

Soares, Samuel Alves. A defesa na política externa da era Lula: uma defesa elusiva a uma liderança proclamada. in Freixo, Adriano et al. (orgs). *A política externa na era Lula*. Rio de Janeiro: Ed. Apucuri, 2011.

Thorstensen, Vera. *O Brasil frente a um trile desafio: as negociações simultâneas da OMC, da ALCA e do acordo CE/MERCOSUL*. IEEI: Lisboa, 2001.

Tota, Antonio Pedro. *O Imperialismo Sedutor: A Americanização do Brasil na época da Segunda Guerra*. São Paulo: Companhia das Letras, 2000.

Tude, João Martins & Milani, Carlos Sanchez. A política externa brasileira em relação ao Fundo Monetário Internacional durante o governo Lula. in *Revista Brasileira de Política Internacional*, vol 56, nº1, 2013.

Vadell, Javier; Lamas, Bárbara & Ribeiro, Daniela. Integração e desenvolvimento no Mercosul: divergências e convergências nas políticas econômicas nos governos Lula e Kirchner. *Revista Sociologia e Política*, Curitiba, v. 17, n. 33, p. 39–54, jun. 2009.

Valdez, Robinson. 2011. *A internacionalização do BNDES no governo Lula*. Dissertação (Mestrado em Relações Internacionais) – Instituto de Filosofia e Ciências Humanas, Universidade Federal do Rio Grande do Sul, Porto Alegre.

Valle, André. Capital financeiro, frações de classe e a crise política de 2015–16. In: A Burguesia brasileira em ação: de Lula a Bolsonaro / organização André Flores Penha Valle, Pedro Felipe Narciso.1. ed. Florianópolis, SC: Enunciado Publicações, 2021.

Vasconcelos, Jonnas. *A agenda regulatória dos BRICS*. Belo Horizonte, Editora Dialética, 2020.

Vigevani, Tullo & Cepaluni, Gabriel. *A política externa brasileira: busca de autonomia, de Sarney a Lula*. São Paulo: Editora Unesp, 2011.

Vigevani, Tullo & Mariano, Marcelo. A Alca e a política externa brasileira. in *Relações Internacionais do Brasil: temas e agendas*. São Paulo: Saraiva, 2006.

Vigevani, Tullo & Ramanzini, Haroldo. Autonomia, integração regional e a política externa brasileira: Mercosul e Unasul. in *A nova política externa brasileira: balanços e perspectivas*. São Paulo: Instituto de Estudos Contemporâneos e Cooperação Internacional. 2013.

Visentini, Paulo Fagundes. Cooperação sul-sul, diplomacia de prestígio ou imperialismo "soft"? As relações Brasil-África do governo Lula. in *Século XXI*, Vol. 1, nº1, 2010.

Waever, Ole, "The Rise and Fall of the Inter-Paradigm Debate". in S. Smith, K. Booth, M. Zalewski (eds). *International Theory – Positivism and Beyond*. Cambridge: Cambridge University Press, 1996.

Waltz, K. *Theory of international politics*. California: Addison Wesley Publishing Company, 1979.

Zibechi, Raul. *Brasil potencia – en la integracion regional y um nuevo imperialismo*. Bogotá: Ediciones desde abajo, 2012.

## Documents, Interviews and Press Reports

Agência Carta Major. *CUT e Via Campesina criticam oferta comercial do Mercosul à UE*. 28 de setembro de 2004.

Barbosa, Rubens. Entrevista. *Rubens Barbosa vê ideologização da política externa brasileira*. Folha de São Paulo/ BBC Brasil, 14 de março de 2008.

Brasil. Texto do Protocolo de Comércio e Cooperação Econômica entre o governo da República Federativa do Brasil e os Estados Unidos da América. 2020. Available at: <www.itamaraty.gov.br/pt-BR/notas-a-imprensa/21867-texto-do-protocolo-ao-acordo-de-comercio-e-cooperacao-economica-entre-o-governo-da-republica-federativa-do-brasil-e-o-governo-dos-estados-unidos-da-america-relacionado-a-regras-comerciais-e-de-transparencia+&cd=1&hl=pt-BR&ct=clnk&gl=br> Consulted on: December 09, 2020.

Camargo, Claudio. O renascimento da indústria de defesa. In: *Revista da Indústria*, ano 7, nº135, jan 2007 e dez 2008.

CEB. *Contribuição para o VII Fórum Empresarial das Américas,* Quito, Outubro, 2002. Available at: <www.cni.org.br/portal.main.jsp>. Consulted on: May 20, 2011.

CEBC. *Carta da China.* Nº53, 2010. Available at: http://www.cebc.org.br/pt-br/projetos-e-pesquisas/projetos-realizados/carta-da-china/carta-da-china-no-53. Consulted on: October 10, 2013.

CEBC. Investimentos chineses no Brasil (2014–2015). 2016. Available at: https://cebc.org.br/2017/07/12/investimentos-chineses-no-brasil-2014-2015/. Consulted on: September 02, 2020.

CNI. Confederação Nacional da Indústria. *A indústria e o Brasil:* uma agenda para o crescimento. Brasília, 2002.

CNI. Confederação Nacional da Indústria. *A indústria e o Brasil*: uma agenda do Crescimento. Brasília, 2002.

CNI. Confederação Nacional da Indústria. *Adesão Venezuela ao Mercosul*: agenda e interesses econômicos do Brasil, Janeiro, 2006a.

CNI. Confederação Nacional da Indústria. *Crescimento*: a visão da indústria. Brasília, 2006b.

CNI. Confederação Nacional da Indústria. *OMC*: o Fracasso da Rodada Doha prejudica o Brasil 2006c.

CNI. Confederação Nacional da Indústria. *Comércio Exterior em Perspectiva.* Informativo da Confederação Nacional da Indústria. Ano 16, nº8.9, maio e junho de 2007a.

CNI. Confederação Nacional da Indústria. *Carta nº089/2009-PRES.* 16 de março de 2009a.

CNI. Confederação Nacional da Indústria. *Carta ºo9o/2009-PRES.* 2009b.

CNI. Confederação Nacional da Indústria. *Medidas unilaterais da Argentina*: uma nova estratégia brasileira, 2009c.

CNI. Confederação Nacional da Indústria. Confederação Nacional da Indústria. *A indústria e o Brasil*: uma agenda para crescer mais e melhor, 2010.

CNI. Confederação Nacional da Indústria. Acordos comerciais – uma agenda para indústria brasileira. 2014. Available at: http://arquivos.portaldaindustria.com.br/app/conteudo_24/2014/07/22/474/V30_Acordoscomerciais_web.pdf. Consulted on: December 09, 2020.

# REFERENCES

CNI. Confederação Nacional da Indústria. Brasil precisa atrair investimento chinês para infraestrutura, diz diretor da CNI. Agência de Notícias CNI (Posicionamento). São Paulo, 29 ago. 2016. Available at: <https://noticias.portaldaindustria.com.br/posicionamentos/brasil-precisa-atrair-investimento-chines-para-infraestrutura-diz-diretor-da-cni/>. Consulted on: November 15, 2019.

CNI. Confederação Nacional da Indústria. CNI e IndustriALL-Brasil pedem a suspensão de proposta para a redução da TEC do Mercosul. 2021. Available at: https://noticias.portaldaindustria.com.br/noticias/internacional/cni-e-industriall-brasil-pedem-suspensao-de-proposta-para-a-reducao-da-tec-do-mercosul/.

CNI. Confederação Nacional da Indústria. *Propostas para a retomada da indústria e geração de emprego.* 7 de dezembro de 2021b.

Confederação da Agricultura e Pecuária do Brasil. *Posição da Confederação da Agricultura e Pecuária do Brasil – CNA. Sobre a Área de Livre Comércio das Américas – ALCA. Setembro 2003.* Available at http://www.ftaa-alca.org/spcomm/soc/thm_meet/cstmi2_p.asp. Consulted on: September 08, 2012.

Conselho Empresarial IBAS. *Declaração do Segundo Encontro*, 16 de outubro de 2007.

COSIPLAN/UNASUR. *Integration Priority Project Agenda*, 2011.

Cunha, Fernanda. Competitividade sem fronteiras. in FIESP. *Revista da Indústria*, Ano 5, nº108, junho de 2005, pp. 30–31.

Cunha, Fernanda. Um bom porto para os negócios. FIESP. *Revista da Indústria*, Ano 4, nº102, dezembro 2004.

CUT. *Carta aos embaixadores na OMC dos países do Grupo NAMA.* 19 de julho de 2007.

CUT. MST e Contag prometem reagir a acordo na OMC. 23 de julho de 2008. Available at <www.cut.org.br/agencia-de-noticias/39868/mst-e-contag-prometem-reagir-a-acordo-na-omc>. Consulted on: October 10, 2013.

CUT. Revisão da Declaração Sociolaboral do Mercosul - CUT - Central Única dos Trabalhadores. Maio, 2015

DG ABC. 30 de março de 2001. CNA vai propor Alca sem subsídios e barreiras. Available at http://www.dgabc.com.br/News/90000198694/cna-vai-propor-alca-sem-subsidios-e-barreiras.aspx?ref=history. Consulted on: September 08, 2012.

Dias, Marina. EUA avaliam leis ambientais que limitam compras do Brasil. Folha de São Paulo, 13 de março de 2021b. Available at: https://www1.folha.uol.com.br/mercado/2021/03/eua-avaliam-leis-ambientais-que-limitam-compras-do-brasil.shtml.

Dias, Marina. EUA pressionam Brasil para acabar com o desmatamento até 2030. Folha de São Paulo, 29 de marco de 2021c. Available at: https://www1.folha.uol.com.br/ambiente/2021/03/eua-pressionam-brasil-para-acabar-com-desmatamento-ate-2030-e-pedem-resultados-ainda-este-ano.shtml.

Dias, Marina & Colleta, Ricardo. Embaixador dos EUA no Brasil anuncia aposentadoria e abre espaço para nova indicação de Biden. Folha de São Paulo, 10 junho de 2021.

Available at https://www1.folha.uol.com.br/mundo/2021/06/embaixador-dos-eua-no-brasil-anuncia-aposentadoria-e-abre-espaco-para-nova-indicacao-de-biden.shtml?origin=folha#.

El País, Quando acaba a saliva tem que ter pólvora diz Bolsonaro para Biden. 10 novembro de 2020. Available at: https://brasil.elpais.com/brasil/2020-11-11/quando-acaba-a-saliva-tem-que-ter-polvora-diz-bolsonaro-para-biden-sobre-amazonia.html.

Ennes, Juliana. Serra se diz cético quanto ao Mercosul. Valor Econômico. 10 de setembro de 2010.

FIESP. Editorial "A defesa da concorrência é fundamental para todos". *Revista da Indústria*. Ano 1, nº5, 05 de agosto de 1996a.

FIESP. *Revista da Indústria*. Ano 1, nº5, 05 de agosto de 1996a.

FIESP. *Revista da Indústria*. Ano 1, nº7, 19 agosto de 1996b.

FIESP. Editorial "Integração sem subordinação". *in Revista da Indústria*. Ano 2, nº42, 19 de maio de 1997.

FIESP. Documento de posição – agenda de integração externa, 2013.

FIESP. Documento de posição. Proposta de integração externa da indústria, 2014.

FIESP. Federação das Indústrias do Estado de São Paulo. TEC do Mercosul: responsabilidade e serenidade. São Paulo. 2019. Available at: https://www.fiesp.com.br/sindoleo/noticias/tec-do-mercosul-responsabilidade-e-serenidade/.

FIESP & CIESP. *O Brasil de todos nós. Proposta da FIESP/CIESP para Discussão com a Sociedade*. Janeiro 2002.

FIESP & ICONE. Análise quantitativa das negociações internacionais – Relatório do Projeto. Available at <http://www.fiesp.com.br/indices-pesquisas-e-publicacoes/analise-quantitativa-de-negociacoes-internacionais/>. Consulted on: September 13, 2018.

Folha de São Paulo. Embaixador repassou a Bolsonaro relatos de fraude nas eleições dos EUA. 16 de dezembro de 2020. Available at: https://www1.folha.uol.com.br/mundo/2020/12/embaixador-repassou-a-bolsonaro-relatos-de-fraude-na-eleicao-dos-eua-diz-jornal.shtml.

Folha de São Paulo. Ernesto Araújo e Ricardo Salles discutem o desmatamento com o enviado de Biden para o clima. 17 de fevereiro de 2021a. Available at: https://www1.folha.uol.com.br/mundo/2021/02/ernesto-araujo-e-ricardo-salles-discutem-desmatamento-com-enviado-de-biden-para-o-clima.shtml.

Folha de São Paulo. Discurso de Bolsonaro não reflete ações do governo. 22 de abril 2021b. Disponível: https://www1.folha.uol.com.br/mundo/2021/04/leia-a-integra-do-discurso-de-bolsonaro-na-cupula-do-clima-com-checagens-e-contextualizacao.shtml.

Fundaçao Dom Cabral. *Ranking das transnacionais brasileiras* 2011. Available at <www.fdc.org.br).

Hamilton, Duda. As bases da Alca estão definidas. *Revista da Indústria*, Ano 1, 09 setembro de 1996.

# REFERENCES

IEDI. Instituto de Estudos Para o Desenvolvimento Industrial. 2017. Indústria Mundial: O Brasil na contramão dos emergentes. Carta IEDI, n. 809, Sao Paulo, agosto.

IEDI. Instituto de Estudos Para o Desenvolvimento Industrial. 2018. Indústria de Transformação por intensidade tecnológica em 2017: aumento generalizado de exportações e importações. São Paulo, fevereiro.

ISTOÉ – Independente "Alca 1 x 0 Brasil", N° Edição: 1713 | 26.Jul.2002.<Available at: http://www.istoe.com.br/reportagens/21692_ALCA+1+X+0+BRASIL>.

Leo, Sergio. Indústria brasileira resiste a acordo com UE. *Valor Econômico*. 15 de setembro de 2010.

Malan, Pedro. *Exposição de Motivos n° 756 /MF*. Brasília 7 de dezembro de 1998. Available at: <http://www.fazenda.gov.br/portugues/fmi/emfmi.asp>. Consulted on: September 06, 2013.

Marques, Delmar & Rios, Manuela. Forças e fraquezas do dragão. FIESP. *Revista da Indústria*, Ano 4, n°102, dezembro 2004.

Ministério da Defesa. *Estratégia Nacional de Defesa*. 2008.

Ministério do Desenvolvimento, da Indústria e do Comércio Exterior. *Balança Comercial (2006 e 2010)*. Available at www.desenvolvimento.gov.br. Consulted in: April, 2012.

Ministério da Fazenda. *Governo divulga os detalhes do acordo do Brasil com o FMI*. 2002. Available at: http://www.fazenda.gov.br/portugues/fmi/pe_acordo_fmi2.asp. Consulted on 06 de setembro de 2013.

Nassif, Luis. Lava-jato: tudo começou em junho de 2013. Jornal GGN, 03/06/2016. Available at? http://jornalggn.com.br/noticia/lava-jato-tudo-comecou-em-junho-de-2013.

Neto, Armando Monteiro. É hora de debater agenda pós Doha. O Estado de São Paulo, 20 agosto 2008.

OGLOBO. Araujo diz que governo Bolsonaro não vai mudar por Biden e que espera compreensão mútua. 15 janeiro de 2021. Available at: https://oglobo.globo.com/mundo/araujo-diz-que-governo-bolsonaro-nao-vai-mudar-por-biden-que-espera-compreensao-mutua-24840047.

PT - Partido dos Trabalhadores. *Carta ao povo brasileiro*. Junho, 2002a. Available at <www.fpa.gov.br>.

PT - Partido dos Trabalhadores. *Programa de governo*, 2002b. Available at <www.fpa.gov.br>.

RADIOBRÁS. MST protesta contra acordo de livre comércio Mercosul-UE. 20 de outubro de 2004.

Skaf, Paulo. Ação conjunta no Mercosul. in FIESP. *Revista da Indústria*, Ano 5, n°108, junho de 2005, p. 78.

Skaf, Paulo, Henrique, Artur & Silva, Paulo Pereira. Um acordo pela indústria brasileira. in Tendências & Debates. *Folha de São Paulo*, dia 26 de maio de 2011.

Tachinardi, Maria Helena. Muita ideologia, poucos resultados. in FIESP. *Revista da Indústria*. Ano.6, nº120, 2006, pp. 23–29.

Teofilo, Sarah & Medeiros, Israel. Brasil sai da Cúpula dos líderes sobre o clima em descrédito. 24 de abril de 2021. Available at: https://www.correiobraziliense.com.br/politica/2021/04/4919936-brasil-sai-da-cupula-dos-lideres-sobre-o-clima-em-descredito.html.

UNASUL. COSIPLAN. *Agenda de Projetos Prioritários de Integração*. 2012. Available at www.unasul.org.br.

UNIDO. United Nations Industrial Development Organization. Country profiles, *MVA* 2018, *quarterly IIP*. Available at: https://www.unido.org/.

Viana, Francisco. O papel da FIESP. FIESP. *Revista da Indústria*. Ano IV, nº31–3º trimestre de 1991.

Viana, N. Maciel, A. Fishman, A. Desde 2015, Lava Jato discutia repartir multa da Petrobras com americanos. Pública [online]. 12 mar. 2020. Available at: https://apublica.org/2020/03/desde-2015,-lava-jato-discutia-repartir-multa-da-petrobras-com-americanos/. Consulted on: July 14, 2020

WikiLeaks. Brazil: Illicit finance conference uses the "T" word, successfully. 2009. Available at: <https://wikileaks.org/plusd/cables/09BRASILIA1282_a.html>. Consulted on: December 09, 2020.

**Consulted Sites**

Agência Brasileira de Cooperação. http://www.abc.gov.br/Projetos/CooperacaoSulSul/Senai.

Cardoso, Fernando Henrique. Entrevista (Veja) FHC, Lula e política externa, 13 de novembro 2009. Disponível em:< (2) FHC, Lula e a política externa (14/15) - YouTube>

FMI. Fundo Monetário Internacional. Balance of Payment Statistics. Available at: http://www.imf.org/.

MDIC. Ministério do Desenvolvimento, Indústria e Comércio Exterior. Dados da balança comercial. Available at: http://www.mdic.gov.br/.

TV Cultura, 28 de maio de 2012. Entrevista com Paulo Skaf <Available at: http://www.youtube.com/watch?v=UVFCUk24JIs>. Consulted on: November 10, 2013.

# Index

agribusiness   2, 61–3, 66, 72, 82, 89, 113–9, 122, 159, 164n3, 168, 176, 179, 182, 186, 198
Alcântara Base   51, 75, 107, 150, 191, 202, 205
Amorim, Celso   49, 95, 100, 104, 107, 118, 124, 176
Araújo, Ernesto   199–200, 205, 207–8
Argentine   66–7, 78, 97, 99, 118, 124–5, 140, 148, 151, 190, 204
associated bourgeoisie   159, 164n2, 166, 175–6, 198. See also purchasing bourgeoisie

Biden, Joe   198–9, 207–10
Boito Jr., Armando   11, 35–6, 41, 43–5, 77, 82–3, 86, 88, 97n5, 113n10, 163–7, 175–6, 191, 197–8, 201
Bolivia   58, 69–70, 75, 99, 101, 123, 126, 127–8, 133–6, 138–142, 153, 156, 172, 205
Bolivarian Alliance for the Peoples of Our America (ALBA)   146, 153–4, 156–8, 173
Bolsonaro, Jair   162, 198–202, 204, 206–10
Brazil-China Business Council (CEBC)   113, 123, 177
Brazilian Business Coalition (CEB)   59, 60, 61, 63, 65, 73, 112–3, 117–8, 147, 179–80
Brazil, Russia, India, China and South Africa (BRICS)   94, 98, 102, 104, 107, 165, 170, 171, 173, 175, 183, 190, 192, 194, 199

Cardoso, Fernando Henrique   1–4, 35, 37, 43, 45–47, 49–50, 52, 54, 64, 69, 71, 73, 79–80, 90, 92, 94, 96, 104, 106, 108, 112, 128, 130, 159, 195, 205
Casarões, Guilherme   47–8
Cervo, Amado Luiz   48, 71, 168
Chile   52, 58, 74, 95n4, 98, 135–138, 140, 153, 171, 184, 190
China   3, 45, 54, 58, 89, 96, 98, 103n, 104–5, 113, 117, 122–3, 131, 137, 140, 174, 177, 189–91, 193, 202, 208–9
Cruz, Sebastião C. Velasco   35–6, 39, 41, 48, 53, 79, 81, 95, 128

Federation of Industries of the State of São Paulo (FIESP)   3, 41, 45–6, 48, 56–60, 69, 73–4, 76–7, 86, 92, 114, 117, 120–4, 127–9, 164, 178–82, 191, 199, 204
Free Trade Area of the Americas (FTAA)   4, 31, 51, 54–5, 57, 59–65, 72–5, 78, 81, 95, 100, 107–8, 112–5, 119, 130–131, 139, 145, 147, 149–54, 157, 159–60, 180
Fund for the Correction of Asymmetries (FOCEM)   99, 119, 140

ICONE   113, 115–6, 128, 179, 180
impeachment   146, 162, 165–6, 169, 175, 183–4, 186, 191n, 199
India, Brazil and South Africa Forum (IBSA)   3, 94, 96, 102
industry   27–8, 38, 43, 58–9, 62–6, 76–7, 82–3, 87, 90–1, 105, 109, 115, 119–21, 123–5, 128–29, 147, 159, 165n3, 171, 175, 179–80, 185–88, 192, 194, 203, 210
Initiative for South American Regional Integration in Infrastructure (IIRSA)   68, 100–1, 139, 141
internal bourgeoisie   2–4, 27–31, 33, 43, 46, 54, 59, 72–6, 81–4, 86, 88–90, 93–4, 96, 97, 99, 110–6, 119–31, 141, 145–7, 159–60, 162–4, 167, 169, 174–9, 181–2, 184–5, 191, 194–9, 204
International Monetary Fund (IMF)   37n, 45, 48, 50–2, 69, 70, 75, 80, 98, 106, 173

Lafer, Celso   51, 71–2
Landless Rural Workers Movement (MST)   39, 74, 88–9, 112–3, 116, 118, 127n, 147, 150–2, 154, 156–8
Lava Jato   165–6, 176, 191n
Lenin   6–8, 133, 196
Lima, Marina Regina Soares de   2, 47–9, 94, 168–9
Lula   1–4, 41, 46, 50, 71, 73, 75, 79, 80, 82–3, 85–7, 90–1, 93–7, 99, 101–7, 110, 112–113, 115–6, 129, 132–4, 138–40, 146, 148, 151–2, 154, 159–60, 162, 165–8, 170, 173–4, 196

Marini, Ruy Mauro   134–38, 195

# INDEX

Mercosur-European Union  55, 57, 64–5, 71, 78, 113, 114, 117, 125–6, 130, 151, 157, 172, 179–82, 185, 190, 197, 203
middle class  30, 41, 89, 91, 134, 162, 165–7, 173, 175, 183–4, 191, 201
Morgenthau, Hans  5–6, 12–4, 17–8

national bourgeoisie  2, 27, 29–30, 112, 144, 164n2, 182, 196
National Confederation of Agriculture (CNA)  3, 62–3, 113, 115–6
National Confederation of Industry (CNI)  3, 45, 56, 60, 62–3, 65, 73, 76–9, 113–4, 116–20, 124–6, 129, 147, 177–81, 199, 203
neo-developmentalism  4, 82–3, 85–7, 87–91, 112, 132, 134, 144, 159–60, 165, 176, 181, 185, 191, 194
neoliberalism  2, 4, 31, 35–41, 43, 46–7, 49, 57, 74–5, 77, 79, 81, 83, 88, 90–2, 99, 126, 148–50, 153–4, 159, 194–5, 206, 210

Organization for Economic Cooperation and Development (OECD)  185, 188, 190, 202–3

Petrobras  44, 69–70, 87, 101, 103, 123, 126–8, 139, 163, 166, 181, 193
Pinheiro Guimarães, Samuel  72, 95, 171
Poulantzas, Nicos  2–3, 5, 9–11, 14–7, 19–20, 23–5, 27–8, 32–3, 42, 141, 159, 164n2, 166n, 186, 201
purchasing bourgeoisie  2, 27, 29–30, 33, 42, 82–3, 144–6, 159, 162, 164n2, 175–6, 181, 191, 198. *See also* associated bourgeoisie

Ramanzini Jr., Haroldo  101, 116, 155
Rousseff, Dilma  4, 131, 146, 154, 157, 159, 162–3, 165, 167–8, 170, 173–5, 186, 191–2, 199

Skaf, Paulo  1, 86, 122, 124, 125n13
Social and Economic Development Bank (BNDES)  43, 49, 59, 82–4, 86–7, 99, 133, 141, 163, 164n3, 173, 175, 191, 196, 199
South Africa  3, 96, 98, 102–3, 117, 119–20, 129–30, 171, 183, 199

Southern Common Market (MERCOSUR)  49, 52, 54–61, 64–8, 71, 73, 78–9, 81, 99–101, 103–7, 113–115, 117–20, 123–6, 128, 130, 139–40, 146, 148–9, 151–7, 159–60, 171–3, 177–82, 190, 199, 203–4

Temer, Michael  161, 162, 184–6, 190–1, 193, 199, 200
Treaty on the Non-Proliferation of Nuclear Arms (NPT)  47, 51, 104, 109
Trump, Donald  167, 187, 191, 195, 198–201, 203, 206–8

Unified Workers Central (CUT)  39, 74, 88, 112, 118–9, 127n, 153–5, 147, 149–50, 152–5, 158
Union of South American Nations (UNASUR)  69, 100–1, 139–40, 144, 151–4, 156, 160–1, 171–3, 177–8, 182n, 190, 199
United Nations (UN)  49, 53, 71, 96, 98, 104, 109, 152, 168, 170, 174, 200–1
United States of America (US/USA)  37n, 39, 47–8, 50–1, 54, 57–60, 62–6, 70–4, 80, 86, 91, 95–8, 101–2, 104–10, 114, 117, 119, 126–8, 130, 132–3, 135, 137, 139–41, 146, 149–53, 161, 166–7, 170–1, 173–4, 181–5, 187, 189–200, 202, 205–9

Venezuela  47n, 70, 75, 81, 95, 99–101, 107–8, 113, 119, 123, 125–8, 135–7, 139–42, 142–3, 146, 148, 153, 156–8, 172, 177–8, 180, 182–3, 185, 190, 193, 199, 202, 204–5
Vigevani, Tullo  1, 51, 71, 101, 107, 122, 168

Workers Party (PT)  1, 4, 41, 73–5, 79–81, 83–5, 88–9, 91, 96, 131, 145–50, 152–4, 156, 159–60, 162, 164n3, 165–6, 168–9, 176, 178–81, 183, 193, 204
World Bank (WB)  37n, 50, 69–70, 192
World Trade Organization (WTO)  37n, 45, 52, 54, 57–8, 60–1, 63–5, 71, 78, 96–7, 102, 105–8, 113–7, 119, 124–5, 151, 172, 181, 188, 200, 202, 207

Printed in the United States
by Baker & Taylor Publisher Services